T0125274

Romance Epic

Romance Epic

ESSAYS ON A MEDIEVAL LITERARY GENRE

EDITED

BY *Hans-Erich Keller*

Studies in Medieval Culture, XXIV
MEDIEVAL INSTITUTE PUBLICATIONS
Western Michigan University, Kalamazoo, Michigan—1987

Copyright 1987 by the Board of the Medieval Institute
Kalamazoo, Michigan 49008-3851

Library of Congress Cataloging in Publication Data

Romance Epic

  (Studies in Medieval culture ; 24)
  1. Epic poetry, French—History and criticism.
2. French poetry—To 1500—History and criticism.
3. Epic literature, Romance—History and criticism.
4. Chansons de geste—History and criticism. I. Keller,
Hans-Erich. II. Series.
CB351.S83 vol. 24 [PQ201]   940.1'7   87-21958
ISBN 0-918720-85-0   [841'.03'09]
ISBN 0-918720-86-9 (pbk.)

Cover Design by Cynthia Tyler

Printed in the United States of America

CONTENTS

Acknowledgment

The great interest which Western Michigan University's Medieval Institute has shown in this endeavor is gratefully acknowledged. I would like to extend my thanks to Otto Gründler, Director of the Institute, to Thomas H. Seiler, Managing Editor of Medieval Institute Publications, and in particular to Juleen Audrey Eichinger, Production Editor, who made many valuable suggestions in matters of detail.

Deep thanks for precious advice on editorial matters is also due to my dear wife Barbara, who gave generously of her time despite demands of her own scholarly work and of pressing family obligations. Without her untiring assistance—both in editing and in word-processing—the publication would have been even more delayed.

The long wait for this volume was worthwhile, however, for the Studies in Medieval Culture series is indeed the appropriate place for a collection of essays exploring the terrain as eminently medieval as the Romance epic.

Columbus, Ohio   Hans-Erich Keller
February, 1987

Introduction

The essays in this volume strikingly illustrate how far we are removed today from the epoch-making studies of a Gaston Paris, Joseph Bédier, Ramón Menéndez Pidal, and Italo Siciliano: while not one of them deals with the genesis and prehistory of the Romance epic, all discuss the actual works as they are read today. Each contributor, convinced of the need to definitely come to grips with problems inherent in the existing literatures themselves, treats one or more of the following questions: the genre *per se* and its form and structure, its spiritual content, the evolution from its first textual inception in the twelfth century, and its rivalry and final absorption—at least in Italy—by the neighboring narrative genre of the *roman*.

The volume constitutes the fruit of the first two symposia devoted to the study of this genre at the International Congresses on Medieval Studies held at Kalamazoo, Michigan, in 1980 and 1981, of which selected, reworked papers are presented here without any attempt to arrive at a consensus of opinion. Unfortunately, it is impossible to also publish the highly spirited ensuing discussions which enabled those in attendance to gain a broader perspective and deeper knowledge of the Romance epic. This knowledge has since been enriched thanks to Daniel Poirion's brillant pages on the subject in his *Précis de littérature française du moyen âge* and those of a more general nature by Paul Zumthor in his *Introduction à la poésie orale* (both 1983), while it is still hoped that the long-awaited third volume of the *Grundriss der romanischen Literaturen des Mittelalters* will provide a thorough treatment of the epic (the first fascicule, containing Jules Horrent's "Chanson de Roland et Geste de Charlemagne" [Heidelberg, 1981; second fascicule, "Partie documentaire," 1985], amounts to not much more than a plot summary of the different *chansons*

ix

de geste). The eighteen essays that comprise this volume afford a complementary and sorely needed tangible idea of the complex character of this chameleon-like genre.

In this respect it is perhaps almost mandatory to quote Marguerite Rossi of the University of Aix-en-Provence, who in her plenary address at the Ninth Congress of the Société Internationale Rencesvals (Padua, 30 August 1982) characterized the Romance Epic as follows:

> Épopée non mythique, elle est inscrite plus que d'autres dans la réalité historique de son lieu et de son temps; elle articule entre eux, différemment selon les cycles et les époques, deux grands thèmes: le thème des relations féodales, essentiellement celles du roi et de ses vassaux, avec leurs crises, leurs problèmes moraux, et le thème de la défense et de l'extension de la chrétienté face aux Sarracins, tâche possible seulement sous condition de l'harmonie interne du royaume de France; à propos de ces sujets, se développe tout une problématique politico-morale: qu'est-ce qui est héroïsme, qu'est-ce qui est démesure? Quand la violence permise devient-elle excès condamnable, la vengeance personnelle, trahison? La révolte se justifie-t-elle par les abus de l'autorité suprême, ou faut-il toujours se soumettre et reconnaître celle-ci, quelles que soient ses insuffisances? Les réponses à ces questions varient selon les époques, mais la réflexion à ce sujet demeure, au moins en apparence, même dans les oeuvres tardives où s'introduisent le romanesque, l'esprit d'aventure ou un certain goût de la parodie; ces tendances engendrent des récits dont le seul but est de divertir, mais qui, pour l'essentiel, respectent les conventions propres à la chanson de geste. Formellement, d'autre part, la chanson de geste se définit par des traits qui évolueront sans disparaître au cours de l'histoire du genre; sa tradition de composition et de style la distinguera jusqu'à la fin d'autres productions narratives, en particulier du roman: stéréotypes et clichés de style permettant la mémorisation, sinon l'improvisation, laisse d'abord assonancée puis monorime comportant un nombre variable de vers, composition qui consiste à combiner des éléments narratifs préexistants.
>
> (*Essor et fortune de la chanson de geste dans l'Europe et l'Orient latin*, 2 vols. [Modena, 1984], 1:248)

Undeniably, then, the core of this genre would seem to have been formed by the French *chansons de geste*; consequently, a great number of the contributions in this volume deal with this type of epic. The Spanish, Occitan, and Italian medieval epics exist, of course, in their own right; yet, the influence of their French counterpart can be detected in works such as the Spanish fragment *Roncesvalles* and the story of Bernardo del Carpio, the Occitan *Ronsasvals* and *Roland à Saragosse*, as well as early

Italian chivalric literature. In this respect, *El Cantar de Mio Cid* resembles a monolith untouched by French literary domination and hence well deserves the attention given to it here by two scholars. Conversely, the Italian chivalric poems of Pulci, Boiardo, and Ariosto have not been taken into consideration: they are products of the Italian Renaissance, which allowed its imagination to roam freely in the glistering worlds of irony and the romantic, combining the matter of Charlemagne with that of King Arthur.

The essays can be divided into seven major groups. In the first, Ruth House Webber explores the specificity of the Romance epic, and William Calin wonders if we actually have the right to call the *chanson de geste* an epic. The peculiar structure of the *chansons de geste* captures the interest of Edward A. Heinemann, Barbara Schurfranz Moorman, and Larry S. Crist, whereas the underlying spirit animating them is the topic of J. L. Roland Bélanger's study and, on a more specific scale, those of Jean Charles Payen and Nancy Bradley-Cromey. Constance B. Hieatt and Alice M. Colby-Hall apply themselves to the reconstruction of lost *chansons de geste* in French and Occitan, while André de Mandach and François Suard trace the evolution of two *chansons de geste* throughout the centuries, the former pulling together all relevant research done in the field, the latter analyzing the continuous transformation and development of the same subject. Particular but very typical topics of the *chansons de geste* challenge Emanuel J. Mickel, Jr., who examines a crucial problem of the *Chanson de Roland*, and William W. Kibler, who studies the introduction of supernatural elements in the *chansons de geste*, whereas Peter S. Noble and Antonio Franceschetti analyze the question of tolerance and understanding for the Saracens in the French and Italian epics. Finally, Aristóbulo Pardo and Miguel Garci-Gómez devote their attention to a special topic dealing with *El Cantar de Mio Cid*, a subject which clearly demonstrates the atypical character of the independently great Spanish epic of the Middle Ages.

A publication such as this one cannot possibly claim to exhaustively examine all of the problems inherent in a literary genre whose form and content ever changed according to period, audience, and region. Nevertheless, it is the coordinator's strong belief that these eighteen essays not only represent an excellent cross-section of all the questions relative to the Romance epic, but also constitute a major contribution to the understanding of a literary phenomenon which until today has consistently eluded definition.

Hans-Erich Keller
The Ohio State University

Towards the Morphology
of the Romance Epic

Ruth House Webber

In any attempt to formulate abstract schema for the description of the medieval French and Spanish epic (the evidence for the early Portuguese epic is inconclusive[1] and the Italian epic is a later development), there is implicit the assumption that there was a Romance epic, an assumption which, however, must be tested at every step. The question is inextricably tied up with theories of epic origin. For the neotraditionalists, Ramón Menéndez Pidal and his supporters, there is no problem: the Romance epic is the continuation of Gothic heroic songs, the Spanish epic representing an earlier more archaic stage than that of the extant *chansons de geste*.[2] For the most part, especially among the individualists, it is not a matter that has been discussed in terms of the concept of a Romance epic. Rather, on the Spanish side the preoccupation has been to demonstrate the independence of the Spanish epic with respect to the French,[3] while among French scholars the focus is often on the indebtedness of the Spanish epic to the French. Even Jules Horrent, mimicking Louis XIV in his declaration "Il n'y a pas de Pyrénées," means that French influence has been dominant in Spain from the beginning, despite admitting in other moments evidence of influence going in the opposite direction.[4] Similarly, in two relatively recent comparative studies, Dorfman's on the *narreme* and Herslund's on epic style, the conclusion is reached that the Spanish epic is modeled on the French.[5]

Therefore, in the course of this scrutiny of French and Spanish epic texts with its assessment of resemblances as well as differences (of which

1

there are more of the former than the latter), we must continually consider whether we are treating parallel but independent phenomena or whether it is indeed a matter of imitation. At the same time we must also ask ourselves whether we are characterizing the Romance epic or whether we are in fact giving a description of all traditional epics.

The French epic texts that will be cited are the *Chanson de Roland*,[6] the *Gormont et Isembart* fragment,[7] *Raoul de Cambrai*,[8] and, from the Guillaume cycle, the *Couronnement de Louis*,[9] the *Charroi de Nîmes*,[10] the *Prise d'Orange*,[11] and the *Chanson de Guillaume*.[12] These seven poems show the highest percentage of semantic formulas on Joseph J. Duggan's list,[13] hence are the most traditional, and are also among the nine poems selected by Jean Rychner for his study.[14]

The Spanish epic offers a serious problem concerning texts. There are only three extant epics: the *Cantar de Mio Cid*;[15] the hundred-verse *Roncesvalles*, the surviving fragment of a Spanish *Chanson de Roland* which is too short to yield valid narrative data;[16] and the *Mocedades de Rodrigo*, a late, much re-worked epic poem on the youth of the Cid.[17] One more poetic text, the *Poema de Fernán González*, is a clerical re-casting of a *cantar de gesta*.[18] The remainder included here have come down to us in other forms but offer evidence both of an early poetic tradition as well as continued life in traditional balladry. They are the *Cantar de Sancho II* of the Cid cycle,[19] the *Siete Infantes de Lara (Salas)*, of which almost seven hundred verses have been reconstructed,[20] *Rodrigo el último godo*,[21] and *Bernardo del Carpio*, the counter-Roland.[22]

It is appropriate to broach the Romance epic question by attempting to discern the essential nature of the epic story. We shall commence with an examination of the role of the hero.

The hero who gives his name to the *Chanson de Roland* is a prodigy of knightly prowess and physical stamina. Yet he does not represent the ideal knight. For that, Roland and Olivier would have to be combined: ''Rollant est proz e Oliver est sage'' (v. 1093). It is Roland's pride, his insistence upon heroism above all else, which brings about the slaughter of his peers and finally his own demise. The same is true of Vivien of the *Chanson de Guillaume*, who is both tormented and doomed by the heroic persuasion. Charlemagne, on the other hand, is a figure of unblemished heroic stature in the *Chanson de Roland*. Blessed by God, he is an aging but still vigorous warrior and leader, conscious of the enormity of his destiny. Guillaume of the *Couronnement* is not only the epitome of the warrior-knight, but he is characterized in particular by his vigor and determination and by his loyalty to and support of his unworthy monarch. This image, however, is modified in other poems: in the *Charroi de Nîmes* he violently accuses the king of ingratitude and indulges in deceit and subterfuge to win a fief for himself; in the *Prise d'Orange* he is the bored, depressed hero who seeks out adventure and romance, while the *Chanson de Guillaume* transforms him into a waning hero who sometimes suffers fatigue, discouragement, and defeat.

The two heroes of the *Gormont et Isembart* poem are both outstanding warriors, yet they make an anomalous heroic pair: the former a noble pagan, an unusual figure in the older French epics, and the latter a rebel and a renegade who ultimately repents. Finally Raoul de Cambrai, another defective hero in the extreme *démesure* of his rebellion and resultant revenge that creates civil war and leaves chaos in its wake, is succeeded by his only slightly modified double, Gautier. Both are in marked contrast to the gentle, contrite Bernier who, however, is not a hero but a hero-slayer.

On the Spanish side the dominant hero is, of course, the Cid, unmatched in prowess, a leader as astute as he is revered, at the same time a devoted family man and an unwaveringly loyal vassal to a rancorous king. He would appear to have little in common with the Rodrigo of the *Mocedades*, an insolent, bumptious hero, whose behavior frightens his pusillanimous king. Favored by God, he upholds democracy, tolerance, and equitable treatment of all except the count of Savoy, the king of France, and the pope. Sancho II is an overweeningly ambitious hero fatally involved in fratricidal rivalries. The figure of Fernán González as it is revealed in the clerical *Poema* is colored with elements from the hagiographic tradition. Nonetheless he emerges as a great warrior in the holy war against the Saracens and a shrewd, calculating schemer in political matters. Rodrigo, the last Visigothic king of Spain prior to the Arabic invasion, changes from version to version from valorous king, victim of dynastic competition, to impassioned lover or impious libertine.

The seven princes of Lara, multiple heroes who function as one, are treacherously led to a death that even their combined valor cannot thwart. They are replaced by their bastard half-brother, Mudarra, model of the implacable avenging hero. Conjectural as is the specific historical source of the barbarous events narrated in the aforementioned *Infantes de Lara*, there is no possible historicity behind the creation of Bernardo del Carpio. The valiant young Spanish warrior who is instrumental in defeating the French at Roncesvalles subsequently turns into a rebellious vassal who defies his king upon discovering the latter's cruel conduct.

It is at once manifest from the foregoing review that there are several different types of epic hero. The epic hero does not resemble the idealized hero of folklore, although sometimes vestiges of the folkloric pattern are to be found, particularly in later manifestations, in such matters, for example, as the hero's illegitimate birth.[23]

3

Closest to the heroic ideal are Roland and Vivien, youthful conquering heroes whose goal in life is the profession of heroism, with the
difference that the heroic imperative leads to death instead of to a rewar-
ding life. The same is true of the seven sons of the Lara family. Rodrigo of
the first part of the *Mocedades* is an exception even though he unquestionably displays the same tragic failing of hubris. In that late epic
dependent upon the *Cantar de Mio Cid*, the canon had to be violated since
the hero's subsequent history was well known. Another degenerate member of the same class is the grotesque Rainouart of the *Chanson de
Guillaume*, who is also permitted to live out his life.

The second category is likewise made up of conquering heroes whose
lives come close to conforming to the traditional heroic pattern, but they
are mature heroes, warriors and at the same time kings or leaders with
additional responsibilities and preoccupations who are able to live on
indefinitely like Charlemagne, the Cid, and Fernán González.

The remainder are heroes with a specific mission; that is, circumstances have forced the heroic role upon them. They in turn are divided,
according to the nature of their mission and how it is carried out, into
praiseworthy heroes and faulty heroes. Among the former are Guillaume,
Bernardo del Carpio, Rodrigo of the second part of the *Mocedades*, and
Mudarra, the avenger of the seven brothers of Lara, all of whom survive
their heroic experiences. Into the second group, the ignoble heroes, fall
the renegade Isembart and the violently implacable Raoul de Cambrai
together with his nephew Gautier. The dissolute king, Rodrigo el godo,
also joins this set because his mission of leadership has been perverted.
Similarly the pagan Gormont must be classified here, owing to the anti-
Christian nature of his mission. Sancho II presents an ambivalent face in
that his motives are reprehensible; yet he is only remembered in the
ballads as the hero assassinated in the course of his mission. Observe that
their fate, except for Gautier's, is the same as that of the noble heroes
guilty of the sin of pride: death.

From the hero, let us turn to a consideration of the epic action, what
form it takes and how the conflict is resolved. With a single exception the
action occurs against the background of the wars between the Christians
and the Saracens, recognizing that in *Gormont et Isembart* "Saracen"
signifies "pagan." It is only in *Raoul de Cambrai* that the holy wars have
no part, an omission which, significantly, is remedied in the continuation.

Roland is the prime example of the hero who is the victim of
treachery which, emanating from personal spite, results in his death and
the defeat of France. The second move ("move" is used here in the
Proppian sense of a part of a story that is complete in itself),[24] the Baligant

4

episode, shifts the hero's role to Charlemagne, permitting the defeat to be replaced by a resounding victory and punishment to be meted out to the traitor by legal (or at least quasi-legal) means. Similarly *Raoul de Cambrai* is an epic narrative of two moves. Raoul's rebellion against the king who has deprived him of his rightful fief sets in motion a devasting war between family factions in which he is killed. The second move is a duplicate of the first with a new hero, his nephew Gautier. It terminates in an uneasy reconciliation of the warring parties united only in a revolt against the king, a non-resolution in epic terms that was destined to be amended in the sequel.

The *Gormont et Isembart* epic appears to be two clearly delineated stories with two heroes, the difference being this time that both are present in each story. In the first part, renunciation of country and faith by the Christian hero leads to conversion to paganism in a strange land at the side of the other hero; in the second part, back in Christendom, their avenging mission is doomed to end in death for the two superb warriors according to the Christian epic ethos.

Guillaume of the *Couronnement* undertakes a dual altruistic quest, that of keeping the French king on his throne and the pope in Rome, in which he is successful. The *Charroi* presents him as a rebel hero in search of a fief, while in the *Prise* he sets out to win another fief together with a wife. This time the fief quests have positive value (in contrast to Raoul's negative one), leading to the greater glory of France and Christendom. It is instructive to observe that if these three texts were considered as one, we would have a narrative of two moves, in the first of which the hero is the defender of the monarchy and Christianity and in the second the seeker of lands and family, all meritorious feudal goals. In each case Guillaume's initiative brings only success without deaths that need to be deplored. The *Chanson de Guillaume* is again of bipartite construction. Vivien is the hero of the first story, who is destined to die as a consequence of the cowardice of his companions and his unswerving commitment to the heroic ideal. Guillaume, the replacement hero of the sequel, with great difficulty and considerable auxiliary help avenges his nephew's death and achieves a victory.

The Spanish *Cantar de Mio Cid* is also a two-move story but with a single hero. At the beginning he is the victim of slanderers who bring about his exile. Later on he becomes the victim of the treason of his sons-in-law (administered vicariously), for which he is avenged through legal procedures that prescribe compensation and retribution but not death, as in the *Chanson de Roland*. The two parts of the *Mocedades* are distinguished by the difference in character of the heroic mission of a single hero. In the first there is heroism for its own sake, and in the second a nationalistic quest as the king's adviser to force the king of France and the pope to recognize the Castilian king's sovereignty. The hero of the intermediate epic of the Cid cycle, the *Cantar de Sancho II*, embarks upon a politically ambitious quest, which leads to death by treachery plotted by his own sister. Like the *Charroi* and the *Prise*, it lacks a second move, for which there is, in fact, textual evidence.[25]

Each of the two moves of the reconstructed epic of the *Siete Infantes de Lara* has a separate hero. The princes are lured to their death in revenge for an incident arising out of a family quarrel. In the second move their half-brother, brought up as a Saracen, sets out on the self-appointed mission to avenge his brothers, in which he is successful.

The story of Bernardo del Carpio, the Spanish rival of Roland, likewise gives evidence of a structure of two moves. At the beginning, similar to Guillaume, his mission is to spur on the king to oppose Charlemagne's invasion of Spain in alliance with the Moors of Zaragoza. In the second move Bernardo wages war with the king to free his unjustly imprisoned father. It terminates in an impasse when the king appears to cede and surrenders the father, a cadaver mounted on horseback.

In the *Poema de Fernán González*, which may or may not represent a modification of the structure of the original epic poem, the hero again has a double quest: to establish the prestige of Castille and win its independence from Leon on one hand and to combat the common enemy, the infidels, on the other. Rather than two moves, the narrative takes the form of alternating lines of action similar to that of the *Couronnement de Louis*. Both goals are accomplished, although the hero has to be rescued from the treachery of his political opponents by the ingenuity of his wife, while divine aid facilitates the defeat of the Saracens.

The story of Rodrigo, the last Visigothic king of Spain, ends with his defeat, metaphorically his death, thus completing a typical first-move pattern. Yet once more the ballads imply the development of a second move, wherein the hero humbly submits to a period of servitude and dies repentant.[26]

Let us now attempt to summarize, then synthesize, these findings. In eight out of the fourteen epics in question, four in French and four in Spanish, the story is composed of two moves. Of the remaining six single-move narratives, the three on the French side belong to the trilogy of the Guillaume cycle (the *Couronnement*, the *Charroi*, and the *Prise*, which may not always have had such an independent relationship to one another).[27] In the *Couronnement,* as we have already noted, the hero has a double mission that converts itself into two alternating, then converging narrative lines, the same form that is found in the Spanish *Fernán*

González. The other two Spanish single-move stories, *Sancho II* and *Rodrigo el último godo*, have been put together on the basis of the insecure evidence of non-epic texts. Nevertheless, one can clearly discern in them all of the narrative elements that are found in the first move of *Raoul de Cambrai*: a defective hero with a perverted mission who meets his death by treachery, which is followed by an embryonic second move.

Within the predominant two-move story form, in three out of the four French examples (the *Chanson de Roland*, *Raoul de Cambrai*, and the *Chanson de Guillaume*), the death of the hero brings to an end the first move, which generates the second with a new hero who avenges that death. The Spanish *Siete Infantes de Lara* repeats the identical pattern. In the remaining three Spanish epics (the *Cantar de Mio Cid*, the *Mocedades de Rodrigo*, and *Bernardo del Carpio*), the same hero performs in both moves and neither one ends in death. The two parts are divided instead by a change of mission and/or a shift in the character of the epic action.

There also appears to be a less-favored alternate of the two-move structure wherein the hero undertakes two different kinds of missions which, instead of being sequential, are developed by turns. This form can be observed in the *Couronnement*, in *Fernán González*, and possibly in *Gormont et Isembart*.[28]

It will be recalled that the heroes who meet their death in these epics, which occurs either at the conclusion of the first move or of the single move of the simple form, are of two sorts: those beset with an heroic impulse (Roland, Vivien, Infantes de Lara), and those with an improper mission (Raoul, Sancho II, Rodrigo el godo). Those who survive are the noble hero-leaders (Charlemagne, the Cid, Fernán González) and heroes with a worthy mission (Guillaume, Bernardo del Carpio, Rodrigo, Mudarra). It is only the aberrant case of *Gormont et Isembart* that mars the almost complete harmony we have found with regard to heroes and structural patterns in the Spanish and French epic in that the two heroes appear in both moves, that both die, and that they die in the second move. At the same time it is conceivable that the importance of Gormont's role in the fragment, which belongs to the end of the poem, is misleading and there was in fact only one hero, Isembart. Pursuing this hypothesis, we would then have the familiar pattern of a narrative of two moves distinguished by different missions, both censurable this time, of a single hero. Furthermore, *Gormont et Isembart* would be seen to have in common with *Rodrigo el último godo* the special way in which the hero dies. Both lose their identity, which is effectively death, at the end of the first move, Rodrigo by his kingdom's being destroyed and Isembart by renouncing his faith, while their physical death comes at the end of the second move accompanied by remorse and repentance.

7

From the vantage point offered by this brief analysis of the hero and the structure of the epic story in these fourteen texts, the case for the Romance epic seems assured. All categories are mutually valid, frequencies of occurrence are approximately the same, structural patterns repeat themselves. Yet enough variants and individual preferences are perceptible that the likelihood of imitation is annulled, at least at this level of analysis.

If then we are willing to accept that there is a Romance epic, what statements can be made to characterize the Romance epic story in such a way as to distinguish it from the epic story in general? Here are four, still subject to further testing, which I should like to offer in combination as a tentative beginning to the morphology of the Romance epic:

1. The Romance epic hero is a redoubtable warrior-knight whose mission may be noble or ignoble, productive or fatal.

2. The Romance epic hero's fate is death if his heroism is tainted with pride or if his mission is unworthy.

3. The Romance epic story is frequently made up of two moves, which may be linked in either one of two ways: by a hero who is killed and then avenged by a second hero, or by a single hero who undertakes two separate missions in succession that involve different epic actions.

4. The backdrop of the Romance epic story is usually the wars between the Christians and the infidels.

Notes

[1] See António José Saraiva, *A épica medieval portuguesa* (Nova, 1979), who cautiously summarizes the problem as follows (p. 91): "Existiu um poema joglaresco provalemente em língua portuguesa, que remonta possivelmente ao ´ltimo quartel do século XII. . . ."

[2] Ramón Menéndez Pidal, *La Chanson de Roland y el neotradicionalismo* (Madrid, 1959); rev. ed., *La Chanson de Roland et la tradition épique des Francs* (Paris, 1960).

[3] See, for example, Américo Castro, *La realidad histórica de España* (Mexico, D.F., 1954), pp. 263-76.

[4] Jules Horrent, *La Chanson de Roland dans les littératures française et espagnole au Moyen Age* (Paris, 1951), pp. 437 ff.

[5] Eugene Dorfman, *The Narreme in the Medieval Romance Epic* (Toronto, 1969); Michael Herslund, "*Le Cantar de Mio Cid* et la chanson de geste," *Revue Romane* 9 (1974), 69-121.

[6] Les *textes de la "Chanson de Roland,"* ed. Raoul Mortier (Paris, 1940-44), 1, *La Version d'Oxford*.

[7]Gormont *et Isembart*, ed. Alphonse Bayot, 3d ed. (Paris, 1931).

[8]Raoul *de Cambrai, chanson de geste du XIIe siècle*, ed. Paul Meyer and Auguste Longnon (Paris, 1882). Only the first part (through laisse ccxlix) is analyzed here.

[9]Le *Couronnement de Louis*, ed. Ernest Langlois, 2d ed. (Paris, 1925).

[10]Le *Charroi de Nîmes*, ed. Joseph-Louis Perrier (Paris, 1931).

[11]La *Prise d'Orange: Chanson de geste de la fin du XIIe siècle*, ed. Claude Régnier (Paris, 1967).

[12]La *Chanson de Guillaume*, ed. Duncan McMillan, 2 vols. (Paris, 1949-50).

[13]Joseph J. Duggan, "Formulaic Diction in the *Cantar de Mio Cid* and the Old French Epic," *Forum for Modern Language Studies* 10 (1947), 81.

[14]Jean Rychner, *La chanson de geste: Essai sur l'art épique des jongleurs*, Publications Romanes et Françaises, 53 (Geneva and Lille, 1955), pp. 7-8.

[15]Cantar *de Mio Cid*, ed. Ramón Menéndez Pidal, 3 (Madrid, 1946; re-ed. Madrid, 1969), 909-1016.

[16]Ramón Menéndez Pidal, "Un nuevo cantar de gesta español del siglo XIII," *Revista de Filología Española* 4 (1917), 108-13.

[17]A[lan] D. Deyermond, *Epic Poetry and the Clergy: Studies on the "Mocedades de Rodrigo"* (London, 1969), pp. 222-77.

[18]Ramón Menéndez Pidal, *Reliquias de la poesía épica española* (Madrid, 1947; re-ed. Madrid, 1951), pp. 34-180.

[19]Carola Reig, "El cantar de Sancho II y cerco de Zamora," *Revista de Filología Española*, 37 (Madrid, 1947).

[20]Ramón Menéndez Pidal, *Reliquias*, pp. 199-239.

[21]Floresta *de leyendas heroicas españolas: Rodrigo el último godo*, ed. Ramón Menéndez Pidal (Madrid, 1973), pp. 5-121, and *Romanceros del rey Rodrigo y de Bernardo del Carpio*, ed. Rafael Lapesa et al. (Madrid, 1957), pp. 3-12.

[22]Jules Horrent, *La Chanson de Roland*, pp. 462-83, and Rafael Lapesa et al., *Romanceros*, pp. 143-52.

[23]See Archer Taylor, "The Biographical Pattern in Traditional Narrative," *Journal of the Folklore Institute* 1 (1964), 114-29.

[24]Vladimir Propp, *Morphology of the Folktale*, 2d ed. (Austin, 1968), p. 92.

[25]See Ferdinand Wolf and Conrad Hofmann, *Primavera y flor de romances* (Berlin, 1856), nos. 47, 47a, 47b, 49, 50, 50a, 52.

[26]See Ferdinand Wolf and Conrad Hofmann, *Primavera*, nos. 6, 7.

[27]See Jeanne Wathelet-Willem, *Recherches sur la Chanson de Guillaume*, 1 (Paris, 1975), pp. 659-85, and Jean Frappier, *Les chansons de geste du cycle de Guillaume d'Orange*, 1 (Paris, 1955), pp. 64 ff.; 2 (Paris, 1965), pp. 9-19.

[28]If the extant verses, which recount the battle of the two heroes against the French and wherein we witness first Gormont's death, then Isembart's, are indicative of the narrative organization of the entire poem, we have here another epic story with two interlaced narrative lines.

Textes médiévaux et tradition:
la chanson de geste est-elle une épopee?

William Calin

La chanson de geste est-elle une épopée? Question sans intérêt, dépassée, et qui ne mérite guère de réponse, affirmeraient plusieurs. Paul Zumthor et Hans Robert Jauß soulignent surtout l'originalité, l'unicité médiévale face au moderne, c'est-à-dire l'altérité de la littérature du moyen âge prise dans sa totalité. Selon ces érudits et selon un nombre considérable de leurs prédécesseurs, le trouvère médiéval était soumis à des conventions thématiques et stylistiques, obligé de puiser dans un fond de registres d'expression. Dans son essence, la chanson de geste serait une oeuvre mi-narrative mi-lyrique, chantée ou chantonnée devant un public, obéissant aux modalités de récitation orale, voire de création orale. Par conséquent, qui assimilerait la chanson de geste à quelque forme épique moderne ou classique serait coupable d'anachronisme, et la notion de ''littérature'' telle que Virgile, Ovide et nous-mêmes la concevons était étrangère aux chanteurs de geste.

Cela se peut. Pourtant, en postulant l'altérité de la poésie médiévale, il nous sied de préciser exactement par rapport à qui et à quoi le moyen âge est autre. La poésie stylisée et archétypique ne se limite pas au seul moyen âge occidental. Elle se trouve chez Ronsard et du Bellay, chez Corneille et Racine, même et surtout chez Lamartine et Hugo. De plus, elle domine les grandes littératures classiques arabe et persane, chinoise, japonaise et sanskrite. Nous voudrions suggérer que, selon un point de vue diachronique mondial, ce sont les trouvères (et non Mallarmé) qui nous fournissent

11

des normes quant à la création artistique. Une constatation primordiale de la critique moderne établit que tout écrivain respire une culture conventionnelle, faite de genres, modes, thèmes, motifs, lieux communs, niveaux de style et archétypes. La nouvelle critique américaine, la nouvelle critique française, les maintes versions de structuralisme et post-structuralisme soulignent la littérarité inhérente à toute littérature. Ne peut-on en conclure que les notions romantiques et post-romantiques de sincérité, d'originalité et d'authenticité que certains attribuent à l'"esprit moderne" en général, sont en fait l'exception et non la norme? Si altérité il y a, c'est nous, pardon ce sont nos grands-pères, qui sont autres. Le champ conceptuel de nos recherches devrait être la poésie mondiale, du *Gilgamesh* à Pierre Emmanuel, plutôt que des théories esthétiques basées sur les cent dernières années et qui nous conduisent à isoler le moyen âge du reste de l'Histoire. L'étude comparative des genres littéraires peut nous aider à réintégrer les oeuvres médiévales dans le courant de la littérature mondiale, à instituer une continuité culturelle dans laquelle le Medium Aevum pourrait occuper une place toute privilégiée. La "génologie" et la périodisation (l'analyse des courants et mouvements littéraires) représentent une orientation particulièrement fructueuse des études comparées actuelles, surtout en ce qu'elles suscitent un renouveau de l'histoire littéraire, discipline restée quelque peu négligée par rapport à la critique et à la théorisation pures.

Première question: qu'est-ce qu'une épopée? Comment la définir? Bon nombre de travaux érudits, de manuels scolaires et de dictionnaires proposent une définition vague et globale: c'est un poème narratif, basé sur les événements "réels", racontant une intrigue martiale et dont le protagoniste se fait "plus grand que la vie". L'épopée manifeste des caractéristiques de grandeur et d'amplitude, témoigne de l'héroïsme et de la dignité de l'homme, incarne une perspective collective et communautaire, est composé *in sermone gravissimo*. Malheureusement, de telles définitions sont normalement formulées à partir d'un corpus de textes trop limité et, par là, prennent un ton de prescriptions normatives. Un grand spécialiste en la matière, angliciste éminent, ayant le triste malheur d'adhérer à ses propres définitions, se voit obligé d'exclure de la communauté épique des auteurs tels qu'Ovide, Lucain, Chaucer, l'Arioste et du Bartas, tout en réservant une place de choix à Hérodote, Xénophon, Bunyan, Fénelon, Defoe et Conrad[1]!

La plupart des spécialistes conçoivent un modèle néo-classique - "de Virgile à Milton" -, un modèle qui convient plus ou moins bien aux XVIe et XVIIe siècles mais qui pose forcément des problèmes quand on envisage d'autres époques. Car l'épopée ne meurt pas avec l'avènement du romantisme - bien au contraire. Toute une génération d'érudits a reconnu la présence épique aux XIXᵉ et XXᵉ siècles, le fait que Lamartine, Hugo, Saint-John Perse, Aragon et Pierre Emmanuel ont créé des épopées. Il est non moins évident que le long poème a beaucoup évolué depuis Milton et Voltaire et que notre nouvel âge d'or épique ne se conforme en rien aux vieilles règles. Les écrivains modernes, conscients d'une tradition classique, désireux soit de la prolonger soit de la répudier, ne peuvent ni ne veulent incorporer à leurs propres textes tous les thèmes et motifs d'un Tasse ou d'un Camoëns. L'épos moderne survit sans prouesses martiales, sans héros sublime et sans "voix chorale". En fait, l'épopée post-classique n'est-elle pas surtout une mise en page de la quête même d'une telle voix, intériorisée, spiritualisée, par le protagoniste poète-narrateur?

Quant au moyen âge, depuis deux siècles on place certains textes héroïques - tels *Beowulf*, la *Chanson de Roland*, *El Cantar de mio Cid*, *Das Nibelungenlied* - à la rubrique "épopée" à côté des poèmes homériques. Pourtant les chansons de geste diffèrent du modèle classique autant que le font *Jocelyn* et *L'Anabase*. Turold n'exhibe ni figures homériques ni motifs traditionnels tel le voyage aux Enfers; on peut même se demander si les textes épiques romans étaient composés dans le "style sublime", si le registre stylistique des jongleurs était censé être élevé à la manière de celui de Virgile, du Tasse et de Camoëns. Il est non moins vrai que les auteurs de "romans" et de "dits" - Chrétien de Troyes, Guillaume de Lorris, Jean de Meun et Guillaume de Machaut - adeptes des lettres anciennes, lisaient Virgile et Ovide dans le texte et parfois les suivaient de près, adoptant une manière d'écrire totalement inconnue aux chanteurs de geste. Chrétien est d'ailleurs non moins "héroïque", non moins "épique", que l'Arioste, ce qui est fort compréhensible, étant donné que Pulci, Boiardo, l'Arioste et même le Tasse héritaient tout autant d'une tradition médiévale d'origine française que d'une tradition latine. Ils sont au moins aussi proches de la chanson de geste tardive, de Chrétien et du *Lancelot en prose* que de l'*Énéide*. Or, les Italiens ont toujours considéré, et à juste titre, leur *poema*, soit *cavalleresco* soit *eroico*, comme l'épopée nationale et comme modèle du genre. En Angleterre, on trouve également un texte épique de la Renaissance, *la Reine des Fées*, qui possède à la fois des affinités avec le *Lancelot-Graal* et le *Roman de la Rose* et avec Virgile. Bien que les médiévistes francophones et anglophones distinguent nettement "épopée" (c'est-à-dire chanson de geste) et "roman", pour nos collègues allemands *die Epik* et *das Epische* nomment et englobent tous les sous-genres narratifs du moyen âge, tels *Heldenepik, höfische Epik, Tierepik, Kleinepik, Spielmannsepos*, etc.... Chez les Allemands, *Epos*, une des trois *Naturformen der Poesie*, désigne le mode narratif en général, par opposition aux deux autres grands modes: le dramatique et le lyrique.

13

Nous voudrions donc inclure la chanson de geste dans la tradition mondiale de l'épopée mais pas forcément à l'exclusion d'autres genres narratifs. Des théories, des formulations qui ne reposent que sur quelques modèles exemplaires, soit classiques (l'*Iliade*, l'*Énéide*) soit médiévaux (disons le *Roland*) risquent, selon nous, d'être incomplètes, voire inadéquates. Notre définition du genre se doit d'être tentative, inductive, provisoire et empirique - *in re* - et non prescriptive, déductive, normative et *ante rem*. Notre définition du genre est obligée de tenir compte de la totalité et multiplicité des poèmes qui, à travers l'espace et le temps, dessinent, gonflent, délimitent l'épique.

Pour toutes ces raisons, sans être helléniste, nous accepterons pour une fois de recourir aux Grecs, pour qui, selon le *Grand Robert*, *épopée* voulait dire "qui fait des récits en vers". Selon Homère c'est tout simplement "une chose dite", c'est-à-dire un "discours"; selon Aristote "la représentation métrique d'actions héroïques". Nous en déduisons que l'épopée est un poème d'une certaine étendue qui, grosso modo, raconte des histoires. Nous aimons également la formulation d'un poète scandinave: "J'ai défini l'épopée comme une narration poétique d'une longueur telle qu'on ne saurait la lire ou la réciter du commencement jusqu'à la fin sans s'arrêter pour manger et dormir"[2].

Étant donné cette prise de position, il est évident que nous voudrions considérer, scruter, examiner et ranger sous la rubrique *epos* la chanson de geste dans sa totalité, les chansons tardives aussi bien que le très classique *Roland*. On y trouve, bien entendu, un nombre de textes qui dérivent du *Roland*, qui ont subi l'influence du chef-d'oeuvre prédécesseur, mais qui se détournent de l'idéalisme et de la ferveur turoldiens pour cerner une autre problématique. Il y a "l'épopée de protestation", les poèmes du cycle de Guillaume, où l'empire se désintègre, le roi Louis s'avérant incapable de faire face à la situation, et donc le comte Guillaume et les membres de son lignage se voient obligés de repousser seuls les vagues d'invasion sarrasine; il y a "l'épopée de révolte", où l'empire est réduit à un univers de chaos et de tyrannie, où les meilleurs êtres gâchent leur vie à lutter inutilement et sans espoir soit entre eux soit contre l'empereur. Ces textes traitent d'une manière plus concrète, plus lucide, plus "réaliste" si l'on veut, les problèmes socio-politiques qui dominent la France des XIIe et XIIIe siècles. Ils expriment également des aspirations vers un individualisme, et c'est là une des grandes contributions de ces siècles à l'histoire culturelle de l'Occident. Ces chansons sont plus problématiques, plus introspectives que le *Roland*; elles n'exaltent plus le mythe de la monarchie centralisatrice ni les valeurs eschatologiques de la croisade. Elles s'ouvrent à d'autres visions du monde, à d'autres mentalités, plus modernes, plus proches de la réalité contemporaine.

Voilà une orientation du genre. Il y en a d'autres. Au cours du XIIe siècle, l'héroïsme traditionnel, mis au service du roi ou d'un grand lignage féodal, se trouve modifié par un phénomène (dépassant des questions d'idéologie ou de politique intérieure) qu'il faudrait rattacher à la grande évolution des mentalités et des goûts, phénomène qui correspond, au XVIIe siècle, à la métamorphose du baroque en classicisme. Dans certaines chansons tardives, on perçoit un raffinement de vie chez les grands barons maintenant capables d'apprécier de beaux habits, des banquets somptueux, de belles couleurs, en un mot le luxe. Les trouvères se lancent dans une profusion de détails descriptifs, ils se mettent à l'école de l'*amplificatio*. Le merveilleux, chrétien et non-chrétien, ajoute au récit. Des différences de classe et de caste apparaissent. Le paysan, le rustre (qu'il soit de naissance princière ou non) a pour antithèse le nouvel aristocrate, grand guerrier, certes, mais, en même temps, *juvenis* élégant, charmant et de beauté insigne, capable de faire des discours et de se conformer à la vie de cour. Surtout, le protagoniste devient amoureux, recherche la compagnie et l'attention des dames, utilisant un vocabulaire et des rites courtois. Il arrive même que le trouvère parodie la *fin'amor* en la juxtaposant aux traditions érotiques antérieures, l'amour de la belle Sarrasine par exemple. Puis, comme dans les romans, le héros subit des aventures, il s'en va en quête, son caractère évolue au cours du récit. Parfois, dans certaines chansons, le trouvère reprend les poncifs du genre avec un sourire, sur le mode ironique, en sapant et démystifiant la littérature antérieure. Ces chansons tardives, qui témoignent d'une transformation des mentalités, représentent-elles un nouvel univers "gothique" par contraste avec la vieille épopée "romane", univers où, pour la première fois, les rêves et tourments de la conscience humaine s'expriment aux côtés des réalités concrètes d'un monde concret?

Voilà que, une ou deux générations après Chrétien de Troyes, Béroul et Thomas, la vitalité d'un genre dit populaire, dit dépassé, survit intacte. Selon Ernst Robert Curtius, l'âge d'or de la chanson de geste se situe cent ans après le *Roland*, qu'il faut considérer comme une ébauche géniale préfigurant les chefs-d'oeuvre du règne de Philippe Auguste[3]. Il est passionnant de constater à quel point les trois grands genres narratifs - chanson, roman et dit allégorique - coexistent, fonctionnent ensemble pendant les mêmes périodes, se faisant concurrence bien entendu, tâchant auprès du public de faire pencher la balance en leur faveur.

Nous voudrions également souligner la haute qualité esthétique de textes tels que *Raoul de Cambrai*, *Garin le Lorrain*, *Renaud de Montauban*, *Ami et Amile* et *Aspremont*, entre autres. Ces chansons tardives peuvent être belles, et, belles ou non, elles sont épiques, aussi épiques que le *Roland* ou le *Guillaume*. C'est s'abandonner à une forme de préjugé romantique en faveur d'un *Urstoff* ou *Ursprung* d'ailleurs largement inventé que de présumer que seule la *Chanson de Roland* ou seule la chanson de geste primitive exemplifie les normes du genre ou un certain idéal héroïque, dont les gestes de la fin du siècle représentent forcément la déformation. Il n'y a pas, il ne saurait exister, un seul modèle "génologique" de la chanson de geste, pas plus qu'il n'y en a un pour le roman moderne. Certes, selon Lukács et ses disciples, *das Epische* incarne une mentalité primitive et spontanée, qui sort d'un âge héroïque précédant le nôtre et qui crée un monde stable, organique et harmonieux, par opposition à la fragmentation et l'aliénation actuelles. Selon cette optique, les chansons tardives représenteraient une sorte de contamination, un mélange des genres, dus à l'influence croissante et écrasante du roman, fiction "à la mode". Pourtant, nous croyons l'avoir déjà indiqué, la pureté du genre n'existe pas, l'intégrité d'un genre n'existe pas. Le roman courtois s'imprègne de la tradition *epos* autant que la chanson de geste, et les caractéristiques dites "romanesques" des chansons tardives puisent leur origine dans la chanson primitive "romane" et dans la nature évolutive de l'épopée *qua* épopée tout autant qu'ailleurs. En effet, l'*Odyssée* est bien une épopée comme l'*Iliade*; pour les Latins, Virgile est un poète épique, mais Ovide également. Pour les Italiens le Tasse *et* l'Arioste; pour les Anglais Milton *et* Spenser; pour les Français du XIXe siècle le Hugo des *Légendes des Siècles* mais aussi le Lamartine de *Jocelyn*. Il se peut même que, à travers toute l'histoire du genre, la structure des aventures et de la quête soit plus importante, plus universelle, plus dominante, que le récit des batailles rangées et l'éloge de la conquête martiale.

De plus, nous aimerions signaler que l'évolution de la poésie narrative médiévale en général, et la chanson de geste en particulier, correspond au développement du même genre sublime pendant la Renaissance et à l'époque baroque. C'est-à-dire, tout commence par l'apparition d'une oeuvre ou d'oeuvres "expérimentales" de grande puissance, pleine d'idéalisme et de force créatrice (*La Chanson de Roland*; les *Hymnes* et *Discours* de Ronsard). Le mode sublime s'oriente ensuite dans des directions quelque peu divergentes: 1) vers une prise de contact avec la vie concrète, réalisme, engagement politique et, en même temps, un certain assouplissement formel (*Raoul de Cambrai* et *Les Lorrains*; *Les Tragiques*); et 2) vers une prise de contact avec Eros et le thème de la quête, donc de la *Wunscherfüllung* romanesque (*La Prise d'Orange, Aymeri de Narbonne, Huon de Bordeaux; Moyse sauvé* et *Saint Louis*). Cet élément romanesque persiste pendant un certain temps mais tôt ou tard cède devant un courant qu'il faut qualifier d'anti-romanesque, où didactisme et satire sociale et littéraire triomphent dans une sorte d'épopée comique ou parodique: *Le Lutrin, Ver-Vert* et *La Pucelle* sous Louis XIV et Louis XV; leurs pendants au moyen âge, *Le Pèlerinage de Charlemagne* et, à la rigueur, *Huon de Bordeaux*, mais surtout des textes comme *Le Roman de Renard*, les compilations cycliques et cette *summa* que représente pour nous *Le Roman de la Rose*. Est-ce pure coïncidence qu'on observe la même évolution, de l'héroïsme à l'érotique, du romanesque au didactique et à la satire, dans la tradition épique persane (les chefs-d'oeuvre de Firdausi, Nizami, Attar, Sadi, Rumi, Jami) qui, d'ailleurs, a fleuri précisément pendant les mêmes siècles qu'en France? Notre hypothèse trouve un dernier appui auprès de la théorie fort répandue concernant l'histoire diachronique des beaux-arts et qui envisage une suite de styles au moyen âge (styles roman, gothique, rayonnant et flamboyant) qui correspondrait aux deux périodes de la Renaissance, au maniérisme et au baroque quelques siècles plus tard.

Enfin, lier la chanson de geste à la pérennité épique peut nous aider à résoudre le problème (à notre avis un faux problème) de l'épopée dite orale. La distinction dans des manuels entre deux sortes d'épopée - orale, authentique, populaire et primitive d'une part; littéraire, artificielle, savante et adulte d'autre part - sort du grand romantisme allemand, est basée sur une opposition Homère-Virgile que nous voudrions voir nuancer. Les romantiques avaient des notions curieusement déformées quant à la création littéraire au moyen âge et dans l'antiquité; de toute façon, Homère et Virgile sont loin d'être les seuls maîtres et modèles du genre. En accord avec René Etiemble[4] et Italo Siciliano[5], nous estimons que l'épopée en général, et la chanson de geste en particulier, sont des manifestations de culture aristocratique, qu'elles n'ont jamais été "primitives" ni "primaires". Nous ne pouvons donc souscrire à la notion de *Volkstimmung* réhabilitée par Menéndez Pidal ou Jean Rychner. L'*Iliade* et la *Chanson de Roland* sont des poèmes aussi complexes, aussi raffinés, aussi structurés que l'*Énéide* et le *Chevalier au lion* ou *Huon de Bordeaux*. Les ressemblances entre ces cinq oeuvres d'art sont beaucoup plus grandes que leurs différences éventuelles. Puis, selon l'argumentation de M. Rychner lui-même, la grande majorité des chansons de geste ont perdu cette structure orale prétendue être à la base du genre. Effectivement, il nous paraît que seul le *Roland* et, à la rigueur, une ou deux autres chansons de la première époque, peuvent être rangées sous la rubrique "épopée spontanée et lyrique"; et là, encore, personnellement, nous estimons que l'épopée romane du moyen âge n'est oralisante que dans le sens de récitation orale, c'est-à-dire vis-à-vis des conditions de consommation littéraire vraies pour toute l'aire médiévale, sacrée et profane, fictive et didactique, en vers et en prose. Puisque la poésie avant Gutenberg était chantée, chantonnée ou lue à haute voix, la différenciation des genres basée sur des critères de "présentation" ou de "performance" devient

17

fort précaire. Des chansons tardives telles que *Renaud de Montauban* et *Huon de Bordeaux* étaient lues à haute voix, lues et non chantées, lues et non improvisées; et elles imitent les textes antérieurs avec autant d'application et autant de recul critique que d'autres genres tels le roman ou l'allégorie. Cette continuité au sein de l'épopée française, de Turold à Bertrand de Bar-sur-Aube ou Jean Bodel, indique combien il est facile qu'un genre oral ou post-oral se transforme en littérature pure, ou plutôt (et c'est là notre avis) que l'épopée est littérature pure et que le stade oral est un rêve d'érudits férus de nostalgie néo-romantique.

A travers les années, à travers les siècles, les chanteurs de geste ont consciemment mis leurs textes au goût du jour, souvent imitant ou subissant l'emprise d'autres genres, surtout le roman. Un trouvère est influencé par le roman, comme un romancier est influencé par des chroniques ou le grand chant courtois. De la même manière, au XVIIe siècle, Pierre Le Moyne, auteur de *Saint Louis, ou la Sainte Couronne reconquise*, subit l'emprise du roman héroïque, du roman pastoral et surtout du théâtre héroïque de Corneille et Rotrou. Et, à l'époque moderne, l'épos se voit formé et modelé par le roman et le lyrisme, se manifeste même (chez Aragon et Emmanuel) comme des suites de poèmes lyriques entrecoupées d'un contre-lyrisme narratif, distanciateur et en prose. Nous croyons fermement que les trouvères, les poètes baroques et les poètes modernes ont raison de vouloir renouveler leurs oeuvres, de les revitaliser en puisant au sein des courants et des modes les plus vivants de leurs temps. Seul un genre mort resterait pur. La chanson de geste, comme tout genre littéraire, évolue selon deux lignes de force. La première est pulsion et cohésion archétypiques à l'intérieur du genre. La seconde est l'évolution inéluctable de l'histoire littéraire, faite d'imitation et de déformation des grandes oeuvres précédentes, subissant l'influence ''extérieure'' venant d'autres genres et accueillant le jaillissement de brusques innovations.

Suivant les préceptes de la *Rezeptionsästhetik*, nous concluons en affirmant qu'un genre tel que l'épopée offre au public et aux auteurs, à des époques différentes, des réseaux de direction différents. Un genre est sans cesse en voie de transformation. Il évolue, et de ce grand courant ouvert au temps, aux traditions aussi bien qu'aux modes et goûts de l'époque qu'il traverse, surgissent régulièrement des chefs-d'oeuvre. Telle est la fragilité et l'évanescence d'un genre, telle est également sa force et sa pérennité[6].

Notes

[1]E. M. W. Tillyard, *The English Epic and Its Background* (New York, 1954).

[2]Björn Collinder, ''On the Translation of Epics'', *Sprachkunst* 3 (1972), 327-32, particulièrement p. 327.

[3]Ernst Robert Curtius, "Über die altfranzösische Epik II", *Romanische Forschungen* 61 (1948), 421-60, particulièrement pp. 423-24.

[4]René Etiemble, "L'épopée de l'épopée", dans ses *Essais de littérature (vraiment générale)* (Paris, 1974), pp. 163-75.

[5]Italo Siciliano, *Les chansons de geste et l'épopée: Mythes, histoire, poèmes* (Turin, 1968).

[6]Une première version de cet article a paru dans *Perspectives Médiévales* 8 (1982), 117-24.

Measuring Units of Poetic Discourse: Analogies between Laisse and Verse in the *chanson de geste*

Edward A. Heinemann

The syntactic ambiguity in the title of this paper is deliberate. "Measuring" is both an adjective modifying "units" and a verb taking "units" as its direct object, and we shall look at both the units which measure and those which are measured. Laisse and verse in the *chanson de geste* function as measuring units against whose regularity the play of other, varying, units produces rhythmic effects which have for the most part passed unperceived, or at least without comment, by critics of the genre. It could be argued that Jean Rychner's classification of the principal syntactic types of the epic verse[1] has documented the rigid monotony of that verse form. Certainly, appreciations which emphasize vigor and austerity suggest that the author of those appreciations would prefer the fluidity of Racine or Baudelaire.[2] The laisse, too, seems to embarrass critics. We recognize easily enough the correspondence between laisse and incident in the *Chanson de Roland*, and, however we may express it, we feel the lyric intensity produced by that correspondence. But Rychner's *reprise bifurquée*[3] or a laisse of some fifty lines or more in *-ant* with its inexhaustible string of present participles does not raise the same ready acknowledgement of artistry.

I do not intend to reveal here the key to hitherto undreamed-of delights in fifty consecutive present participles. I do think, however, the

21

chanson de geste derives much poetic effect from the rhythmic modulation arising out of the play between units of measure and units of discourse.

The view presented here is a general one; it assumes that recognition of laisse and verse presents no difficulties and that the effects pointed out in the examples are for the most part self-evident. It would exceed the scope of this article to examine the details.

I shall use the categories which Rychner set out in describing laisse and verse[4] as a guide in our measuring elements of poetic discourse, but classification is not my goal. Rychner's categories result from a metric rule in the grammar of the *chanson de geste* which highlights various aspects of the language produced by that grammar, and the categories are an invaluable aid to perceiving these effects. The forms of highlighting which we shall examine are length (the number of metric units, including fractions, to a discourse unit), intensification (the "sympathetic vibrations" arising from a match between metric and discourse units), and re-ordering (the shift of hierarchy among discourse units produced by the impact of metric units).

Two brief points should be made about the units in question. First, the measuring units are not all fixed in length. While the verse is indeed fixed at ten syllables (leaving aside the dodecasyllable and paroxytonic hemistichs), the hemistich comes in two sizes, four and six syllables, and the laisse has no fixed length whatever. Although the length of the measuring unit may vary, however, all units of the same level are equivalent. A short laisse is equivalent to a long one. This variable length of the measuring unit will be of some importance for the measurement of the length of discourse units.

The second point is that discourse breaks into certain "natural" divisions: word, noun phrase, predicate, clause, sentence, idea, incident, episode, etc. Modern typography recognizes some of the units with punctuation, paragraph indentation, and chapter headings, and just as these newfangled contraptions can show quite a bit of latitude in highlighting the units of discourse, so too the units of measure in the *chanson de geste* will vary widely from one passage to another in the units of discourse they set off and the effects they produce.

Length

The most straightforward measuring function is that of measuring the length of discourse units as so many metric units, or fractions of a unit, long. The clauses in the first example range in length from one hemistich to two verses:

1)	Or escoutés	com il fu esragiés	385
	En cel bois fu	Tiehars uns pautoniers	386
	Et Amouris	uns culvers renoiés	387
	En sa compaigne	ot .C. larrons proisiés	388
	Illuec estoit	li culvers herbregiés	389
	Les gens desrobent	qui vienent des marciés	390
	Rainuart oent	qui mout est revoisiés	391

Moniage Rainouart I (MR I), XVII[5]

I have boxed off each clause to make graphic the rhythmic structure of the passage, based on the length of the clause, one hemistich long in v. 385, then two verses long (vv. 386-87), one verse long (vv. 388 and 389), and again one hemistich long (vv. 390-91). A proper appreciation of the rhythms in this passage would require detailed consideration of re-ordering; let the passage merely stand here to illustrate the clause as unit of discourse and the measurement of length as a matter of hemistich, verse, and groups of verses.

In the second example, the contrast between verse-long clauses and hemistich-long clauses sets off vv. 71 and 72 as a conclusion to the preceding lines:

2)	Si t'ai forni	maint fort estor chanpel	68
	Dont ge ai morz	maint gentil bacheler	69
	Dont le pechié	m'en est el cors entré	70
	Qui que il fussent	si les ot Dex formé	71
	Dex penst des armes	si le me pardonez	72

23

Charroi de Nîmes (CN), I[6]

The third example uses the same kind of contrast to mark an articulation in the story line as Guillaume passes from observing to acting:

3)	Et Herneïs	por son riche lignage	170
	Vot la corone	par devers li atrere	171
	Quant ge le vi	de bel ne m'en fu gaire	172
	Ge li doné	une colee large	173
	Que tot envers	l'abati sor le marbre	174
	Haïz en fui	de son riche lignage	175
		(CN), VI	

The two clauses of v. 172 stand in marked contrast to the two-verse clause of vv. 170-71 on the one hand and the one-verse clauses of vv. 173-75 on the other.

The texts so far have contrasted adjacent clauses of various lengths. To give an idea of other forms of measuring length, let us look at a pair of details, perception and reaction. First, three examples illustrate the usual form of the details, in a single line of verse:

4)	La dame l'ot	si gita un soupir	1359
		(Prise d'Orange [*PO*] [*AB* version]), XLIV[7]	
	Arragons l'ot	le sens cuide changier	1482
		(PO [*AB* version]), L	
	Ot le Guillelmes	a pou d'ire n'enrage	1556
		(PO [*AB* version]), LIV	

Passage 5 shows the amplification of this unit of discourse to five verses in length:

5)	Qant Olivier	s'oï si menacier	4201
	De pandre au forches	come larron fossier	4202
	Et qant ill ot	de Girart le guerrier	4203
	Que il menacent	de la terre a chacier	4204
	Tel duel en a	le sans cuide changier	4205
		(Girart de Vienne), CXVII[8]	

The effect of amplification in this passage comes not from contrast to adjacent segments of the text but rather from reference to occurrences of the detail in other texts, from reference, as it were, to the *langue* rather than to the *parole*. This, of course, is the kind of reference involved in the motif as it is generally understood. It is worth insisting on the point that a feature may refer to either *langue* or *parole*, but that subject would exceed the limits of this paper.[9]

At the level of the laisse, modulation of length in the number of laisses relating a unit of discourse is striking in the contrast of single laisses, paired laisses, and tripled laisses in the opening phases of the battle of Roncevaux.[10]

Length is a measure of importance; amplification is a means of emphasis. Single combat between champions, for example, being an important moment in the story line, spreads over several laisses, as in *Rol* CCLVIII-CCLXII (Charlemagne and Baligant) and CCLXXX-CCLXXXVI (Tierri and Pinabel) or *CL* (*AB* version) XIX-XXVII (Guillaume and Corsolt).[11]

Amplification can be used, too, to articulate the narrative. Michael Holland has examined the number of syllables given to the naming of Charlemagne and Pinabel in the *Chanson de Roland* and observed that the longest identifications occur at such important moments as the opening line, Marsile's first mention of Charles, and the climax of judicial battles.[12] The amplification we saw in example 5 opens a laisse. The principle of relative length may well be quite general at laisse boundaries, as the boundary between laisses XI and XII in the *Chanson de Roland* illustrates:

6)	Desuz un pin	en est li reis alez	165
	Ses baruns mandet	pur sun cunseill finer	166
XI	Par cels de France	voelt il del tut errer AOI	167
XII	Li empereres	s'en vait desuz un pin	168

(*Chanson de Roland*), XI-XII

Ignoring vv. 166 and 167, we find Charles designated twice, as *li reis* in v. 165 and as *li empereres* in v. 168. The first occurrence, two syllables long, is a part of the hemistich in which it occurs. The second, four syllables (plus a posttonic syllable), fills the hemistich in which it occurs. Two points arise, the rhythmic effect here and the difference between the four- and the six-syllable hemistichs.

Writing about the laisse-introductory line in the *Prise d'Orange*, Rychner observed the frequency with which a character is named in the first verse of a laisse.[13] The proper noun is longer than the pronoun; *Gillebert* is longer than *li mes*, which in turn is longer than *il*. Rychner described the pausing effect, or *palier*, at laisse boundaries as a repetition from the conclusion of the first laisse to the introduction of the second laisse in which a slight change of aspect occurs. The repetition slows the advance of the story line, but the slight change of aspect prevents a complete halt.[14] We may add that in the case of example 6 the pause effect

25

derives also from this longer identification of a character. The lengthening of the designation of Charlemagne in v. 168 underscores the repetition which v. 168 makes of v. 165 and emphasizes the slowdown in the story line which results from the repetition. Lengthened designation of characters seems to be a laisse-introductory device.[15]

The second point is that, although the hemistich is measured by the number of syllables, the measuring unit is the hemistich and not the syllable. Holland's count of syllables should be expressed as numbers (including fractions) of hemistichs. The two hemistichs are equivalent even though they differ in length. The point is important, for the six-syllable hemistich may swallow up an element of discourse which would predominate in the four-syllable hemistich. As we shall see below in the discussion of re-ordering (example 11), meter highlights among the "natural" divisions of the sentence those parts which correspond to the hemistich. Compare the adverbial phrase *desuz un pin* in vv. 165 and 168 of example 6. The phrase fills a hemistich in v. 165 and ranks as one of the two principal elements of discourse in that verse. In v. 168 the same four syllables are merely part of a larger element, the predicate. In this light I advance example 7 with the question whether the name Guillaume is more prominent in the first hemistich than the second:

7)	Ferir quida	Guillaume en mi le vis	1479
			(*MR I*), LXVII
	Fierent Guillaume	el costé et el pis	1852
			(*MR I*), LXXXVI

These two lines do not constitute any particular echo in the *Moniage Rainouart I* of which I am aware, but an affirmative answer to the question may mean that the place of a proper noun, in first or second hemistich, may have esthetic implications. Further to the difference between the four- and six-syllable hemistichs, an element of discourse which predominates in a six-syllable hemistich carries more weight than one which predominates in a four-syllable one.

8)	D'Orenge issi	Guillaume li marchis	1340
			(*MR I*), LXI
	Li quens Guillaume	Rainuart apela	1663
			(*MR I*), LXXVII

Example 8 illustrates how the naming of Guillaume can be made to occupy a four- or a six-syllable hemistich, and it would be difficult to decide whether it is the postposition of the subject or the length of the subject which contributes more to the particular difference of effect in these two lines. Again, the first- and second-hemistich positions of the proper noun show potential esthetic significance. (Nor is the proper noun the only part of speech implicated.)

The length of the laisse, almost completely free, is a more familiar trait of esthetic potential than the length of the hemistich. In the first battle at Roncevaux, Roland, Oliver, and Turpin lead off the battle in three long laisses, and the following combats are dispatched in very short laisses, echoing the accelerated rhythm of the melee as well as reflecting the hierarchical importance of the combatants.

Intensification

When the unit of discourse repeatedly coincides with the metric unit, the effect is similar to the familiar troop of Boy Scouts marching across the suspension bridge: the resultant sympathetic vibrations intensify the impact of each individual unit. We know the intensely lyrical laisse of the *Chanson de Roland*. Incident matches up with laisse, content with form, narrative with song, and the result is the intensification of the musical effect of the laisse and of the dramatic effect of the narrative.

In the *Chanson de Roland* it is not just incident and laisse which coincide. Verbal echoes between laisses or between incidents reinforce the match still further, whether in *laisses similaires* or only in such devices as parallel laisse introductions.

9)	Oliver sent	que a mort est ferut	1952
		(Rol), CXLVI
	Oliver sent	qu'il est a mort nasfret	1965
		(Rol), CXLVII

Laisses CXLVI and CXLVII are not particularly similar in the incidents they relate, but they are marked by parallel introductions which reinforce the intensification produced by the match between unit of discourse (incident) and unit of meter (laisse).

This triple match is not, of course, necessary. As Barbara Schurfranz Moorman has pointed out, an echo network independent of laisse structure plays an important role in organizing the telling of the *Prise d'Orange* (A version), emphasizing as it does parallels and contrasts in situations.[16] It is worth adding to her observations that this echo structure stands alongside a fairly strong laisse structure, for incident and laisse show a great tendency to match up in this text. The measuring unit matches up with the discourse

27

unit, but their combination plays *against* the strongly marked echoes of the text, which highlight *other* discourse units.

Example 10 illustrates the match of discourse unit and measuring unit at the level of the verse and shows the intensity which that match can create even in the absence of verbal echo. Vv. 5-12 in the prologue of the *Charroi de Nîmes* (version *A*) match one clause to each verse and provide a strongly marked frame within which some fairly elaborate semantic rhythms develop.

10)	C'est de Guillaume	le marchis au cort nes	5
	Conme il prist Nymes	par le charroi monté	6
	Aprés conquist	Orenge la cité	7
	Et fist Guibor	baptizier et lever	8
	Que il toli	le roi Tiebaut l'Escler	9
	Puis l'espousa	a moillier et a per	10
	Et desoz Rome	ocist Corsolt es prez	11
	Molt essauça	sainte crestïentez	12
	Tant fist en terre	qu'es ciels est coronez	13

(*CN*), I

(Notice that the conclusion in v. 13 breaks the pattern with two clauses to the verse for a concluding effect.)

Re-ordering

When the measuring units and the discourse units do not quite mesh, meter overrides discourse and re-orders the hierarchy of the "natural" units. We saw above that the adverbial phrase *desuz un pin* is one of the two principal components of the clause in *Rol* 165, but subordinated to the predicate in *Rol* 168. Text 11 gives a striking example of the metric unit overriding the discourse unit at the level of the verse:

| 11) | Rainaurs vest | l'auberc qui fu mailliés | 372 |

(*MR I*), XVII

A grammatical analysis would place the principal division between the main clause and the subordinate clause; the metrical rule converts the main division to lie between the verb and its direct object.[17] The metrical units re-order the discourse units.

This re-ordering is responsible for the semantic rhythms in example 10 to which we alluded above. We might add that those rhythms are based on the semantic function of the hemistich, but we cannot go into further detail here.

Items 12 and 13 show this re-ordering at the level of laisse and incident. They refer to laisses V to VIII of the *Charroi de Nîmes* (*A*

28

version), the passage in which Guillaume lists his past services to the king. The past service is the unit of discourse in question, and in each instance it is related according to the pattern of verbal and referential echoes listed under 12.

12)   Structure of the *mi grant servise* units
       1. Vocative

Looys sire	dist Guillelmes le ber	133 (1)
Looys rois	dit Guillelmes li sages	153 (2)
Looys sire	dit Guillelmes li prouz	182 (4)

       2. Guillaume calls on Louis to remember

Dont ne te menbre	del grant estor chanpel	134 (1)
Rois quar te menbre	d'une fiere bataille	157 (2)
Dont ne te menbre	del cuvert orgueillous	183 (4)
Rois quar te menbre	de l'Alemant Guion	203 (5)
Rois quar te menbre	de la grant ost Oton	213 (6)

       3. Description of the service (no verbal echo)
          a. Offense or threat to Louis: (3) 163-71; (4) 183-87; (5) 204-06; (6) 229-37.
          b. Intervention of Guillaume: (1) 135-38; (2) 158-59; (3) 172-79; (4) 188-90; (5) 207-09; (6) 238-50.
          c. Grave consequence for Guillaume: (1) 139-49; (3) 175; (4) 191-98; (5) 210-12.
          d. Physical presence of the defeated man: (2) 160-61; (4) 199-200.
       4. Royal ingratitude
          a. Service

De cest servise	ne vos remenbre gueres	180 (3)
De cel servise	ne vos remenbre il prou	201 (4)

          b. Compensation

Quant vos sanz moi	voz terres	181 (3)
Quant vos sanz moi	terres fetes don	202 (4)

The numbers in parentheses refer to the occurrences in which the elements appear. Not all the elements appear in each occurrence of the service unit; the vocative, for example, appears in the first, second, and fourth occurrences. The diagram in 13 shows more graphically the distribution of the elements listed under 12, and it also shows the relation between the six units of discourse (the six services) and the four units of measure (the four laisses).

The diagram shows that, whether we look at discourse unit or measuring unit, the two do not match up except in laisse VI, which is coterminous with the combination of services 2 and 3. The first service occurs in laisse V along with other matters.

29

13) *CN* V-VIII, Relation of Discourse Units to Metric Units

V 115- 152			116-128	I, 46-57
	(1)	1 2 3b 3c	133 134 135-138 139-149	
			150-152	IX, 265-67
VI 153- 181	(2)	1 3b 3d	153 157 158-159 160-161	
	(3)	3a 3b 3c 4a 4b	163-171 172-179 175 180 181	
VII 182- 219	(4)	1 2 3a 3b 3c 3d 4a 4b	182 183 183-187 188-190 191-198 199-200 201 202	
	(5)	2 3a 3a 3b 3c	203 204-206 204-206 207-209 210-212	
	(6)	2	213	
VIII 220- 255	(6)	 3a 3b	 229-237 238-250	
			253-255	IX, 257-59

30

Services 4 and 5 occur in laisse VII, but so too does a part of service 6. Service 6 overlaps the boundary of laisses VII and VIII but does not quite fill laisse VIII, which ends on other matters.

If, however, we look at discourse units and measuring units simultaneously, a pattern appears of increasing intensification.

The passage begins with an introductory laisse V. Vv. 116-28 echo a passage from laisse I, closing off the development of laisses III-IV with this reference back to the initial action of the poem and marking an articulation in the story line.[18] Then, in the same way as Guillaume turns to face Louis, the laisse turns to a recitation of a first service rendered to the king. The laisse then ends on three lines, vv. 150-52, which will be echoed in laisse IX, closing off our passage. Thus the laisse reproduces on a small scale the structure of the passage as a whole.

At laisse VI the essential repetition of the passage begins. The text picks up elements from the interior of the preceding laisse and converts them to structural elements of the laisse by coordinating them to the introduction and development of the laisse. The introduction of the discourse unit matches the introduction of the measuring unit, and so on. The effect of repetition is triple: recurrence of laisse, of discourse unit, and of wording.

The repetitive effect of laisse VI is reinforced by a second occurrence of the discourse unit in the same measuring unit. A variant introduction,

14)   Aprés celui   vos refis ge une autre   162
                                                                 (CN), VI

making explicit referential allusion without any verbal echo (in the place of elements 1 and 2), brings in the recitation of a third past service. This occurrence of the discourse unit, in addition to emphasizing by repetition, emphasizes by amplification. Besides sheer numbers of verses, it adds new structural elements, 3a (referential) and 4a-b (verbal).

We count three intensifying effects produced by laisse VI: emphasis by repetition (three occurrences by the end of the laisse), emphasis by amplification (from occurrence 2 to occurrence 3), and emphasis by sympathetic vibration. The pair of discourse units matches up with the measuring unit and raises the service to the king to an element of form.

Laisse VII then builds on this pattern. Service 4 shows all three intensifying effects, by repeating the discourse unit, coinciding with the opening of laisse VII, and giving for the first time (and indeed the only time) the complete set of structural elements, 1, 2, 3a-d, and 4a-b. Occurrence 5 marks a departure from the pattern. It recalls occurrence 3 by its appearance as an emphasis by repetition within the laisse. It does not,

31

however, amplify but rather compresses. By this point repetition has fully established the patterns and now proceeds by shorthand allusion, using only elements 2 and 3a-c. Further, instead of coinciding with the end of the laisse, occurrence 5 is wholly interior, and the beginning of yet another occurrence occupies the end of laisse VII.

Occurrence 6 carries disjunction from the measuring unit one step further, matching up with no laisse boundaries. Further, the reinforcing effect of verbal echo is reduced to element 2. But the emphasis by amplification in sheer numbers of lines receives very strong reinforcement from precisely that mismatch between discourse unit and measuring unit. The pause or discontinuity between laisses puts a moment of suspension if not suspense into the narration of Guillaume's last service to the king.

15)	Mes cors meïsmes	tendi ton paveillon	218
VII	Puis te servi	de riche venoison	219
VIII	Quant ce fu chose	que tu eüs mengié	220
	Ge ving encontre	por querre le congié	221

(CN), VII-VIII

The moment is scarcely dramatic in itself, but the discontinuity, the almost imperceptible halt and restarting draws out this final occurrence of the service unit and intensifies it with a new kind of amplification.

The final three lines of laisse VIII will be echoed by the opening of laisse IX, and this phase of the story is closed off. By joining occurrence 6 to the conclusion, laisse VIII serves a conclusional function similar to the introductory function of laisse V.

Modulating rhythms, length as a measure of importance and as an articulatory device, intensification from match between discourse unit and metric unit, re-ordering by mismatch between discourse unit and metric unit, this rapid survey has allowed us to evoke some of the devices dependent on the verse and laisse. We have seen rather more musicality of language in the genre than is traditionally admitted, and that musicality may be attributed to measuring units of poetic discourse.

Notes

[1]Pp. 168-70 in Jean Rychner, "Observations sur la versification du *Couronnement de Louis*," in *La Technique littéraire des chansons de geste*, Actes du Colloque de Liège (septembre 1957), Bibliothèque de la Faculté de Philosophie et Lettres de l'Université de Liège, 150 (Paris, 1959), pp. 161-78.

[2]As, for example, Pierre Le Gentil, in *La Chanson de Roland*, Connaissance des Lettres, 43 (Paris 1955): "Il ne faut surtout pas demander à la langue et au

mètre dont notre auteur se servait une richesse, une variété et une souplesse qu'ils ne possédaient pas encore" (p. 171); "Tant d'austérité ne pouvait certes aller sans quelque raideur, ni tant de régularité sans quelque monotonie" (p. 172); "Le vers, avec ses deux accents privilégiés sur la quatrième et la dixième syllabes, progresse avec majesté, sans toutefois s'interdire ça et là une démarche plus souple" (p. 177). See, however, the studies of syntactic flexibility in Leopold Peeters, "Syntaxe et style dans la *Chanson de Roland*," *Revue des Langues romanes* 80 (1972), 345-54.

[3]Jean Rychner, *La chanson de geste: Essai sur l'art épique des jongleurs*, Publications Romanes et Françaises, 53 (Geneva and Lille, 1955), pp. 80-82, 107.

[4]For the laisse, see chapter 4 of *La chanson de geste*, "La structure strophique des chansons," pp. 68-125, esp. 69-107. For the verse, see pp. 168-70 of "Observations."

[5]*Le Moniage Rainouart I, publié d'après les manuscrits de l'Arsenal et de Boulogne*, ed. Gerald A. Bertin, Société des Anciens Textes Français (Paris, 1973).

[6]*Le Charroi de Nîmes: Chanson de geste du XIIᵉ siècle éditée d'après la rédaction AB avec introduction, notes et glossaire*, ed. Duncan McMillan, 2d ed., rev. and corr., Bibliothèque Française et Romane, Série B, 12 (Paris, 1978).

[7]*Les rédactions en vers de la "Prise d'Orange,"* ed. Claude Régnier (Paris, 1966).

[8]*Girart de Vienne par Bertrand de Bar-sur-Aube*, ed. Wolfgang Van Emden, Société des Anciens Textes Français (Paris, 1977).

[9]See, for a sample analysis of this question, "Linguistic Counterpoint in *Roland*, XII: Expressions of Parallel Alignment in *Langue* and in *Parole* and the Place of Convention and of Construction in a Semantic Set," *Olifant* 8 (1980-81), 115-29.

[10]Pp. 403-404 in Michael Holland, "Rolandus *resurrectus*," in *Mélanges offerts à René Crozet* (Poitiers, 1966), pp. 397-418.

[11]We use Joseph Bédier's *La Chanson de Roland publiée d'après le manuscrit d'Oxford et traduit par J.B.*, édition définitive (Paris, 1937) and Yvan G. Lepage's *Les rédactions en vers du Couronnement de Louis*, Textes Littéraires Français, 261 (Paris and Geneva, 1978). In Ernest Langlois' *Le Couronnement de Louis: Chanson de geste du XIIᵉ siècle*, 2d ed., rev., Classiques Français du Moyen Age (Paris, 1968), the combat occupies laisses XX-XXVIII. Holland, "Rolandus *resurrectus*," pp. 405-07, points out the amplification of judicial combat in the *Chanson de Roland*.

[12]Holland, "Rolandus *resurrectus*," p. 412.

[13]Rychner, *Chanson de geste*, p. 72.

[14]Ibid., p. 78.

[15]On laisse-introductory devices see also pp. 43-47 of "Some Reflections on the Laisse and on Echo in the ThreeVersions of the *Prise d'Orange*," *Olifant* 3 (1975), 36-56.

[16]Barbara Schurfranz, "Strophic Structure versus Alternative Divisions in the *Prise d'Orange*: Laisses versus Similar and Parallel Scenes and the *Reprise bifurquée*," *Romance Philology* 33 (1979), 247-64.

[17]The verb includes an expansion of the grammatical category of person, the subject noun: *Rainuars vest*. The direct object too includes an expansion, the relative clause: *l'auberc qui fu mailliés*.

[18]The writer gives a rough breakdown of the phases of the first half of the poem as well as a rundown of the echoes of laisse I in "'Composite Laisse' and Echo as Organizing Principles: The Case of Laisse I of the *Charroi de Nîmes*," *Romance Philology* 37 (1983-84), 127-38. The breakdown is slightly more detailed than that of D. D. R. Owen, "Structural Artistry in the *Charroi de Nîmes*," *Forum for Modern Language Studies* 14 (1978), 47-60.

A *l'altre feiz*: Narrative and Structural Patterns in the *Chanson de Guillaume*

Barbara Schurfranz Moorman

Repetitions of various kinds are common to both the *chanson de geste* and traditional oral narrative. It is above all the unusually important role that repetition assumes in the *Chanson de Guillaume* (in particular the first 1980 lines, or *William 1*), which has prompted the feeling on the part of some critics that the poem resembles more closely a popular and/or orally transmitted work than does the *Chanson de Roland*, for example. This characteristic of the work is evident in at least two aspects of its style and structure and in one major principle of its narrative organization, all of which call for description, for an examination of their roles in the *William 1* and *2* respectively, and for an inquiry into what they may imply about the poem's development and meaning.

One of two dominant compositional devices used remarkably often in *William 1*, and much less so in *William 2*, is the set piece, a group of two or more lines repeated at least once in the poem, conveying the same idea each time, following one pattern (using most of the same narrative elements in much the same order, including at least three hemistichs of exact repetition, and lastly, ending on the same assonance each time it occurs).[1] I have dealt with these set pieces at greater length in another paper[2] and, thanks to Edward A. Heinemann, have, I hope, refined my definition of them and re-evaluated some. Nonetheless, my conclusion remains the same: that they are used far more often in *William 1* than in *William 2* and that those found in *1* do not carry over to *2*.

35

An example of such set pieces is the leader's urging of the secondary hero to fight beside him:

> "Trai vus ça, Girard, *devers mun destre poig.*
> Alum *ensemble*, si met *tun gunfanun*;
> *Si jo t'a, ne crem malveis engrun.*"
> *Il s'asemblerent, le jur furent barun,*
> *En la bataille dous reals cunpaignuns*;
> Paene gent mistrent en grant errur,
> *Lunsdi al vespre.*
> Dolent est le champ senz le cunte Willame.
> (vv. 465-74)[3]

Lines 1672-79 repeat the underlined portions of the above passage, but now William and Gui are involved rather than Vivien and Girard.[4]

The last of the *William 1* set pieces ends at line 1978. But if one relegates to a particular type of "ballad" sequence the continuing exchange between William and Gui (beginning with the latter's first appearance, and several segments of which end with the words "cors as d'enfant e raison as de ber," then the last of the *William 1* set pieces ends at v. 1731 ("le soleil raed . . ."); the last *extensive* one ends at v. 1703, the conclusion of the description of the Saracens after William and his troops have arrived on the field.

Mildred K. Pope, Jean Jacques Salverda de Grave, Jean Rychner, and others have referred to the "ballad"-like nature of certain passages in the *William*, especially in *William 1*.[5] The inference (occasionally the argument) has been that certain dialogues and monologues are reminiscent of English or Scottish ballads and therefore reveal a close connection between the *William* and popular oral literature. Aside from the fact that origins and composition of this type of ballad are a hazy matter, no precise description of stylistic or structural features characterizing exclusively the "ballad" has been formulated, so that a comparison of parts of any medieval epic with the English (or more generally the European) ballad must itself remain somewhat vague.[6]

Rather than begin with what I confess is a much-needed definition, I should like to argue that the *William* contains a large number of passages that, with some justification, might be labelled "ballad"-type sequences, though some merit this description for different reasons than others do. All consist of a series of units (groups of lines) in which verbal and syntactic repetition are a prime structural factor. Four examples in *William 1* are the following:

1. Girard's exclamations as he throws down his armor and the narrator's description of the action (vv. 716-30);

36

2. Vivien's preface to his request that Girard carry a message to William (vv. 623-33);
3. the message itself, as Vivien presents it to Girard (vv. 635-88);
4. the message, as Girard delivers it to William (vv. 978-1002).

Each of these passages consists of a series of at least four groups of lines. Since each group is defined by its own assonance, I shall refer to them as laisses, whether or not the scribe indicated such a division. In each laisse at least two lines are parallel to their counterparts in the other laisses of the series, and the correspondences are emphasized by "consecutive repetition," especially "syntactic repetition" and "exact repetition" as defined by John S. Miletich.[7] They are also presented primarily as speech (dialogue or monologue), with each unit presented in the same manner as the preceding.

Although I would not claim that this suggests a "primitive" stanzaic structure involving laisses of equal numbers of lines, each line corresponding perfectly to a counterpart, I do believe (somewhat as Paul Zumthor does about certain *chansons de toile*)[8] that this structure is latent and, in Girard's exclamations, almost perfectly realized.

These passages not only display a particular form, but all have a similar effect on the movements of the narrative. While all involve a series of items (the introduction of each new item corresponding to a change of assonance), and while this in itself marks a slight internal progression, the dominant effect is to stop the forward motion of the story and to prolong the moment.

Instances of this pattern are less well defined elsewhere in the poem, but other series in the *William 1* are obviously of a related type. Despite their brevity, Tiebald's questions and the answers he receives (vv. 46-49, 252-55) should be included, as should the two-stanza dialogue in which William asks Guiborc why she is acting as his doorkeeper (vv. 1275-87), and Gui's lament on the battlefield over his weakness from hunger (vv. 1737-68). This last moment is prolonged throughout, which is true as well of the William-Guiborc dialogue. The four laisses constituting Gui's complaint do not appear at first glance to be parallel, the ordering of the elements within them changes, and at one point there is a three-line interruption. Nevertheless, the same device observed in other passages underlies their composition: that is, there are latent here four laisses with corresponding lines of verbal and syntactic repetition. Gui's speech is especially noteworthy because it may reveal a "transition" from a stanzaic series of correspondences to a less rigidly ordered grouping of laisses containing a repetitive pattern, but in which syntactic and exact repetition are no longer perfectly matched to stanzaic substructure.

37

There are other examples in *William 1* of what is at least potentially the same type of sequence but without any indication at all in these passages that the series of parallels was to be divided into laisses of different assonances. The meal that Guiborc serves to Girard (vv. 1045-57) and later to William (vv. 1404-30) is, again, a case of repetition: the same list is presented three times. But there are three different manners of presentation. The first time, Guiborc brings the meal (action related by the narrator):

> Ele li aportad un grant pain a tamis,
> E desur cel dous granz gastels rostiz,
> Si li aportad un grant poun rosti,
> Puis li aportad un grant mazelin de vin.
> (vv. 1407-10)

The second time, the hero consumes the meal (a different action related):

> Mangat Willame le pain a tamis,
> E en apres les dous gasteals rostiz;
> Trestuit mangat le grant braun porcin,
> E a dous traiz but un sester de vin,
> E tut mangad les dous gasteals rostiz.
> (vv. 1412-18)

And the third time, Guiborc comments on the hero's appetite:

> . . . .
> Qui mangue un grant pain a tamis,
> E pur ço ne laisse les dous gasteals rostiz,
> E tut mangue un grant braun porcin,
> E en aproef un grant poun rosti,
> E a dous traiz beit un sester de vin,
> Ben dure guere deit rendre a sus veisin.
> (vv. 1425-30)

The elements of repetition again correspond imperfectly, material without counterparts is included, and—it is worth emphasizing again—the repetitive groups are not defined by different assonances. Nor do repetitive groups of lines constitute separate laisses in the two death scenes of Girard (vv. 1146-63) and Guischard (vv. 1186-207). Each scene begins with at least three questions whose wording is repeated in the next group of lines—the negative responses to these questions. This is followed by a third, longer, group within which there are three lines whose content

38

corresponds to the three questions and answers, though very little verbal repetition is present. Similar to these two scenes is the beginning of the William-Gui dialogue when Gui first makes his appearance (1433-83). William's question, "Who will hold my land if I die?," is answered in the next group of lines (on the same assonance) by Gui, who uses similar words. In a third group, William angrily retorts that Gui will neither hold his land nor protect Guiborc. And in a fourth group, William accepts Gui as his heir. Repetition, not assonance, is here again the delineator of line groups.

In the passages discussed, the constant factor is "prolongation of the moment" through verbal and syntactic repetition that sets off one group of lines from another. Except for the fact that the repetitive groups do not in all instances constitute laisses, they could be termed *laisses similaires* or *laisses parallèles*.

While the disappearance after line 1978 of a repertoire of set pieces indicates a discrepancy between the techniques of *William 1* and *2*, and while the four- to six-part stanzaic ballad sequence is confined to lines 623-1002, the more loosely organized ballad-type exchange is characteristic of both parts of the poem. At least three passages in *William 2* are readily identifiable as related in style to the ballad sequences of *William 1*. On William's second return home, immediately after he has been forced to prove his identity, Guiborc asks him a series of questions concerning the young men who have not come back (vv. 2337-77). Despite the expansion of the third and fourth, five groups of syntactic repetition are present, the first three on the same assonance. At Laon, when William's relatives offer to come to his assistance (vv. 2541-72), what is potentially a strophic arrangement is blurred by the imperfect correspondence of elements and the use of the same assonance for two successive repetitive groups of the four.

The sequence in which Guiborc persuades Reneward to accept conventional arms (vv. 2831-45) is a convenient transition to a discussion of another type of sequence. Twice Reneward refuses arms; the third time he accepts. There is a definite progression in the narrative, and had the passage been longer, the technique of incremental repetition so often found in ballads might have been more obvious.[9] Suggestions of this technique are present in earlier passages already discussed: the meal sequences, the death of Girard, the death of Guischard, and Gui's argument with William over who will protect William's wife and land. In all these examples there is a progression leading to a reversal or conclusion.

This incremental repetition is most obvious in the *William* when the author deals not with a prolongation of the moment, but instead with a series of moments that repeat each other. The scene portraying the deaths of both Girard and Guischard illustrates that, in cases of the repeated moment (marked progression or incremental repetition), the structure may be not single consecutive laisses repeating each other, but *groups* of laisses repeating each other, so that instead of the pattern A, A^1, A^2, etc., we find ABC, $A^1B^1C^1$, $A^2B^2C^2$, etc. Not only are groups of laisses now involved, but it seems the rule rather than the exception for material extraneous to the basic progression to be incorporated into the series, as in Reneward's freeing of the captives (vv. 3024-156). This passage (composed on only three different assonances) consists of five repetitive units, although their elements are by no means in perfect order and correspondence. The progression is as follows: Bertrand asks to be freed, Reneward kills some Saracens and frees him. Bertrand thanks him and asks him to free the other prisoners. When Reneward has done this, Bertrand asks him to get them horses, and finally when this too is done, Bertrand asks Reneward to lead them all to William. Once the series is ended, a reversal has occurred as the number of heroes has increased steadily and the entire family is re-united. Similar progressions are evident in Gui's exchanges with William, where he is at first rejected, then put to several tests, and finally accepted as both wise and an excellent fighter (vv. 1433-83; 1615-71; 1961-79). Another rather lengthy passage of progressions (or of what seem intended as progressions) is Guiborc's testing of her returning spouse (vv. 2214-328). In all these sequences, divisions are marked by repetition, only rarely by assonance.

An examination of the ballad-type sequence thus brings to the fore-ground the problem of the composite laisse—one that depicts more than one *moment* (in Rychner's sense of the word) and which contains more than one group of lines introduced by a typical *vers d'intonation* and ending with a typical *vers de conclusion*.[10] This tendency is manifest very early in the poem. Rychner has noted three examples in *William 1*, but close examination of the repetitions and progressions of the ballad se-quences indicates there are more,[11] and certainly the composite laisse begins to predominate from around the point at which we find a prepon-derance of laisses, often consecutive, assonating in *-é* (particularly in *William 2*, from laisses 152-53 on, but also earlier, as in laisses 111-12).[12]

The best guides to structural or compositional divisions in the *William* are, first, the syntactic and verbal repetitions characterizing all the ballad passages, and, second, the progressions associated with incremental repe-tition. One might, therefore, approach the poem taking as a serious possibility that, while the laisse in many sections of it has very little force as an organizational or compositional element, this does not necessarily imply structural disintegration. Relaxing an overly intent pursuance of laisse boundaries and their significance, and turning instead to an examina-

40

tion of the types of parallel and repetition the *William* shares with ballads (and other forms of orally transmitted, popular narrative), the movement of certain passages becomes much clearer. As only one of several possible examples, let us mention the group of laisses 13-17, in which three times Tiebald looks in the direction of the enemy, describes what he sees, and receives from Vivien a comment on the situation. Two of these laisses Rychner mentions as composite. He accepts the notion of the intentionally composite laisse, but proposes no alternative to the "pure" laisse that the poet may have been using as an organizing device.

While I am not sure what this says about the relative chronology of stanzaic and anti-stanzaic sequences, I would maintain that the ballad-type pattern and not the laisse is the prevailing compositional unit of the *William* as it is preserved. In *William 1*, where both the set piece, the prolonging pattern, and the progressive sequence are present, the first two tend to rigidify the structure and to slow the rhythm in places, while the third gives the impression of a looser organization and more rapidly moving narrative. In *William 2* the notions of set piece and stanza are extremely weak and the ballad *pattern* prevails, with progression predominating over repetition, a fact that has led some critics to consider the second part of the poem more "narrative" and less well organized than the first.

To turn now to the articulation of the *William* in terms of purely narrative elements, the entire poem shares with folk and fairy tales the tendency to repeat the same episode, to multiply one character into several, and thus, even in the case of additions or continuations, to follow a pattern inherent in the tale.[13] The *William* narrative can be viewed as one story pattern repeated at least four times.[14] The pattern or episode is divisible into two parts: I) before the battle, and II) the battle.

Part I consists of the following elements:
  1. the setting: a leader in peacetime pursuits
  2. the disturbing factor: announcement of an attack or of a battle having occurred
  3. a question: arguments for and against participating in defense or retaliation (the leader at first opposes participation)
  4. the deciding factor: help is offered (troops are made available or the assistance of an important relative is offered)
  5. the preparations: one of the heroes dines, sleeps, awakens, arms, and sets out for the battlefield
  6. the emergence of the secondary hero: an unlikely hero makes himself known

41

Part II is made up of 10 elements:
1. the setting: a description of the enemy
2. a question: a difference of opinion (latent or actualized) between the leader and his men
3. danger from within: cowardice threatens to become an issue, and solidarity is menaced
4. help: the secondary hero appears on the field; solidarity is insured
5. successive losses and subsequent reduction to one, two, or three heroes
6. lack of food and drink hinders a hero's progress
7. an attempt (successful or not) to leave the field
8. the leader (or a hero) is attacked
9. a hero is killed or defeated
10. the report of the battle: news (involving a need for reinforcements) is carried from the field.

Only the final episode will be a victory, and then the progressions (successive losses and reduction to three or fewer heroes) will be reversed.[15]

In the fourth episode, beginning with William's second return home (the return from Larchamp to Orange) there are three variations on the Part I pattern before the author introduces Part II:

1. William and Guiborc at Orange; William sets out for Laon;
2. William at court; William, his relatives, the army, and Reneward set out for Orange;
3. William, Guiborc, and Reneward at Orange; William and his army set out for Larchamp.

In addition, the presentation of Part II in Episode 3 (the battle fought by William and Gui) shows a definite interruption of the Part II pattern, which elsewhere is fairly regular. Elements of the pattern are doubled here: the hero is attacked twice in precisely the same way at two different times; the hero is once victorious and once defeated; there are two instances of "leaving the field"; and there are two reductions to two heroes or one. Finally, the combat against Alderufe is entirely superfluous within this pattern at this point.

These observations aside, from a narrative point of view, the *William* (in its entirety) is uniform and consistent—far more so than can be indicated within the limits of this article. But I should like not to stop here with a description of the episode pattern, for it appears that the pattern, once perceived, suggests certain hypotheses about the poem's composition.

42

The sometimes mystifying correspondences between characters and events can perhaps be explained by this "replaying" of essentially the same story again and again. The author's ability to "get away" with abrupt transitions, with sudden unexplained appearances and disappearances of characters, with cryptic remarks and actions by some of these same characters may be ascribable to the fact that an underlying story pattern is strong enough to support such inconsistencies or apparent relaxing of the author's attention. The death scene of Guischard foreshadows the scene in which William is forced to leave Vivien's body behind; the queen at Laon is the exact reverse of Guiborc in the "question" segment of the episode's Part I; Gui's sudden appearance is not unlike Reneward's or even Girard's, and the resemblance between Gui and the young squire of the journey to Laon is not accidental; the heat of the sun at midday and lack of food or drink trouble every secondary hero; the progression involved in the Gui episode (from insolent ash-boy to wise young knight) is echoed by that in the Reneward episode (from uncouth pagan kitchen boy to victorious Christian knight of royal background), though it is clearer in the latter that we are faced with a folktale motif;[16] and hints of the same progression are discernible in Girard (with a reversal in Guischard); and so forth.

Turning to another implication of the episodic pattern, as already stated, this type of work can be added to at the beginning, the end, or even internally. Second, there is a point in the poem where we note some irregularities in the pattern. And finally, it seems not entirely unreasonable to wonder if the reversal we note in the Reneward battle—the freeing of the captives and the restoration of the original number of heroes—might well, at one time, have been the movement of the Gui episode. The many parallels between Gui and Reneward tend to confirm this hypothesis. An argument to the effect that, at one time, the second episode of the *William* was not the battle involving Girard and Guischard, but, instead, a battle involving several young relatives of William captured by the enemy, would allow for their release in a later episode by Gui, who, like Reneward, began as an unlikely hero and emerged finally as the liberator and avenger.In this context, "a l'altre feiz"[17] in the present episode 3 is a most appropriate remark, for the Saracens on their boats, about to depart, would be the same as those who had captured the prisoners and who will now be forced to relinquish them. While space will not permit a detailed argument along these lines, I believe a convincing one could be presented that would resolve many inconsistencies and contradictions.

Other studies (of vocabulary, of the refrain types, of proper names, of assonance, etc.) indicate that there were at least two authors of the *Chanson de Guillaume*. The analysis of set pieces, ballad-type patterns,

43

and the recurring episode supports this contention. There is, however, no clean-cut division at line 1980.[18] One abrupt change in technique occurs at line 1978 (the last of a body of set pieces); other changes occur gradually (v. 623, the first stanzaic ballad sequence of more than two laisses; v. 1002, the last well-ordered stanzaic ballad sequence of this type and the beginning of longer and more frequent composite laisses in -é; v. 1433, the incremental pattern becomes prevalent; v. 1863, irregularities in the episode pattern begin—to list only those problems discussed in this study).[19] But despite a lack of uniformity in some aspects of style and structure, the ballad pattern persists, and the same narrative elements continue to reappear in roughly the same order, with a ballad-type reversal near the end. Certainly we observe in the ballad pattern a compositional technique common to both authors and in the handling of the episode pattern a thorough comprehension on the continuator's part of the first author's narrative technique. And this writer believes both tendencies indicate the authors were at least as well grounded in folk narrative style as in that of a literary epic. It is this that makes the *William* appear unique among French epic poems, and I believe as well that the poem requires analysis from this point of view before it will cease to be a thorn in the side of students of the *chanson de geste*.

Notes

[1] What John S. Miletich, "Elaborate Style in South Slavic Oral Narrative and in Kačić Miošić's *Razgovor*," *American Contributions to the Eighth International Congress of Slavists* (Columbus, Ohio, 1978), 1:524, terms the "repetitive group" ("a combination of five or more immediately successive units which is repeated at least once at some point within a given text") is similar to the set piece. Miletich's findings indicate that this type of repetition is "second highest in frequency in the oral poems [and] much less frequent in the learned imitation."

[2] "Repetitions and the Divisions of the *Chanson de Guillaume*," paper read at SAMLA, Atlanta (Georgia), October 1979.

[3] All quotations from the poem are based on *La Chanson de Guillaume*, ed. Duncan McMillan, 1 (Paris, 1949).

[4] Other set pieces from *William 1* occur within these line boundaries:
12-18; 38-44
50-52; 168-70
54-58; 178-82; 906-08
68-69; 207-08
132-40 + 144-46; 1073-86; 1497-1508
194-95; 256-57
219-31; 1108-19

232-33; 1730-31
297-99; 1437-39
321-27; 441-47
374-81; 642-48
437-39; 786-88
465-71; 1672-78
533-34; 1168-69; 1298-99 (1168-71; 1298-1301)
709-13; 838-46
773-79; 1212-17
855-56; 1815-16
1007-08; 1328-29; 1474-75; 1621-22
1020-21; 1344-45
1042-58; 1401-19 + 1425-31
1065-73; 1484-97
1087-1107; 1562-64 + 1680-1703 (1100-01; 1234-35) (1090-91; 1341-43)
1233-37; (1353-55 + 1358)
1146-54; 1186-92 and 1158-59; 1194-95
1373-77; 1598-1603
1478-80; 1636-38; 1976-78
1526-29; 1640-43
1557-59; 1661-63
1824-28; 1829-34 (consecutive segments in a composite laisse)

[5]Jean Rychner, *La chanson de geste: Essai sur l'art épique des jongleurs*, Publications Romanes et Françaises, 53 (Geneva and Lille, 1955), p. 92; Mildred K. Pope, "Four Chansons de Geste: A Study in Old French Epic Versification," *Modern Language Review* 8 (1913), 364-66. Jean Jacques Salverda de Grave, "La chanson de geste et la ballade," in *Mélanges de philologie et d'histoire offerts à M. Antoine Thomas par ses élèves et ses amis* (Paris, 1927), pp. 389-94.

[6]This is a problem to which Miletich refers in "The South Slavic Bugarstica and the Spanish Romance: A New Approach to Typology," *International Journal of Slavic Linguistics and Poetics* 21, 4 (1975), 54-55, and one cannot argue with his comments elsewhere to the effect that more material known to be oral must be analyzed before we can draw sound conclusions about the degree to which written epic reflects or is part of an oral tradition.

[7]John S. Miletich, "Narrative Style in Spanish and Slavic Traditional Narrative Poetry: Implications for the Study of the Romance Epic," *Olifant* 2 (1974), 110-15.

[8]Paul Zumthor, "La chanson de Bele Aiglentine," in *Mélanges de linguistique, de philologie et de littérature offerts à Albert Henry* (Strasbourg, 1970), pp. 325-37.

[9]See Ruth Finnegan, *Oral Poetry, its Nature, Significance and Social Context* (Cambridge, 1977), p. 105: "Many forms of oral poetry make use to some degree of the same principle of parallelism in consecutive stanzas, a literary device which can build up successive layers of insight and meaning around the central theme and manifest a unity as well as an opportunity for development in the poem

itself. It is well known, for example, in English and Scottish ballads. Here the unfolding of a story often involves repetitions of a theme with slight variations, 'thereby,' as Karpeles puts it, 'creating a feeling of tension, and gradually leading to the dénouement.'. . . This type of parallelism is often known as 'incremental repetition' and is well illustrated in the famous ballad of *Lord Randall*.''

[10]Rychner, *La chanson de geste*, p. 166; Pope, "Four Chansons de Geste," p. 360.

[11]Rychner (*La chanson de geste*, p. 167) maintains that there are remarkably few composite laisses in the *William 1*; I would disagree. Using the criteria I am trying to establish in this discussion, the following laisses from *William 1* are composite: VI, XIII, XIV, XXVIII, XXXIII, XL, XLVII, LIX, LXIII, LXVa, LXIX, LXXXIII, LXXXV, XCII, XCIV, XCVI, CI, CIII, CIV, CVII, CXII, CXIV, CXVII, CXX.

[12]Only the refrains "Joesdi al vespre" and "Lunsdi al vespre," with their attendant decasyllables in $a \ldots e$ or $e \ldots e$ keep laisses CIV-CV and CX-CXI from being consecutive -é laisses.

[13]Fairy tale propensity for re-telling the same adventure, if not the same episode, is described by Max Lüthi in a discussion of "The Dragon Slayer," in *Once Upon a Time: On the Nature of Fairy Tales* (Bloomington, Ind., 1976), p. 53: "... the fairy tale cannot resist its innate propensity for repetition ... the almost word-for-word repetition conforms very closely to the rigid style of the fairy tale. We must not blame it on the clumsiness of the teller. It is the fairy tale's own innate stylistic urge for rigidity of form through repetition. ... The same changelessness is expressed in the inflexible repetitions of entire sentences, indeed whole sections, found in the tales of all peoples. . . ." See also Francis Lee Utley's introduction to this same work, p. 13: "Episodes are tripled, form is rigidified, and scenes isolated (as in the ballad's famous technique of 'leaping and lingering'); the tempo is retarded for suspense and speeded up for action; the whole tale betrays a feeling for 'the sacral, the stylized, and the abstract.'" Albert B. Lord, in *The Singer of Tales* (New York, 1978), pp. 200-01, makes related observations a propos of different material: "A glance at Parry 6580 ... will show how easy it is for the singer to continue to narrate about a hero or about action leading out of incidents that would perhaps in normal performance close a song. In other words, in dictating, a singer would very possibly continue narrating, let us say, about Beowulf, about a third encounter with a monster and about the hero's death, thus perhaps adding one song to another. . . . I believe that when the singer does add material it is because of an association that often goes deeper than association of one rescue with another, or of one monster-fight with another.''

[14]This story pattern has some kinship to the Action Patterns outlined by Lonnroth and Andersson; however I see only one, bipartite pattern in the *William*, with no others used concurrently or woven in with this basic one; see Lars Lonnroth, *Njals Saga: A Critical Approach* (Berkeley, 1976), Theodore M. Andersson, *The Icelandic Family Saga: An Analytic Reading* (Cambridge, Mass., 1967). As for the divisions of the poem, one cannot divide the work (as do Wathelet-Willem, Rychner, and Valtorta in their outlines) at line 1980 simply

46

because an earlier *William* may have ended near that point; the battle continues, and the fourth episode does not begin until William returns to Orange. See Rychner, *La chanson de geste*, pp. 40-42; Jeanne Wathelet-Willem, *Recherches sur la Chanson de Guillaume*, 1 (Paris, 1975), pp. 281-388; Bruna Valtorta, "La Chanson de Willelme," *Studi Romanzi* 28 (1939), 33-34. John D. Niles has already made the point that the battle involving William, Gui, Deramed, and Alderufe was intended to be taken as one single battle, in "Narrative Anomalies in *La Chanson de Willame*," *Viator* 9 (1978), 259-62.

[15]Viewed according to this pattern, the episodes of the *William* are the following:

Episode I,	Part I:	Laisses III-XII
	Part II:	Laisses XIII-LXXIIIb
Episode II,	Part I:	Laisses LXXIIIb-LXXVIII
	Part II:	Laisses LXXXVIII-XCV
Episode III,	Part I:	Laisses XCVI-CX
	Part II:	Laisses CX-CXL
Episode IV,	Part I:	Laisses CXL-CLXV
	Part II:	Laisses CLXVI-end

[16]Both John D. Niles and Gustav Adolf Beckmann have investigated different aspects of the folk tale motifs in the *William*. Niles, "Narrative Anomalies," p. 262, has explained the revival of Vivien as one of the fairy tale segments in Propp's study: "... the author of *La Chançun de Willame* pleased himself and his audience ... by shaping his tale in accord with a common folktale pattern...." Beckman, "Das Beispiel Renewart: Geschichte und Folklore als Inspirations-quellen der altfranzösischen Epik," *Romanistisches Jahrbuch* 22 (1971), 54-59, while maintaining that Reneward owes his place in the poem to a historical model, nonetheless outlines the many fairy tale elements incorporated into his story.

[17]"La bataille out vencue Deramé,
A l'altre feiz que Williame i fu al curb nies.
Si out pris l'eschec e les morz desarmez."
(vv. 1680-82)
The entire passage (a set piece) and its counterpart from Episode 2 consist of the following lines: 1680-1704 and 1083-1107.

[18]Wathelet-Willem, *Recherches*, p. 647, has already made this clear, but she posits one author for the entire present version, an author who took his inspiration from two separate poems; my suggestion is that a second author recomposed part of *William 1* and added a continuation, which itself included at least narrative elements from an original *William 1*.

[19]Even these line references are at best vague divisions; it is not easy to say exactly when a particular trait begins to dominate, though I believe that the introduction of Gui (v. 1433) with the loosely ordered ballad type of progressive sequence is a significant point.

On Structuring *Baudouin de Sebourc*

Larry S. Crist

Baudouin de Sebourc is an epic, of the sub-genre *chanson d'aventures*, of the French "third generation" of medieval epics, i.e., fourteenth century.[1] More precisely, it can right now be dated approximately in the sixth decade (1350-60).[2]

Its 25,770 verses include, as one might guess, a large number of episodes. In his secondary thesis, *Étude sur Baudouin de Sebourc, chanson de geste* (Paris, 1940), Edmond-René Labande takes twenty-seven pages for his *analyse* (pp. 23-50). The section headings in themselves, of course, do not necessarily show much of the structure (as system) of the poem; they serve mainly to break down the story into more easily handleable parts and give us some idea of what the central figures are. Nonetheless, since the resumé is the product of a scholar who had worked ten years on the poem, we could do worse than to take a second look at it. That is what we have done in the parentheses, expanding the titles somewhat so as to tell the main story for those unfamiliar with it.[3]

(1) La trahison de Gaufroi
   (Senechal of Ernoul de Nimegen, father of Baudouin; he turns the king over to the Saracens, then marries his "widow" and takes over the kingship).
   I,1 - II,289 / 1-1761 / / 1761 vv.
(2) Les aventures d'Eliénor
   (Saracen princess in love with Esmeré, eldest son of Ernoul whom she meets in her father's prison; she finds Esmeré in Nimegen,

49

interrupts his marriage, and sets voyagers out to the Holy Land).
II,290 - III,421 / 1762-2459 / / 698 vv.

(3) Exploits de jeunesse de Baudouin
(In Sebourc, taken in by the lord, and kept in ignorance of his ancestry; acquires *trente bastards*, plus one of the daughters of the lord of Sebourc).
III,422 - III,222 / 2460-3257 / / 801 vv.

(4) Les aventures d'Esmeré
(Divers and sundry; imprisoned by the Saracens).
III,1223 - VI,254 / 3258-5171 / / 1914 vv.

(5) L'enlèvement de Blanche
(Sister of Robert, count of Flanders; by Baudouin de Sebourc, who has become Robert's marshal).
VI,256 - VII,481 / 5172-6267 / / 1096 vv.

(6) La vie errante de Baudouin et de Blanche
VII,482 - VIII,1248 / 6268-7918 / / 1651 vv.

(7) Baudouin à Luzarches
([6-7] Baudouin taken prisoner by Gaufroi).
VIII,1249 - X,1023 / 7919-9820 / / 1902 vv.

(8) Les merveilleuses aventures de Baudouin en Orient
(Baudouin's ship sent by storm to Orient, where he does many things).
X,1024 - XIV,1046 / 9821-13689 / / 3869 vv.

(9) La mission de Baudouin
(He will go fetch help from the Lowlands for the imprisoned Esmeré).
XIV,1047 - XVII,20 / 13690-16531 / / 2842 vv.

(10) Le lion d'Abilant
(Gives Baudouin de Sebourc the Holy Blood; Baudouin de Sebourc does penance as a hermit).
XVII,21 - XVII,809 / 16532-17313 / / 782 vv.

(11) Les exploits du bâtard de Sebourc
(Wounds Gaufroi, delivers his captured relatives, Baudouin's brothers and uncle).
XVII,810 - XXI,95 / / 17314-20711 / / 3398 vv.

(12) Le comte de Flandre retrouve Baudouin
(Grants him Blanche, having learned who he is; tells him his true origins).
XXI,96 - XXII,1203 / 20712-22606 / / 1895 vv.

(13) Derniers crimes et châtiment de Gaufroi
(Finally defeated by Baudouin and hanged at Montfaucon).
XXIII,1 - XXIV,1128 / 22607-24703 / / 2097 vv.

(14) Baudouin retrouve son fils. Epilogue.
(Outremer, where the Bastard gains Edessa from a bad Christian. The whole family—Baldwin, sons, brothers—will go to conquer Rochebrune and Mecca with king Baldwin of Jerusalem).
XXIV,1129 - XXV,1042 / 24704-25770 / / 1067 vv.

Already, from this very rough outline and section titles, several structuring elements can be noted:
(1) misdeed → (13) misdeed punished, (but, (1) against Ernould de Beauvais, (13) by Ernoul's *youngest* son).
To this stands a corollary:
(1) Nimegen *lost* by Ernould de Beauvais → (13/14) (?). Nimegen *restored* to Ernould. If the pattern of loss/restoration, as linked with villainy (or misdeed)/villainy punished (Propp's base)[4] were central, the structurally essential character would be the eldest son, Esmeré, to whom, Ernoul once dead, the fief should belong. But this element is far from foregrounded.

What then is central? Not even the enfieffing of Baudouin de Sebourc, as a heir of Ernoul, for that never takes place in the poem; nor is the potential inheritance of Flanders, through Blanche, even mentioned.

The beginning of *Baudouin de Sebourc* tells us that the eponymic hero was eventually king of Nimegen, then of Jerusalem (vv. 80-83) (historically, Baudouin II du Bourg, 1118-31). Nothing of this is accomplished in the poem, which ends, as does the *Chevalier au Cygne et Godefroi de Bouillon*,[5] with a preparation for the expedition to Rochebrune and Mecca.

The action proper of *Baudouin de Sebourc* begins with a statement concerning the treacherous senechal Gaufroi's love for his lord's wife, Rose, and his desire to poison the king and kill his four sons at the first opportunity (vv. 175-76). He is defined by the narrator as "traïtrez, renoyez" (v. 96), even *before* we see him in thought or in action. He is essentially (vs. existentially) traitor, anti-subject (is main subject of the dysphoric narrative trajectory). With him proleptically as traitor, then, we "know"—by our competence as *connaisseurs* of stories—that he "must" be punished.

But the *occasion* for his realizing (carrying out) the treachery is more interesting, since it opens a larger dynamic: A messenger brings Ernoul the news that his brother, Baudouin de Beauvais, has been taken prisoner by Corborant d'Oliferne at the battle of Mount Civetot (historically, the final defeat of the People's Crusade on 21 October 1096); Godefroi de Bouillon otherwise occupied in leading a crusade, Ernoul should go help his brother captive in Oliferne.

51

The success of Godefroi's Crusade (the first), Godefroi's death, and the succession of Baudouin de Bouillon as first king of Jerusalem, all happen "off-narrative," and, if mentioned, are only referred to as *faits acquis*. And so is Corborant's conversion, recounted in the first cycle's branch 9, the *Chrétienté Corborant*, the last properly called a branch, coming just after the *Conquête de Jérusalem*.[6]

But it is the capture of Baudouin de Beauvais which makes Ernoul set out for the Holy Land, and allows Gaufroi to betray him to the Saracens. And this betrayal sets the events of the *Baudouin de Sebourc* proper in motion.

No mention is made of Baudouin de Beauvais's captivity subsequently. He simply appears (v. 17604),[7] having escaped from Corborant, who is thus not yet Christian at the time. Captured by Gaufroi, he is, with the other prisoners, delivered by the Bastard of Sebourc in the castle of Sebourc. Thus the first event, which sets off all the other events, is prediegetic, recounted to Ernoul by a messenger.

On several occasions, but with special emphasis at the end of the work (vv. 15110, 15726),[8] it is announced that Corborant will be killed during the Christian in-fighting in the Holy Land after Tancred has been hanged in Boulogne for having poisoned Godefroy, and that from this self-caused weakness and distress, Saladin will rise and the Christians will lose the Holy Land. Thus the last event promised is post-diegetic, will end the Christian kingdom, bring the cycle full turn, and be "caused" by Corborant:

BEGINNING of the cycle of the crusade properly speaking

Corborant *Sar.*-defeats, imprisons > Baudouin de Beauvais *Chr.*

-DEFEAT OF CHRISTIANS-

Godefroi *Chr.* ⋂Holy Land ⋃Sar.) } recounted
[in possession of] [separated from]
-SUCCESS OF CHRISTIANS-

then _____

Corborant *Chr.* < defeat, kill - other *Chr.*

(*Chr.*⋃) Holy Land (⋂Saladin) *Sar.* } promised
-DEFEAT OF CHRISTIANS-

END of cycle

52

The action of *Baudouin de Sebourc* takes place between these two enunciatory events, between one defeat of Christians, origin of the Crusade, and another defeat of the Christians by the Saracens, end of the Christian success (of the kingdom of Jerusalem) in the Holy Land. In this sense, *Baudouin de Sebourc* takes place outside of chronological (*i.e.*, "real historical") time.

As mentioned earlier, one would "expect" the kingdom wrongfully acquired by Gaufroi to be restored to its rightful heir. But the eldest son, Esmeré, is never shown installed in his rightful position as king of Nimegen. (We could presume that in the post-diegetic *histoire*, between the expedition to Rochebrune [inchoative in *Baudouin de Sebourc*], and Baudouin being king of Nimegen [promised by the narrator], Esmeré would indeed "normally" occupy that position. But in the actual state of our texts, that is mere speculation, and probably quite idle). But he is the centre of another cycle in the small sense of a *boucle*, one begun in the poem, but whose end is only promised:

- Eliénor, daughter of the Rouge Lion, Ernould of Nimegen's emprisoner, goes to Nimegen to seek Esmeré, with whom she fell in love on hearing Ernoul tell her about him while in the Rouge Lion's prison;
- She brings with her an object of /knowledge/ (*vulg.* piece of information), concerning Gaufroy's treachery, and arrives in Nimegen just as her yet unseen beloved is about to marry the lady of Ponthieu.
- Endowed with this /knowledge/, Esmeré has the /wanting/(will)
- and the familial /having-to/(duty) - to punish the traitor; his attempt causes a battle, during which he and his two brothers flee the town, while his mother Rose, his new beloved, Eliénor, and his former fiancée, the lady of Ponthieu, flee in the same boat towards Boulogne.
- The ever-ready storm drives their boat to Babylon; there the sultan weds the lady of Ponthieu, who has become Saracen for him. Thus a simple equilibrated change has been accomplished:

> Eliénor: *Sar.* — for marriage → *Chr.*
> Lady of Ponthieu: *Sar.* ← for marriage — *Chr.*

- From this union will come the great Saladin, whose retaking of Jerusalem—as noted a moment ago—will dysphorically end the cycle of the Crusade.

The "inverted content" (loss of inheritance/fief/ possession) manifested at the beginning of the story in Gaufroy's seizing of Nimegen is never explicitly "posed" at the end.[9] The explicit reversal (or posing: "setting to right") is in events referred to or promised, not shown. This frustration of expectations in the first case (underscored by the completed misdeed/misdeed punished sequence personed in Gaufroy), serves to emphasize what has the most of reversal(s) in it: the Crusade fortunes. There the "inverted content" recounted at the beginning of the story is inverted again at the end. In Bremond's terms, the story moves from a (prediegetic) situation of degradation, through an (extra-diegetic) process of improvement (amélioration), to a (post-diegetic) process of improvement (amélioration), to a (post-diegetic) process of degradation.[10]

I would postulate, very tentatively, that the effect produced by these three sequence-cycles serves two purposes: 1. It makes of *Baudouin de Sebourc* very much a cyclic entity, not an entity in itself, thus motivating its consumers to seek its "continuations"; 2. It emphasizes the need for restoring the historically principal loss, and thus would serve as propaganda for a new crusade, much talked about in the fourteenth century.

Notes

[1]*Li romans de Bauduin de Sebourc, IIIe Roy de Jhérusalem; poème du XIVe siècle, publié pour la première fois d'après les manuscrits de la Bibliothèque Royale*, ed. Louis-Napoléon Boca, 2 vols. (Valenciennes, 1841). A new critical edition by the present author with the collaboration of Robert Francis Cook, University of Virginia, is nearly finished.

[2]A very approximate dating. See Robert F. Cook and Larry S. Crist, *Le Deuxième Cycle de la Croisade: Deux études sur son développement. Les textes en vers* (Geneva, 1972), pp. 36 ff. and 146 ff. We have not yet progressed beyond the agnosticism professed there. Suzanne Duparc, in a long and careful review of our joint effort, "Les poèmes du 2e Cycle de la Croisade: Problèmes de composition et de chronologie," in *Revue d'Histoire des Textes* 9 (1979), 141-81, maintains that *Baudouin de Sebourc* was written after the *Chevalier au Cygne et Godefroi de Bouillon [CCGB]*, thus after 1355. This does not seriously conflict with our dating.

[3]The first set of numbers following each section show, first, the Boca edition numbers (Roman numeral for the *chant*, Arabic for the line within the *chants*), then the Crist-Cook edition line numbers, and, finally, the total of lines in each section.

[4]Vladimir Propp, *Morphology of the Folktale*, trans. Laurence Scott, 2d ed. (Austin, Tex., 1968), chap. 3: "The Functions of Dramatis Personae," pp. 25-65.

[5]Discussion in Crist, "Étude sur *Saladin*," in *Deux études*, pp. 94 ff.

[6]For a succinct description of the first Cycle of the Crusade, see our *Deux études*, pp. 80-81. A table of manuscripts and branches is also provided in Geoffrey M. Myers' introductory essay, "The Manuscripts of *The Cycle*," in *The Old French Crusade Cycle*, ed. Jan A. Nelson and Emanuel J. Mickel, Jr., 1, *La naissance du Chevalier au Cygne* (Birmingham, Ala., 1977), p. xvi.

[7]Boca, *Li romans*, pp. xviii, 32.

[8]Ibid., pp. xxv, 491, 1000.

[9]Reference is made here to A. Julien Greimas' canonical schema in "Pour une théorie de l'interprétation du récit mythique," in his *Du sens* (Paris, 1970), p. 198; originally in *Communications* no. 8 (1966), rpt. Coll. Points, 129 (Paris, 1981), p. 43.

[10]Claude Bremond, "La logique des possibles narratifs," in *Communications* no. 8 (1966), pp. 62 ff.; "Morphology of the French Folktale," *Semiotica* 2 (1970), 251 ff.; "Les rôles narratifs principaux," in *Logique du récit* (Paris, 1973), pp. 162 ff.

"Au commencement était l'école (de théologie)": A New Paradigm for the Study of the Old French Epic

J. L. Roland Bélanger

Debate on a possible school influence on the Old French epic has centered mainly on the use of rhetorical devices. Sarah Kay has recently well summarized the main contributions to this debate in her article, "The Nature of Rhetoric in the *chansons de geste*,"[1] concluding that the nature of the rhetoric of the schools and the rhetoric of the *chansons* is significantly different. She disclaims any other conclusion, but the reader is certainly left to infer that there is probably no school influence on the Old French epic, as ascertained by studies of style. This paper will approach school influence from a different angle, namely, that of religious data, and will propose for consideration a new paradigm, to use the word of Thomas S. Kuhn,[2] for the study of the French *chansons de geste* as "positive"[3] literature: "Au commencement était l'école." I certainly do not believe that all or even most of the elements found in these epics spring from school influences; not at all. Nevertheless, there are without a doubt numerous elements that clearly have been inspired by the schools, and such a paradigm will provide a useful focus for ordering a maze of presently discrete items.

A perusal of the bibliography on the *chansons* reveals almost no entries on school influence other than those concerning arts of rhetoric.

57

Yet, is it really preposterous to opine that—then as now—the authors, though not quoting *verbatim* ideas being daily discussed and even hotly debated in the schools, were certainly conditioned by these ideas and introduced them into their work in progress? The majority of Old French epics took their present shape in the twelfth century and the beginning of the thirteenth. This is precisely when theology underwent its greatest development.[4] Divergences of opinion flourished in this "open" twelfth century,[5] scholars took sides, and our authors, militantly or not, consciously or not, reflected contemporary theological themes and theses. The belief in school influence receives ample support from an investigation of the religious context of the Old French epic.[6]

Theological renewal, then as now, is predicated on Biblical study. The essential intellectual exercise of the twelfth century school was to read the "divina pagina" and to comment on it. Emile Lesne goes so far as to state: "Au XIIe siècle, la 'divina pagina' prend possession des écoles."[7] We are all familiar with the host of Biblical figures in our epics: Adam and Eve, Cain and Abel, David and Goliath, Samson, Solomon, Jonah, Jonas, Longinus recur frequently.[8] Entire passages even are freighted with Biblical lore, as, for instance, in the Oxford *Roland*:[9]

> 3096 Li emperere de sun cheval descent,
> Sur l'erbe verte se est culchet adenz,
> Turnet su vis vers le soleill levant,
> Recleimet Deu mult escordusement:
> 3100 "Veire Paterne, hoi cest jor me defend,
> Ki guaresis Jonas tut veirement
> De la baleine ki en sus cors l'aveit,
> E esparignas le rei de Niniven
> E Daniel del merveillus turment
> 3105 Enz en la fosse des leons o fut enz,
> Les .III. enfanz tut en un fou ardant!

For her pioneering treatise on *The Study of the Bible in the Middle Ages*,[10] Beryl Smalley was led to devote fully half of her text to the twelfth century, mainly to the brilliant school of Saint Victor in Paris with its shining lights Hugh (d. 1131), Richard (d. 1173), and Andrew (d. 1175), the latter the most notable Biblical scholar of the mid-twelfth century.[11] Paul Franklin Baum demonstrated years ago that Saint Victor was also responsible for the spread of the Judas legend late in the twelfth century.[12] School exegesis on the Bible found its way to the market-place. The anagogical concept of architectural ornamentation launched by Abbot Suger of Saint Denis in the middle of the twelfth century did much to popularize this Biblical knowledge.[13] Otto von Simson is of the opinion that Suger "very likely" derived his views, particularly his use of the stained-glass window as a visual "demonstration" of Dionysian theology, from his friend Hugh of Saint Victor.[14] Amelia Klenke made much of Suger's aesthetics in her study of Chrétien's *Perceval*,[15] especially of the Synagoga-Ecclesia *topos*.[16] In his *Exégèse médiévale*, Henri de Lubac devotes some two hundred fifty pages to expounding the four levels of meaning in the Bible: *historia, allegoria, tropologia*, and *anagogia*.[17] In any case, suffice it to register that contemporary artists transposed to page and stone the rich Biblical lore of the monastic and cathedral schools.

The pervasive influence of the schools is also seen in a study of the names and epithets of God. The six names most consistently used to refer to God in the Old French epics studied are *Damedieus, Créateur, Paterne* and *Père, Sire*, and *Trinité*.[18] The prominence of the first five would seem to have developed from the liturgy, the sixth from theological speculation. The reader has to be struck, for instance, by the fact that the only three uses of *Trinité* in the entire 3,554 verses of the *Chanson de Guillaume* all appear within 97 verses (vv. 802, 897, 899).[19] Is it that, at the precise moment of the composition of this passage, school debates on the Trinity were present in the poet's mind? There is no doubt that the Trinity was very well expounded in the twelfth century. Early in the century Rupert of Deutz (d. 1130) saw universal history as the unfolding of the Trinity[20]; later, the theological school of Saint Victor was at the height of its brilliance with Hugh of Saint Victor, whose essential work is a treatise on the Trinity.[21] Still later in the century, Peter Lombard devotes the entire First Book of his *Sententiae* to God, One and Triune.[22] Compositions on the Trinity proliferated,[23] and much of the investigation seems to have been linked to the wild disputations on universals.[24] No schoolman-author would have been unaware of such speculation.

Among the names of God that we found appearing somewhat later than others in the Old French epic are *roiamant, Sauveur, Souverain*, and *Saint-Esprit*;[25] the latter could very well have been inspired by the schools. The great Anselm of Canterbury (d. 1109) had formulated as early as the end of the eleventh century a new theory of world history which he saw as continual progress under the inspiration of the Holy Spirit.[26] But the thought of the Holy Spirit was injected into common consciousness more particularly by Joachim of Fiore (d. 1202) in the last third of the twelfth century. Joachim vehemently proclaimed the imminent coming of the third epoch of mankind, that of the Holy Spirit.[27] In any case, it does seem that at a given moment in the composition of the epics there was a greater consciousness than previously or subsequently of the Third Person of the Blessed Trinity. Such an increase in consciousness certainly stemmed from the schools and possibly from the apocalyptic Joachim of Fiore.

Not only do certain names and epithets of God fade in and fade out, for whatever reason, but a change of tone is also noticeable. There is initially a certain simplicity of thought and sentiment. God is first seen as *Damedieus, Createur, Paterne*; as *glorieux, vrai, fort, grand*; later, God is more frequently envisaged as *Fils de Marie, Jésus, Roi*; as *beau, doux, droiturier*.[28] God, simple and personal, is gradually "fractured" into multiple terms and traits as the schoolmen dissect and label. A great controversy on *Deus-Deitas* and on the axiom *Quidquid de Deo dicitur est Deus* rages in the twelfth century and into the thirteenth.[29] Abelard (d. 1142) defends the inaccessible mystery of God against the grammatical anthropomorphism of Ulger of Angers, who uses the rules of Donatus and Priscian to study the nature of God.[30] Gilbert de la Porrée (d. 1154) sides with Abelard; one of his major themes is the absolute simplicity of *Dieu-Un*.[31] The *Sententiae* of the School of Laon also abet this "negative theology."[32] Nonetheless, schoolmen continue their dissecting and dessicating, and popular Franciscan affectivity will soon be born to counter school intellectuality.

Thus, theodicy and the Bible give plausibility to school influence on the Old French epic. Such plausibility is strengthened when one looks at the data on the sacraments as practiced in these epics. To be baptized is expressed in the *Roland* as "to receive the law of Christians";[33] to confer Baptism is "to put in Christianity."[34] A few decades later, in *Hervis de Metz*, to baptize is "to regenerate,"[35] a new expression that indicates a deepening awareness of the theology of Baptism under the influence of the schools.[36]

The expression used for marriage is added indication of school debate. In *Garin le Loheren*, Pepin gives Duke Millon's daughter in marriage to Garin with the words, "Tenez ma niece, la bien faite Aeliz."[37] George H. Joyce has an interesting passage in his *Christian Marriage: An Historical and Doctrinal Study* which clarifies the use of "tenir" for marrying. Joyce informs us that this very word was crucial in Church legislation to determine the binding power of betrothal: Innocent III (1198-1216) declares the tie indissoluble if a man has promised to "hold" (tenere) the woman, dissoluble if he promised only to "marry" (ducere) her. The legislation stemmed from earlier situations (c. 1050 A.D.) when the Latin use was simply *habere*.[38]

Our epics also tell us that the married couple immediately consummated their marriage. The expression, "L'ore fu bone," signals the telescoping of time between the conception and the birth of children right after marriage. Two schools of thought existed in the twelfth century on the indissolubility of marriage. The one represented by Gratian (d. ca. 1160) taught that indissolubility depended on consummation; the other, headed by Peter Lombard (d. 1159) but based on Hugh of Saint Victor (d. 1141), maintained that it depended on validity of consent. Pope Alexander III himself (1159-1181) at one moment followed Gratian; later he followed Peter Lombard and the Paris school.[39] In the midst of such floating doctrine and with so much at stake, feudal knights took no chances and immediately consummated their marriage and begot children as proof certain. Marriage was totally bound up with inheritance, and no knight was taking any chances on losing out. On his very wedding night he engenders children:

> Premiere nuit qu'avoec li se coucha,
> L'ore fu bone; .i. fil engendré a.[40]

Epic data on symbolic reception of Holy Viaticum at the moment of death on the battlefield reinforces the data on baptism and marriage. When Begon is dying in *Garin le Loheren*,

> 10621 .III. fuelles d'erbe a pris entre ses piez,
> Si les conjure des trois vertus dou ciel,
> Por le cors Dieu les commence a mengier.

In *Raoul de Cambrai*,[41] the dying Bernier is served by the faithful Savari:

> 8441 .III. fuelles d'erbe maintenant li ronpi,
> Si le resut por *corpus Domini*,
> Ses .ij. mains jointes anvers le ciel tendi,
> Bati sa corpe et Dieu pria mercit:
> Li oel li torblent, la color li noircit,
> Li cors s'estent et l'arme s'en issi.[42]

The three blades of grass recall the rite in the Mass. As early as the ninth century it was the custom to put three pieces of the Consecrated Host into the casket, together with three grains of incense and some relics; though fought by canonists, the practice continued into the fourteenth century.[43] The meaning of these three parcels became a "classic question" in the twelfth century. Honorius of Autun, ubiquitous and ineluctable in all study of religion in this great century, opens his treatise on the Eucharist by discussing the *trifarie corpus Domini*, and he affirms that the parcels are the Body of Christ born of the Virgin Mary, the Body present on the altar, and the Mystical Body, viz., the Church.[44] This *trifarie corpus Domini* fascinated Yvo of Chartres, Hugh of Saint Victor, and Peter Lombard. Joseph de Ghellinck affirmed: "Il n'est guère de théologien, de canoniste

61

ou de liturgiste qui ne l'invoque d'une certaine façon.''[45] The priestly gesture of the dying knights, particularly in *Garin* and *Raoul*, which are dated in the last third of the twelfth century, necessarily triggers questions on school debates concerning the universal priesthood of all Christians. We will touch upon this shortly.

School influence in epic compositions is also easily discernible in matters that concern moral guilt and the sacrament of Penance. Jean Charles Payen has given us a solid study on this motif in medieval French literature: some one hundred pages deal with the epic.[46] Attention is called here only to a few matters not highlighted therein. In the Old French epics the word *péché* means at times 'mishap' or 'misfortune';[47] at others it stands clearly for sin.[48] This blurring of meaning, confounded in the *Roland*, in *Gormont et Isembart*, and in *La Chanson de Guillaume*, is progressively clarified in the schools of theology, and by the thirteenth century the *grand péché* of *Roland* 2370, *Garin* 14353, and *Raoul* 1305, for instance, has become the clearly defined 'péché mortel' of *Anseÿs* 7367 and *Hervis* 4926.[49]

Not only was sin debated in the schools, ''good intentions'' were as well, as in the passage in *Anseÿs de Metz* where Morant dies:

14060 Or muert li bers, Dieus li fasse pardon.
Envers Dieu ot moult bonne entencion.[50]

This matter of ''good intentions'' directly reflects a debate opened early in the twelfth century by Abelard and prolonged into the thirteenth. Abelard, reacting against Jewish legalism as well as against the discipline of the Penitentials, both of which were but very little concerned with inner dispositions, taught that what counts is the intention to do good or to do evil; guilt and merit spring from one's intentions.[51] He concluded that external acts have no intrinsic moral import, that they are in themselves indifferent.[52] His view was condemned at Soissons in 1131 and again at Sens in 1140. Hugh of Saint Victor, while accepting the important role of intention and consent, held that the external act is not negligible but rather adds effectively to our inner disposition.[53] Where Abelard is primarily a logician, Hugh is a psychologist. Peter Lombard maintains the general truth of Abelard's position but excludes acts intrinsically evil in themselves.[54] At the end of the twelfth century Alan of Lille, speaking for the Porretan school, counters the Lombardians and maintains the total indifference of all acts.[55] In any case, the isolated mention of ''good intentions'' in *Anseÿs*, though too terse to afford any conclusion as to Abelardian or Lombardian inspiration, does nonetheless reveal a clear school influence.[56]

The influence of theological schools is also seen in the manner of confessing. When Roland dies, "Durement en halt si recleimet sa culpe" (v. 2014). Confession definitely had to be made at the moment of death; Paul Anciaux has clearly demonstrated this at length.[57] And theologians of the twelfth century maintained that, in the absence of a cleric, confession was still required to a layman or, as in Roland's case, directly to God. This confession, furthermore, had to be made "en halt," out loud. Theologians of the twelfth century came to agree that the root evil in all sin, whether that of the angels or man, was pride. Consequently, public confession was necessary to atone for this pride,[58] whence in the Old French epic such expressions as "en halt" and "clamer sa colpe."

Of particular interest is the practice of confessing to one's fellowman in the absence of a priest. Bernier, dying, calls his faithful friend Savari:

> 8438 De ses peciés a lui confès se fit,
> Car d'autre prestre n'avoit il pas loisir.[59]

The expression, "no *other* priest," poses the question of contemporary theological thinking on the innate priesthood of every Christian, seen above under symbolical lay communion. Amédée Teetaert studied in detail the practice of confessing to a layman at the hour of death if there is no ordained priest available.[60] Originally based on a passage in the letter of James 5:16, "So confess your sins to one another, and pray for one another, and this will cure you,"[61] further authority was later found for it in Saint Augustine. The practice was firmly accepted in the eleventh century,[62] and was repeatedly upheld by twelfth century authors.[63]

Confession to one's fellowman leads to the last point of this paper: the debate about universal priesthood. The participation in and even actual administering of sacraments by the unordained Christian has been the subject of much debate both historically and in our own time.[64] It is most interesting to read that, in discussing confession to lay people, Yves Congar wrote: "Among theologians, Saint Thomas took an exceptionally favourable attitude to this practice and he expressly bracketed it with the administration of baptism: it appeared to him that in both cases necessity for salvation justified maximum facilities."[65] The daring twelfth century had gone further than Aquinas. In the penultimate laisse of the *Roland*, Charlemagne has broken the temporal power of the Saracens; he must now complete his task by breaking their spiritual power. This total victory will be symbolized by the baptism of the widowed Saracen queen, Bramimonde:

> 3975 Quant li empereres ad faite sa venjance,
> Sin apelat ses evesques de France,

> Cels de Baviere e icels d'Alemaigne:
> "En ma maisun ad une caitive franche.
> Tant ad oït e sermuns e essamples,
> 3980 Creire voelt Deu, chrestïentet demandet.
> Baptizez la, pur quei Deus en ait l'anme."
> Cil li respundent: "Or seit faite par marrenes,
> Asez cruiz e linees dames."
> As bainz ad Ais mult sunt granz les c...
> 3985 La baptizent la reïne d'Espaigne,
> Truvee li unt le num de Juliane.
> Chrestïene est par veire conoisance.

Three verses particularly of this laisse have puzzled editors and commentators since Francisque Michel's discovery of Digby 23 in the summer of 1835. The verses in question are

> 3982 Cil li respundent: "Or seit faite par marrenes,
> Asez cruiz e linees dames."
> As bainz ad Ais mult sunt granz les c...

Only the first of these is germane to our present discussion: "Or seit faite par marrenes." There has been unanimous agreement among scholars on the reading of this lesson.[66] Why is it, then, that all scholars—most recently, Gerard J. Brault —translate this as "Let her have godmothers"? It is because the Christian mindset against the role of women in the Church has been so strong since Lateran IV and more so since the Reformation and Vatican I that modern scholars simply cannot accept the fact that Charlemagne's bishops actually authorized women to administer the sacrament of baptism in ordinary circumstances. I believe that the man—or the woman—who wrote or at least inspired the end of the *Song of Roland* struck a coup for women's rights in the Church clearly as bold as, if not bolder than, Sister Theresa Kane's confrontation of Pope John Paul II in our day. Mindset has dictated reading the lesson of v. 3982 as, "Let her have godmothers"; philology dictates, "Let it be done by godmothers." And the bishops' own authority is adduced to support the role of women in the Church.[67] The coup does stagger the Roman Catholic mind, but it is there, unmistakably. In the twelfth century both Gratian and Peter Lombard strongly repeat prohibition against women ministers of baptism "unless there is urgent necessity."[68] Their very emphasis against baptism by women suggests an equally strong move for just that.[69] The marriage formula in our epics, "a moillier et a per," tersely states the case for equal rights.[70]

The great personalist thrust of the twelfth century naturally led to a clear stance for human rights and equal opportunity. The schools were in the forefront of this move. Maurice de Wulf has written: "Notwithstanding their various shades of difference, the theory of *respectus* advanced by Adelard of Bath in Laon and Paris, the doctrine of *status* taught by Walter of Mortagne, the so-called 'indifference-theory' and the 'collection-theory' re-echoed by the anonymous author of the *De Generibus et Speciebus*—all of these theories mentioned by John of Salisbury in his *Metalogicus* [II:17] agree in maintaining that universal essences could not exist, and that only the individual possesses real existence."[71] Wulf notes the convergence of law to abet philosophy: "Roman civil law and canon law and feudal law—the three forms of jurisprudence that developed so rapidly from the eleventh century onward—had come to a remarkable agreement regarding the existence of natural right; and in the name of this right, based on human nature, they had proclaimed the equality of all men."[72] Again, "Hence the human perfection which constitutes *human reality* is of the same kind in each person—king or subject, seigneur or vassal, master or servant, rich or poor, these all have a similar essence. The reality that constitutes the human person admits of no degrees. According to scholastic philosophy, a being is either man or not man."[73] Ironically, Wulf here makes no mention of the equality of man and woman, but it is most certainly supposed. And this equality, by the evidence of the *Roland*, led to a demand for or a recognition of woman's right to the ordained priesthood[74] or, at the very least, to administer the sacrament of baptism even in ordinary circumstances.

A few years ago in a colloquium on the thought and influence of Abelard in the twelfth century, Jean Charles Payen cautioned:

> Pour être sûr que cette influence se fût réellement exercée, il faudrait que l'on trouvât dans les oeuvres françaises ou occitanes des passages qui fussent des traductions ou des commentaires d'écrits abélardiens. Or, à ma connaissance, il n'y a pas de référence directe à l'abélardisme dans les ouvrages en langue vulgaire avant Jehan de Meung. Il n'est donc possible, en toute rigueur, que de procéder à des rapprochements dont l'exacte portée demeure hypothétique.[75]

This *caveat* applies to our present work. Although we have adduced considerable circumstantial evidence of the influence of schools of theology on the Old French epic, we have not yet been able to pinpoint precisely a particular quotation from a particular teacher. The ground has merely been broken. This study has aimed at raising the reader's consciousness to the undercurrents of many passages in the epics that would otherwise be passed over without sufficient attention and comprehension.

Notes

[1]*Zeitschrift für Romanische Philologie* 94 (1978), 305-20.

[2]Thomas S. Kuhn, *The Structure of Scientific Revolutions*, 2d ed., enl. (Chicago, 1970). Kuhn (p. 10) uses the word throughout his study. A "paradigm" must have two characteristics: be "sufficiently unprecedented to attract an enduring group of adherents," and be "sufficiently open-ended to leave all sorts of problems for the redefined group of practitioners to resolve."

[3]The term "positive" literature is used in the same sense by Amédée Teetaert in *La confession aux laïques dans l'Église latine depuis le VIIe jusqu'au XIVe siècle: Étude de théologie positive* (Bruges, 1926). This sense is literature as scientific composition rather than imaginative creation.

[4]This is the opinion, among many, of George H. Joyce, S.J., *Christian Marriage: An Historical and Doctrinal Study*, 2nd ed., rev. and enl. (London, 1948), p. 58; Paul Anciaux, *La théologie du sacrement de pénitence au XIIe siècle* (Louvain, 1949), pp. 76, n. 2, 608; and Henry Charles Lea, *A History of Auricular Confession and Indulgences in the Latin Church*, 1 (New York, 1896), pp. 136-37.

[5]The expression is Friedrich Heer's in *The Medieval World: Europe 1100-1350*, trans. Janet Sondheimer (New York, 1961), pp. 146, 215, 287. Victor Murray also uses it in his precise theological brief, *Abelard and St. Bernard: A Study in Twelfth Century 'Modernism'* (Manchester, England, 1967), p. 159: "Everything seems to have been treated as an open question...."

[6]I initiated such a study in my *Damedieus: The Religious Context of the French Epic*, vol. 1, *The Loherain Cycle viewed against other early French Epics*, Histoire des idées et critique littéraire, 152 (Paris and Geneva, 1975). The present article builds on some of the material therein.

[7]Émile Lesne, *Histoire de la propriété ecclésiastique en France* (Lille, 1940), p. 643.

[8]See, for example, Bélanger, *Damedieus*, pp. 248-52.

[9]The quotations of the *Roland* are taken from Gerard J. Brault, *The Song of Roland: An Analytical Edition*, 2 (University Park and London, 1978).

[10]Beryl Smalley, *The Study of the Bible in the Middle Ages* (Oxford, England, 1952). This presentation must now be supplemented by Henri de Lubac, S.J., *Exégèse médiévale: Les quatre sens de l'Écriture*, 2,1 (Paris, 1961). Hugh of St. Victor is extensively treated in Lubac's chapter 4 (pp. 287- 359), and the Victorine School in chapter 5 (pp. 361-435). Andrew occupies only pp. 361-67 here, no doubt so as not to needlessly repeat much of Smalley's entire chapter on him (pp. 112-95).

[11]"At St. Victor was Master Andrew, typical of all specialists and scholars,

but sharing in the definite, daring quality which distinguished St. Bernard, Abailard, Henry II and St. Thomas Becket. Andrew applied his Hebrew studies to Scripture as Abailard applied logic to the principles of faith; and he had fewer predecessors than Abailard. Master Andrew of St. Victor is so forgotten and yet so important a figure, his influence so decisive in the history of biblical studies, that it is not disproportionate to allot him a whole chapter, a sixth of our total space" (Smalley, p. xvii).

[12]Paul Franklin Baum, "The Medieval Legend of Judas Iscariot," *Publications of the Modern Language Association of America* 31 (1916), 485, 515.

[13]In his study of the origins of Gothic architecture, Otto von Simson, *The Gothic Cathedral* (Princeton, 1956), p. 22, defines the medieval sense of "anagogical" as "leading the mind from the world of appearances to the contemplation of the divine order." He writes (p. 108): "What concerned Suger was the façade as the entrance to his sanctuary, entrance in the physical but also in the symbolic sense. St.-Denis is the first church where the façade is designed to evoke the idea that the sanctuary is, in the words of the liturgy, the gate of heaven. It is the motif that the cathedrals were to take up thereafter. Here in St.-Denis, as we know from Suger's own testimony, it is inspired by the idea that Christian art be 'anagogical' in the Dionysian sense, a gateway leading the mind to ineffable truths."

[14]Simson, *The Gothic Cathedral*, p. 120.

[15]M. Amelia Klenke, "Chrétien de Troyes and the Abbot Suger," in Urban T. Holmes, Jr. and Sister M. Amelia Klenke, *Chrétien, Troyes, and the Grail* (Chapel Hill, N.C., 1959), pp. 108-22.

[16]Klenke (p. 117) uses the expression "tropological iconography" of Suger. She did not have available at that time (nor did Simson) the astounding precisions of terminology which Lubac, *Exégèse médiévale*, 1/2, subsequently gave researchers. A full sixty pages study the etymology, history, and meaning of the word *anagogia* (pp. 621-81). This "philological barbarism" (p. 621) means "leading higher" (p. 622), "from the visible to the invisible" (p. 623). Where *tropologia* leads to individual moral perfection, *analogia* leads to universal salvation. The noted scholar also finely distinguishes *anagogia* from *eschatologia* (pp. 621-81 passim), a distinction just hinted at in Simson (p. 119). The reader will recall that in our time Northrop Frye, *Anatomy of Criticism: Four Essays* (Princeton, 1957), 2d essay: "Ethical Crtiticism: Theory of Symbols," indicated levels of meaning similar to those of the twelfth century. Frye equates anagogy with "universal meaning" (p. 116). He also writes (p. 120): "Anagogically, then, poetry unites total ritual, or unlimited social action, with total dream, or unlimited individual thought." And further (p. 122): "The anagogic view of criticism thus leads to the conception of literature as existing in its own universe, no longer a commentary on life or reality, but containing life and reality in a system of verbal relationships."

[17]Lubac, *Exégèse médiévale*, 1,2:425-681.

[18]Bélanger, *Damedieus*, pp. 17-19.

[19]*La Chanson de Guillaume*, ed. Duncan McMillan, 2 vols. (Paris, 1949-50).

[20]Marie-Dominique Chenu, O.P., *La théologie au douzième siècle*, 2d ed. (Paris, 1966), p. 82.

[21]Joseph de Ghellinck, S.J., *L'essor de la littérature latine au XIIe siècle*, 2d ed. (Paris, 1955), p. 59: "... il laisse surtout un grand ouvrage théologique très original, souvent plus voisin des Grecs que des Latins, le *De Trinitate*, très apprécié par Vincent de Beauvais et Alexandre de Hales."

[22]See Joseph de Ghellinck, *Le mouvement théologique du XII[e]siècle. Sa préparation lointaine avant et autour de Pierre Lombard, ses rapports avec les initiatives des canonistes; études, recherches et documents*, 2d. ed., enl. (Bruges, 1948), p. 223. Ghellinck would go so far as to entitle book one *De deo uno et trino* (p. 380). Lombard's *Sententiae* have been dated with more and more certainty as around 1150-51 (see Ghellinck, *Le mouvement théologique*, p. 222).

[23]Maurice de Wulf, *Histoire de la philosophie médiévale*, 1, 6th ed., rev. (Louvain, 1934), notes the following: Boethius' *De Trinitate* at Chartres (p. 179), probable commentary of Thierry of Chartres on the *De Trinitate* (p. 181), Clarembaud of Arras' commentary on the *De Trinitate* (p. 186), Gautier of Mortagne's *Tractatus de sancta Trinitate* (p. 197), Abelard's *De unitate et trinitate divina* (p. 201), Gilbert de la Porrée's commentaries on the *De Trinitate* (p. 212), Richard of St. Victor's *De Trinitate* (p. 222), a *Liber de Trinitate* erroneously attributed to Alan of Lille (p. 228), and Anselm of Laon's *Sententiae* (p. 247-48).

[24]Wulf, *Philosophie médiévale*, 1:208.

[25]Bélanger, *Damedieus*, pp. 20-21.

[26]Heer, *The Medieval World*, trans. Sondheimer, p. 131.

[27]Chenu, *La théologie*, p. 82: "Mais cette vision théologique de l'économie prendra soudain, dans le dernier quart du siècle, par une extrapolation violante qu'opérera Joachim de Flore, une valeur historique considérable, matérialisant dans des espaces chronologiques les données bibliques primitives. On sait quelle séduisante et déconcertante élucubration amena Joachim et ses disciples à considérer l'âge de l'Esprit comme devant succéder prochainement à l'âge du Fils, décidément périmé et clos." See also Raymonde Foreville and Jean Rousset de Pina, *Du Premier Concile du Latran à l'avènement d'Innocent III (1123-1198)*, pt. 2 [=Augustin Fliche and Victor Martin, *Histoire de l'Église depuis les origines à nos jours*, 9] (Paris, 1953), p. 360.

[28]Bélanger, *Damedieus*, pp. 26-28.

[29]Chenu, *La théologie*, p. 105.

[30]Ibid., p. 104. This recalls R. Buckminster Fuller's modern thought: "For, to me, it seems, God is a verb, not a noun."

[31]Ibid., p. 105.

[32]Yves Lefèvre, *L'Elucidarium et les lucidaires* (Paris, 1954), p. 104 n. 2, uses the expression "théologienégative."

[33]"Si recevrez la lei de chrestïens" (v. 38); "Que recevez la lei de chrestïens" (v. 471).

[34]"En Bramidonie ad christïentet mise" (v. 3990).

[35] *Hervis von Metz: Vorgedicht der Lothringer Geste nach allen Handschriften*, ed. Edmund Stengel (Halle a. S., 1903), v. "Et en sains fons mon cors regenerer."

[36] I am convinced that the *Roland* expression "the law of Christians" also derives from the schools, but this remains to be confirmed.

[37] *Garin le Loheren, according to Ms. A. (Bibliothèque de l'Arsenal 2983)*, ed. Josephine E. Vallerie (Ann Arbor, Mich., 1947), v. 7128.

[38] Joyce, *Christian Marriage*, p. 89.

[39] Ibid., pp. 58-64 passim.

[40] *Garin le Loheren*, vv. 785-86; see also vv. 2840-41, 71881-82.

[41] Raoul *de Cambrai, chanson de geste du XIIᵉ siècle*, ed. Paul Meyer and Auguste Longnon (Paris, 1882).

[42] J. D. M. Ford, "'To Bite the Dust' and Symbolical Lay Communion," *Publications of the Modern Language Association of America* 20 (1905), 197-230, studied this matter of symbolic communion in detail. He noted the peculiarity that in French passages grass is always used and never earth. This article was supplemented by George L. Hamilton, "The Sources of Symbolical Lay Communion," *The Romanic Review* 4 (1913), 221-40. The only possible school influence Hamilton suggests (p. 226) is from Gregory the Great's commentary on Job 9:24 where "terra" is symbolic of "caro Christi." Hamilton's source is PL 75:882, to which must be added 883. Gregory's *Moralia in Job* were in fact greatly studied and disputed in the twelfth century, particularly at St. Victor in Paris; see Chenu, *La théologie*, p. 174: "Ses *Moralia in Job*, conçus tout entiers sur la base de la tropologie, suscitent, non sans l'appesantissement de la vulgarisation, une littérature abondante...."

[43] Émile Bertaud, "Dévotion eucharistique," in *Dictionnaire de spiritualité*, 4/2 (Paris, 1961), col. 1624.

[44] *Eucharistion, seu Liber de Corpore et Sanguine Domini*, PL 172:1250: "Trifarie itaque corpus Domini dicitur. Primo id quod de virgine incarnatum, ... Secundo: ... ex substantia panis et vini mysterio sacerdotum quotidie conficitur, ... Tertio: Corpus Domini tota Ecclesia praedicatur, quae de omnibus electis ut de multis membris in unum compaginatur."

[45] Ghellinck, "Eucharistie au XIIᵉ siècle en Occident," in *Dictionnaire de théologie catholique*, 5/2 (Paris, 1924), col. 1274.

[46] Jean Charles Payen, *Le motif du repentir dans la littérature française médiévale (des origines à 1230)*, Publications Romanes et Françaises 98 (Geneva, 1967). Pages 108-228 deal with the *chansons de geste*.

[47] *Roland*, v. 16: "Oëz, seignurs, quel pecchet nus encumbret"; *Roland*, v. 3646: "Morz est de doel, si cum pecchet l'encumbret"; *Gormont*, vv. 327, 414: "Ceo fut damages e pecchiés"; *Guillaume*, v. 2376: "'Deus,' dist la dame, 'quel duel et quel pechié!'"

[48] *Roland*, v. 1140: "Ben sunt asols e quites de lur pecchez"; *Roland*, v. 1882: "Si prierat tuz jurz por noz peccez"; *Gormont*, v. 573: "Deo ceo fist il

pechié et mal''; *Guillaume*, v. 2044: "Del mal que ai fait, des pecchez e dé lassetez!''

[49]*Roland*, v. 2370: "De mes pecchez, des granz e des menuz''; *Garin*, v. 14353: "Grant pechié faites, cant voz n'estez ici''; *Raoul*, v. 1305: "Grans pechiés faiz se nos lais essilier''; *Hervis*, v. 4926: "Qui que met guerre, ceu est pechiez mortez''; *Anseÿs*, v. 7367: "L'on ocit l'autre dont font pechié mortal.''

[50]*Anseÿs de Mes*, according to Ms. N *(Bibliothèque de l'Arsenal 3143): Text, published for the first time in its entirety, with an introduction*, ed. Herman J. Green (Paris, 1939).

[51]Robert Blomme, *La doctrine du péché dans les écoles théologiques de la première moitié du XIIe siècle* (Louvain, 1958), pp. 104, 108, 206, 217. For the precise meaning of *intentio*, see pp. 136-37.

[52]Odon Lottin, O.S.B., *Psychologie et morale aux XIIe et XIIIe siècle*, 4/3 (Louvain, 1954), pp. 311-12. The debate on moral intention from Abelard to Aquinas covers pp. 309-486.

[53]Blomme, *La doctrine du péché*, p. 315.

[54]Lottin, *Psychologie et morale*, p. 319.

[55]Ibid., pp. 320-21.

[56]Much of the foregoing is also treated in Payen's discussion of contritionism in Abelard (pp. 59-63), Saint Bernard (pp. 63-66), and Hugh of St. Victor (pp. 66-70).

[57]Anciaux, *Sacrement de pénitence*, pp. 164-253.

[58]Ibid., p. 193.

[59]*Raoul de Cambrai*, vv. 8438-39.

[60]Teetaert, *La confession aux laïques*.

[61]Alexander Jones, gen. ed., *The Jerusalem Bible* (Garden City, N.Y., 1968).

[62]E. Vacandard, "Confession du Ier au XIIIe siècle de l'Église latine," in *Dictionnaire de théologie catholique*, 3/1 (Paris, 1923), col. 877.

[63]Anciaux, *Sacrement de pénitence*, p. 34. There seemed to exist a divergence of opinion, however, on its necessity. Anciaux states (p. 607) that such a confession could be made at the hour of death. Others affirm that it was not simply permissible and advisable but obligatory; such was the opinion of the Pseudo-Augustine (ca. 1100), Peter Lombard, and Aquinas (cf. Vacandard, "Confession," col. 877-78). The texts we studied convey the impression that the knights felt obliged to confess to a layman at the moment of death if an ordained priest was not available.

[64]Most popularly by Hans Küng, in *The Church* (1967; rpt. Garden City, N.Y., 1976); see esp. pp. 473-95.

[65]Yves M. J. Congar, *Lay People in the Church*, trans. Donald Attwater (London, 1957), p. 218.

[66]Professor Brault informs me that this is so; I personally am not a specialist in paleography.

[67]Let it be recorded in passing that the sacerdotal character of Charlemagne is heightened by the fact that he absolves from sin even in the presence of Archbishop Turpin, cf. *Roland*, vv. 340, 3066.

[68]G. Bareille, "Baptême d'après les Pères grecs et latins," in *Dictionnaire de théologie catholique*, 2 (Paris, 1905), col. 188.

[69]This contention would have to be supported by a detailed history of women in the Medieval Church. This is evidently not possible within the present confines; a few brief notes will have to suffice. René Metz has given a very helpful summation of "Le statut de la femme en droit canonique médiéval," in *Recueils de la Société Jean Bodin pour l'histoire comparative des institutions*, 12, 2 (Brussels, 1962), 59-113. There has been, to our very day, a "perpetual contradiction" (p. 60) between the Christian New Testament egalitarian position (e.g., Gal. 3:26-28, Eph. 6:25-32, 1 Cor. 11:11-12) and the Jewish Old Testament and Early Church cultural position of "female" inferiority (e.g., 1 Cor. 11:7-10, 14:34-35, 1 Tim. 2:11-14). Paulinian ambivalence is continued in the Fathers of the Western Church and in medieval theologians and canonists (p. 69). Augustine accounts for 582 out of the 1200 patristic texts in the Decree of Gratian (p. 73 n. 2); though his *De Trinitate* unequivocally affirms the equality of the sexes (p. 71), his other treatises support the inferiority of women, due to their weaker human nature (p. 72). "Anatomy is destiny," we would say today. Roman law, the Decree of Gratian, and the Code of Napoleon are the pernicious path to legal inferiority of woman (cf. Régine Pernoud, *La femme au temps des cathédrales* [Paris, 1980], pp. 19-20). While the twelfth-century debates are going on in the schools of theology, real society is experiencing a "feminist" irruption: "la courtoisie" is being promoted by the long-lived Eleanor of Aquitaine (1122-1204), "one of the greatest women Maecenases who ever lived" (Rita Lejeune, "La femme dans les littératures française et occitane du XIe au XIIIe siècle," *Cahiers de Civilisation médiévale* 20 [1977], 205). Eleanor appoints a woman head of the immense abbey of Fontevrault, then numbering some 5,000 souls, according to Abbot Suger (Pernoud, p. 131). We can only conclude that such a humanist society surely tried to change women's legal position in the Church as well. Newton's third law of motion is fully applicable here: "To every action there is always opposed an equal reaction" (Sears-Zemansky-Young, *University Physics*, 6th ed. [Reading, Mass., 1982], p. 23). The very vehemence of the prohibitions imply an equal insistence on participation. Michelle Augier's affirmation that "Il va de soi que nous n'aurons guère l'occasion de rencontrer dans ces oeuvres des controverses théologiques subtiles" ("A propos de quelques conversions féminines dans l'épopée française," *Mosaic* [1975], 98), appears too general a remark. While noting the "evident religious intention" in matters pertaining to Bramimonde (p. 102), Augier seems not to suspect any underlying feminist issue relating to canon law.

[70]Bélanger, *Damedieus*, pp. 94, 234-35.

[71]Wulf, *Philosophie médiévale*, 1:195-99, outlines these theories.

71

[72]Maurice de Wulf, *Philosophy and Civilization in the Middle Ages* (Princeton, 1922), p. 55.

[73]Ibid., p. 58.

[74]Congar, *Lay People in the Church*, pp. 120-36, discusses the Scriptural texts which indicate the royal priesthood of all Christians. The most important of these is 1 Pet 2:4f, 9: "He is the living stone, rejected by men but chosen by God and precious to him; set yourselves close to him so that you too, the holy priesthood that offers the spiritual sacrifice which Jesus Christ has made acceptable to God, may be living stones making a spiritual house.... But you are a chosen race, a royal priesthood, a consecrated nation, a people set apart to sing the praises of God who called you out of the darkness into his wonderful light." Other texts are Apoc. 1:5-6; 5:9-10; 20:6. Paul Dabin, S.J., *Le sacerdoce royal des fidèles* (Paris, 1950), has collated relevant texts on this subject from the birth of Christianity to our day. Of the texts given for the twelfth century, Abelard's is the only one which speaks of the role of women, but this role was to minister to Christ only, whereas men minister to the faithful (pp. 229-40). Furthermore, James E. Rea has given an excellent study on the royal priesthood in *The Common Priesthood of the Members of the Mystical Body* (Washington, D.C., 1957). He states (p. 144) that the "first great teacher of the doctrine of the common priesthood among the Fathers was St. Augustine." Pertinent passages in Augustine are from his *Enarrationes in Psalmos* and *De Civitate Dei*. The prominence of Augustine in the twelfth century allows one to believe his thoughts on the common priestood would also be known and discussed at that time; Hugh of St. Victor was, in fact, surnamed *secundus Augustinus*, see Philippe Delhaye, "Augustinisme," in *Dictionnaire des Lettres françaises: Le Moyen Age* (Paris, 1964), p. 87 c. Nevertheless, James E. Rea, *The Common Priesthood*, p. 171, notes that "the doctrine of the common priesthood as such does not enjoy a position of prominence in the writing of the early scholastics," and there was no documentation useful to our investigation. However, Rea does have an interesting quotation from Peter Damian (d. 1072) concerning women (p. 163): "... in the very celebration of Mass, to the words, *Memento, Domine, famulorum famularumque tuarum*, is added, *pro quibus tibi offerimus, vel qui tibi offerunt hoc sacrificium laudis*. In these words it is clearly shown that sacrifice of praise is offered by all the faithful, not only by the men but also by the women, although it is seen to be specially offered by one priest." Cf. original text in PL 145:237-38.

[75]Jean Charles Payen, "La pensée d'Abélard et les textes romans du XIIe siècle," in *Pierre Abélard - Pierre le Vénérable: Les courants philosophiques, littéraires et artistiques en Occident au milieu du XIIe siècle* (Paris, 1975), p. 513.

L'hégémonie normande dans la *Chanson de Roland* et les *Gesta Tancredi*: De la Neustrie à la chrétienté, ou Turold est-il nationaliste?

†Jean Charles Payen

Que la *Chanson de Roland* exprime un certain sentiment national va de soi: les nombreuses mentions qu'elle fait de "France la Douce", ou encore la façon dont elle exalte la valeur des Francs, témoignent d'une conscience déjà vive de la communauté française, encore que cette communauté ne soit perçue que dans un cadre chevaleresque: ce sont les chevaliers de France dont le poète chante la gloire et non l'ensemble du peuple qui est bien évidemment absent des batailles et du récit. Mais sans revenir sur l'épineuse question des origines, force est de reconnaître que les éléments idéologiques de la chanson ne sont pas homogènes: elle garde la nostalgie des temps carolingiens; elle peint selon des modalités assez utopiques une chrétienté étroitement unie contre l'Islam et victorieuse; elle trace de la France capétienne une image un peu mouvante, tantôt réduite au seul Bassin Parisien, tantôt élargie jusqu'aux Pyrénées, quand elle n'englobe pas les Pays-Bas et la Bavière, en se souvenant alors des conquêtes de Charlemagne, qu'elle étend même, dans certains passages, à la Bretagne, à l'Angleterre et à l'Italie du Sud. Elle superpose dans ces épisodes l'image de Guillaume le Conquérant et de Robert Guiscard à celle de l'empereur à la barbe fleurie, et il ne fait aucun doute que l'appartenance

73

normande de Turold n'ait infléchi par moment le texte dans le sens d'un particularisme normand de type prénationaliste. Il existe un orgueil normand, souvent flatté par les chroniqueurs du Bâtard (comme Guillaume de Poitiers) ou par ceux qui ont relaté l'épopée méditerranéenne de Tancrède de Hauteville et de ses compagnons (et je pense ici à Guillaume de Pouilles)[1].

Cet orgueil, je le retrouve dans les *Gesta Tancredi* de Raoul de Caen: cette apologie concerne le petit-fils de Tancrède de Hauteville, Tancrède le Croisé, l'un des vainqueurs de Jérusalem en 1099, et elle a la particularité d'avoir été écrite du vivant même de son héros et peut-être sous sa dictée[2]. La comparaison entre la *Chanson de Roland* et les *Gesta Tancredi* n'est pas une entreprise arbitraire, et quelques indices permettent de penser que les deux oeuvres ont plus d'un point commun. L'une et l'autre traitent de la croisade; l'une et l'autre font apparaître le glissement de l'Histoire à la Légende[3]; et surtout l'une et l'autre mettent en oeuvre un nationalisme latent où se mêlent et l'éloge de la grandeur normande et l'admiration respectueuse des Francs: pour Raoul de Caen, devenu l'intime d'un prestigieux chevalier venu de Pouille et de Calabre, l'adversaire est le Sarrasin ou le Grec, mais aussi le Méridional, qu'il méprise, alors qu'il excepte de ce mépris tous les hommes de la Neustrie. C'est ce "nationalisme" déjà affirmé que je voudrais étudier ici, par rapport à l'idée de croisade, et sans occulter ce qui sépare une chronique encomiastique d'une chanson de geste. Comment se présente, à la lumière de ces deux ouvrages, le sentiment national normand ou français au début du XIIe siècle?

Dans la *Chanson de Roland*, les Francs sont les champions de la chrétienté militante[4]. Le droit est de leur côté, et le tort du côté des païens, qui vont être punis de leur haine de Dieu[5]. Charlemagne a pour mission constante de défendre les chrétiens en péril[6] et de promouvoir la vraie foi par les armes. Il rassemble dans ses armées des chevaliers venus de tout son Empire, mais de cette *ost* immense, les *Franceis de France* constituent le fer de lance, l'élément le plus dynamique, la voix collective la plus écoutée lors des conseils[7]. Les Normands, dans l'affaire, ne semblent pas avoir le pas sur eux. Ils forment la *quinte eschele* de l'expédition vengeresse (laisse CCXX, v. 3045); ils sont prestigieux et vaillants, et Richard le Vieux les dirige[8]; mais leur éloge est à peine plus marqué que celui des Bretons, des Poitevins et Auvergnats, des Frisons et Flamands ou des Bourguignons et Lorrains[9]. C'est ailleurs, et de façon plus discrète, que la *Chanson de Roland* glorifie leur grandeur: elle y parvient au prix d'une déformation de l'Histoire, lorsqu'elle superpose aux conquêtes de Charles l'expansion des Normands en Armorique, en Grande Bretagne, en

Méditerranée[10]. Tout se passe comme si le texte d'Oxford révélait des strates successives qui se référeraient tour à tour à l'Empire carolingien, à la France capétienne, à l'impérialisme normannique. Et ces strates sont particulièrement sensibles lorsque l'on examine les allusions géographiques du poème.

L'Empire de Charlemagne: où il apparaît de la façon la plus nette, c'est dans l'épisode de Baligant, lors de la description des *escheles* (laisses CCXVIII-CCXXV). La nature du récit (préparation d'une puissante bataille affrontant deux civilisations) appelle le recensement de cette "Grande Armée" aussi composite que celle de Napoléon en Russie. Mais peut-être joue aussi dans ce passage une réelle nostalgie de l'Europe impériale, un instant reconstituée lors des expéditions vers Jérusalem avant et après 1099. Dans cette foule de guerriers farouches, les *baruns de France* ont droit à la laisse ultime, la plus longue, la plus laudative (CCXXV). Quelle France? Je laisse la question en suspens et la traiterai plus loin. Ce qui m'importe à présent, c'est de relever la présence des Bavarois (laisse CCXVIII), des Allemands (laisse CCXIX) et des peuples que je viens de mentionner dans le précédent paragraphe: de ces peuples, seuls les Bretons n'ont pas participé aux guerres de Charlemagne. Et je note aussi que le texte ne dit rien ni des Gascons, ni des Provençaux, ni des Italiens, comme si la prouesse chevaleresque n'avait plus cours au-delà de l'Auvergne: argument *a silentio* en faveur d'une *superbia nordica* il est vrai démentie par la présence, à la tête de la septième "échelle", de deux vaillants vassaux dont l'un, Godselme (ou Gaucelm) porte un nom manifestement occitan et dont l'autre s'appelle Jozeran de Provence, "homme de confiance de l'Empereur au même titre que Naimes de Bavière"[11]. Un autre baron méridional est nommé au v. 3938: Willalme de Blaive, mais Blayes est un sanctuaire rolandien, où selon la légende avaient été enterrés les paladins morts à Roncevaux - et Blaye est ville française, où malgré le souvenir de Jaufré Rudel, jamais l'occitan n'a prévalu sur la langue d'oïl.

Dans cet empire de Charlemagne, une place privilégiée est conférée à "France la douce". Cette formulation est toutefois absente de la laisse LXVI, où les Français retrouvent la *Tere Majur*, la Terre des Aïeux, en apercevant la Gascogne du haut des Pyrénées. Plus généralement, aucune occurrence de la *Tere Majur* n'est associée au terme de France, comme si le poète ne faisait pas coïncider les deux notions. Aix-la-Chapelle, au contraire, est dès le vers 135 considérée comme une ville française ("En France, ad Ais, devez bien repairer"): à cet égard, le domaine carolingien semble bien se superposer au domaine royal, et l'axe wallon-mosan se révèle être le lieu d'une souveraineté qui s'étend à travers des provinces vassales jusqu'aux confins de l'Espagne.

Tout à coup apparaît dans cet espace une réminiscence de l'antique Neustrie: la laisse CX relate les signes qui accompagnent la mort des preux à Roncevaux. D'épouvantables orages ravagent le pays entre le Mont-Saint-Michel, Xanten[12], Besançon et Wissant (vv. 1428-29), en même temps que des tremblements de terre ébranlent les demeures. Ce passage se souvient des prodiges qui avaient marqué la Passion du Christ; mais ce qui avait alors frappé Jérusalem atteint "la *Francia* sur laquelle ont régné (plus ou moins effectivement) les derniers Carolingiens"[13]. Cette *Francia* occupe, en gros, tout le Bassin Parisien; elle englobe la Normandie, qui était neustrienne avant le traité de Saint-Clair-sur-Epte en 911, où Charles le Chauve abandonne à Rollon les territoires hauts-normands; elle avait constitué à partir de Chilpéric le plus puissant des royaumes francs à l'époque mérovingienne.

Reste à savoir qui sont les "Francs de France". Pour Gérard Moignet, il s'agit des seigneurs d'Ile-de-France[14]. Mais les choses ne sont pas si simples. Les termes *Francs* ou *Franceis* sont dans la *Chanson de Roland* énoncés sans être associés à une localisation précise, sauf dans un seul passage: encore une fois la description des *escheles*. Il s'agit de la laisse CCXXV dont je parlais tout à l'heure. Leur chef, Geoffroi d'Anjou, dont le nom évoque les ancêtres des Plantagenêts, n'a rien à voir avec la région parisienne! Et pourtant il porte l'oriflamme de Saint-Denis, et cette oriflamme s'appelle désormais *Monjoie*. Voilà qui fleure la France capé-tienne, celle qui s'étend de Laon à Orléans . . . Et pourtant, les Français de la *disme eschele* ne peuvent, comme Dieu, se définir que négativement: ce sont des gens qui ne sont ni Normands, ni Bretons, ni Poitevins, ni Auvergnats, ni Lorrains, ni Bourguignons, avec pour chef un Angevin, comme si la Neustrie avait été amputée de sa province normande, ou comme si le domaine royal s'étendait sur l'Anjou! La vérité, me semble-t-il, est tout simplement que le poète n'a pas fait de détails et ne s'est pas encombré de considérations politiques: il se contente de faire la part belle à ceux qui ne sont pas Normands dans cette communauté neustrienne dont on garde encore le souvenir au début du XIIe siècle, et paraît bien nommer *Franceis* ceux que Raoul de Caen appelle *Gallos*, les chevaliers d'entre Belgique et Loire qui n'appartiennent pas à la communauté normannique et que leur exceptionnelle valeur au combat met au-dessus de tout éloge.

Je parlais tout à l'heure de strate normande: ce n'est pas tant dans ce passage qu'elle est visible, mais lorsque Blancandrin évoque les conquêtes de Charlemagne en Italie du Sud et en Angleterre (vv. 370-73), ou lorsque Roland, se lamentant sur Durendal son épée, se remémore ses campagnes qui l'ont conduit en Bretagne, en Anjou, dans le Maine et jusqu'en Ecosse (comment ne pas penser à Guillaume le Conquérant?). Les vers 2322-34 de la laisse CLXXII impliquent indiscutablement que le poète projette sur

Charlemagne la figure du vainqueur de Hastings, alors que l'allusion faite par Blancandrin à l'expédition de Pouille et de Calabre peut être une simple réminiscence d'un *Girard de Vienne* antérieur à la *Chanson de Roland*: la légende selon laquelle Charlemagne serait allé guerroyer au sud des Apennins est en effet le sujet d'*Aspremont*, dont Girard est une des figures les plus marquantes. Mais la référence à un *Aspremont* ou à un *Girard de Vienne* perdus n'expliquent pas les vv. 372-73:

> Vers Angletere passat il la mer salse,
> Ad oes seint Perre en cunquist le chevage[15].

D'autre part, Moignet fait remarquer à juste titre que dans la *Chanson de Roland*, le personnage de Richard de Normandie est peut-être l'avatar poétique de Richard Ier, également appelé Richard le Vieux comme lui, et qui fut enterré en 996 à l'abbaye de Fécamp où fut moine un certain Turoldus ...[16]. Dès 1960, David Douglas avait avancé que la version d'Oxford s'était inspirée de la conquête de 1066[17]; mais on peut aller beaucoup plus loin et soutenir qu'au cours de la réécriture anglo-normande de la Chanson (par Turold?), celle-ci cesse d'être une glorification exclusive de la chevalerie franque, et fait la part belle à la *superbia normannica*, dans une apologie plus globale d'une chrétienté chevaleresque dont les barons de Neustrie sont les modèles. Nous nous retrouverions dès lors dans un climat idéologique très proche de celui qui baigne les *Gesta Tancredi* que je vais examiner maintenant.

Les *Gesta Tancredi* constituent une chronique en prose, entremêlée de longues parties en vers, composées par un clerc-chevalier nommé Raoul du vivant même de Tancrède, dont l'auteur était apparemment un intime. Raoul, né à Caen vers 1080, a fait ses études dans sa ville natale. L'écolâtre Arnulfus y fut l'un de ses maîtres, et c'est à ce personnage, devenu patriarche de Jérusalem, qu'il dédie son livre. Lui-même, comme Arnulfus, a sans doute définitivement quitté la Normandie. Il s'est voué corps et âme aux Normands venus d'Italie du Sud: avant de se rendre en Orient, il a combattu sous Boémond lors du siège de Durazzo, et sa fidélité au lignage de Tancrède de Hauteville et de Robert Guiscard a d'importantes conséquences, comme nous le verrons, sur sa façon de concevoir ce que j'appellerai sa ''normannité''. Quoi qu'il en soit, son dévouement fut payant: le Raoul qui devint gouverneur d'Acre vers 1110 est probablement notre chroniqueur, enfin récompensé après une longue série de loyaux services[18].

Ce qui m'intéresse présentement dans les *Gesta Tancredi* est l'expression assez ingénue d'un nationalisme normand qui se révèle avec netteté dans quelques passages: le chapitre VIII (message de Boémond à l'empereur Alexis), le chapitre XXI (première bataille avec les Turcs), le chapitre LXI (dénonçant le comportement des "Provençaux" lors du siège d'Antioche), le chapitre XCVIII (querelle entre Tancrède et Raimond de Saint-Gilles) et le chapitre CXIX qui relate les origines de cette querelle. Ces passages révèlent chez Raoul de Caen (et chez Tancrède) une hostilité fondamentale pour le monde méditerranéen, qu'il s'agisse des Grecs ou des Occitans, en même temps qu'une fierté normande qui n'exclut pas, bien au contraire, une vive estime des Francs de la France du Nord.

Dans le chapitre VIII, Boémond rappelle à l'empereur de Byzance ses conquêtes en Macédoine. Puis il ajoute (je cite la traduction de François Guizot):

> Autrefois en effet la Normandie lui [à Boémond] fournissait des cavaliers, la Lombardie des hommes de pied; les Normands allaient à la guerre pour remporter la victoire, les Lombards pour faire nombre: de ces deux peuples, l'un venait comme guerrier, l'autre comme serviteur. En outre, levés à prix d'argent, forcés par un édit, ils ne marchaient point volontairement, ils ne combattaient point par ardeur mais pour la gloire. Maintenant au contraire la race entière de la Gaule s'est levée et s'est associée dans sa marche toute l'Italie ... Tous ceux qui servent dans le camp du fils de Guiscard [Boémond] sont ardents, belliqueux et savent supporter les fatigues. Ajoutez-y d'autres hommes de la race de Guiscard, Tancrède et les deux frères Guillaume et Robert, dont le courage est pareil à celui des lions de Phénicie, et qui sont alliés à Boémond autant par les liens du sang que par leur ardeur à faire la guerre[19].

Le chapitre XXI (et les chapitres qui suivent) relatent le premier affrontement direct contre les Turcs. Il souligne la valeur des Normands, qui repoussent dans un premier temps l'adversaire[20]. Puis les chrétiens sont mis en déroute. Intervient alors le comte Robert de Normandie (chapitre XXII):

> Là enfin le fils de Guillaume, au sang royal, se rappelant ce qu'il est, son origine, et qui il combat, découvre sa tête, s'écrie à haute voix: *Normandie!* et gourmande en ces mots Boémond, son collègue [*sic*] et bien plus, son compagnon de fuite: "Holà, Boémond, pourquoi cette fuite? La Pouille est loin de nous, Otrante loin de nous, et loin de nous tout espoir d'atteindre aux confins d'une région latine. C'est ici qu'il faut demeurer; ici nous attend ou la glorieuse mort des vaincus, ou la glorieuse couronne des vainqueurs"[21].

Le chapitre LXI décrit les moeurs des Méridionaux, qui sont peu soigneux de leur personne, peu belliqueux et surtout habiles à trouver de la nourriture. Et Raoul de citer un dicton: "Les Français pour les combats, les Méridionaux pour les vivres"[22]. Le drame est que lors du siège d'Antioche, lesdits Méridionaux, ajoute notre chroniqueur, se livraient au marché noir, vendaient du chien pour du lièvre ou de l'âne pour du chevreau, et tuaient traîtreusement chevaux et mulets pour tirer profit de leur viande...

Je passe sur le chapitre XCVIII, où l'on voit Tancrède, avec quelques compagnons, entrer secrètement dans la même ville d'Antioche, désormais tenue par Raimond de Saint-Gilles, pour en expulser les Méridionaux et restituer la citadelle à Boémond. Et Raoul nous rappelle alors, dans le chapitre XCIX, comment la dispute entre Normands et Méridionaux avait éclaté lors du premier siège, précisément à propos de denrées mal partagées. Il apparaît que l'armée était le lieu d'un conflit ouvert entre gens du Nord et gens du Midi, auquel assistaient plus ou moins passifs les Bretons et les Impériaux que Raoul égratigne au passage parce que ce sont des barbares qui ne parlent pas les langues romanes.

> Les gens de Narbonne, les Auvergnats, les Gascons, et tous ceux de même race, tenaient pour les Provençaux [=Méridionaux]; le reste de la Gaule, et principalement les Normands, étaient prononcés pour les hommes de la Pouille. Quant aux Bretons, Suèves, Huns, Ruthènes et autres, leur langage barbare les protégeait même en dehors du camp[23].

Ce texte définit donc une solidarité normande, entre chevaliers d'Outre-Epte et d'Angleterre d'une part, et d'autre part les gens de Tancrède et de Boémond. Les *Galli* ou autres Neustriens ont spontanément pris le parti de ceux qui, malgré leurs origines nordiques, sont censés participer à une sorte de communauté franque. Français et Normands sont les champions les plus actifs de cette épopée vivante qu'est l'ost: *Gesta Dei per Francos*.

Guibert de Nogent ne distingue guère non plus les *Normanni* des *Galli* lorsqu'il célèbre les qualités militaires et chrétiennes des conquérants d'Antioche et de Jérusalem[24]. Guibert est un Français d'Ile-de-France, bien que Laon soit à la limite du parler picard. Mais l'oeuvre commune de la croisade fait oublier un instant un lourd contentieux. Guillaume de Poitiers relatant les démêlés de Guillaume le Bâtard avec Henri Ier n'est certes pas tendre avec le roi de France[25], pas plus qu'Orderic Vital n'épargne Philippe Ier soutenant contre son père le jeune Robert, fils du Conquérant[26]. Inversement, la littérature française ultérieure, lorsqu'elle émanera de poètes étrangers à la Normandie, ne sera pas tendre non plus à l'égard des Normands[27]. Mais pour l'instant, et dans le contexte de la chrétienté en armes contre l'Islam, les rancoeurs se sont tues, et les préjugés s'abolissent. L'union sacrée se réalise dans le cadre de la *Pax Dei*, mais cette paix de Dieu implique la suprématie franco-normande sur l'Occident en lutte pour la *Christianitas*.

Des éléments idéologiques communs rapprochent donc la *Chanson de Roland* sinon de toutes les chroniques de la première croisade (il faudrait, pour pouvoir l'affirmer, appliquer les précédentes analyses à Foucher de Chartres, à Robert le Moine et à maint autre texte), du moins des *Gesta Tancredi* qui ont cette particularité d'avoir été rédigés par un Normand à la gloire d'un autre Normand (et peut-être pour un public normand; disons que le dédicataire, le patriarche Arnulfus, est lui aussi originaire de Normandie). Sans revenir sur les problèmes posés par l'identité de Turold[28], il est à peu près indéniable que ce nom est lui aussi normand (et j'ai personnellement eu pour étudiants à l'Université de Caen plus d'un ou d'une Turoude ou autre Thoroude); la version d'Oxford est d'autre part copiée en anglo-normand, et je crois avoir tout à l'heure confirmé l'existence dans le poème de strates normanniques. Il reste que les *Gesta Tancredi* n'ont pas grand'chose à voir avec la chanson de geste et que la *Chanson de Roland* n'est pas un livre d'histoire composé à la gloire d'un chef encore vivant. Ceci contribue à expliquer qu'entre le prénationalisme normand de Raoul et l'orgueil normanno-franc du chef d'oeuvre épique se révèlent quelques différences, sur lesquelles je voudrais insister maintenant.

La *Chanson de Roland* met en avant la communauté des chevaliers français et n'évoque la grandeur normande que de manière indirecte, par une confusion sans doute volontaire entre les conquêtes de Charlemagne et celles des guerriers normands. Elle demeure donc une oeuvre plus française que normande, et l'on peut soutenir que lorsqu'elle consent à glorifier le monde normannique, il s'agit d'additions ou de remaniements. La version de Turold est ''normannophile'', mais non la matière originelle qu'elle refond. Le ou les premières *Chanson de Roland* perdues seraient bien originaires de la Neustrie non normande, voire (pourquoi pas?) du Nord-Est de la Neustrie où s'est diffusée aussi la *Vie de saint Alexis*[29]; donc en pleine aire carolingienne, mais aussi en contact avec l'Ile-de-France; et dans le contexte d'une réconciliation entre Capétiens et Carolingiens, mais cette hypothèse - plausible - appellerait bien d'autres travaux[30].

Les *Gesta Tancredi*, au contraire, font passer les Français au second plan. Estimés par Raoul et par son héros, les *Galli* sont les alliés efficaces des Normands, mais la première croisade est délibérément présentée ici comme une sorte d'entreprise à la fois familiale et nationale dont la direction de fait incombe au lignage de Tancrède l'aïeul. Les vrais meneurs d'hommes sont ici Tancrède le Croisé et son cousin Boémond. Quand, à partir du chapitre XIV, sont énumérés les chefs des assiégeants devant Nicée, la première place est donnée à Godefroi de Bouillon, qui est déjà de fait le commandant de l'ost, mais tout de suite après viennent Robert, comte de Normandie, et Boémond; Étienne de Blois, gendre de Guillaume II le Roux, qui règne alors sur l'Angleterre (lui-même sera roi d'Angleterre à partir de 1135) n'est dissocié d'eux que par une courte mention concernant Hugues le Grand, frère du roi de France Philippe Ier. Je note que cette liste des chefs témoigne d'une certaine objectivité: Raoul reproche à Robert de Normandie ses démesures[31] et sa coupable indulgence en matière de justice[32]. Et lorsqu'à la fin du chapitre XI, il décrit, *the last but not the least*, le brillant personnage de Raimond de Saint-Gilles, c'est pour faire de lui un éloge sans réticences, malgré les événements à venir et que Raoul connaît déjà, puisqu'il n'entreprend pas ses *Gesta* avant 1107 (date de sa venue en Orient), donc près de dix ans après le déclenchement de la querelle entre les Normands et les gens d'Occitanie[33].

Il n'en reste pas moins que Raoul perçoit la première croisade à travers les exploits de Tancrède, qui est le premier à franchir le fleuve Bardal (chap. IV), le premier à tuer un Turc lors de l'assaut contre Nicée (chap. XVI), le chevalier le plus actif devant Tarse (chap. XXXIV), etc. Ici, la prouesse individuelle prévaut sur l'ardeur collective, qu'elle galvanise ou fait renaître à l'heure de l'échec provisoire et du découragement. C'est que les *Gesta Tancredi* participent d'une littérature particulière: celle du panégyrique, de la louange encomiastique du prince guerrier qui se voit doter de tous les charismes. L'apologie du chef inspiré semble traditionnelle en milieu normand, du Conquérant selon Guillaume de Poitiers au Rollon que décrit Wace dans son *Roman de Rou*, et il ne fait pas de doute que cette pratique est d'origine scandinave: la fonction royale, chez les Nordiques, est plus sacralisée que dans le Midi; de même la dignité du chef de guerre ou celle de l'évêque. Celui qui commande et dont on fait l'éloge brille donc à la fois par sa *fortitudo* et par sa *sapientia* (et c'est ce que Raoul dit de Tancrède dès son chap. I)[34]; il est aussi un modèle de *pietas*, et sur ce point je citerai deux faits: la mauvaise conscience de Tancrède en face de la violence à laquelle est condamnée la chevalerie (d'où sa joie lorsque la guerre sainte rend cette violence licite)[35], et surtout cette scène étonnante des chapitres CXII et CXIII où on le voit méditer dans le Jardin des Oliviers sur Jérusalem à conquérir et sur la Passion de Jésus-Christ, puis s'entretenir avec un ermite qui lui prédit un destin plus prestigieux encore que celui, déjà grandiose, qu'il a vécu jusqu'alors. La *pietas* justifie que l'élu soit *felix*, favorisé par la Providence, et la chance de Tancrède éclate à chaque instant, lorsqu'il revient indemne d'épreuves redoutables[36].

La *Chanson de Roland* dissocie la *fortitudo* de Roland et la *sapientia* d'Olivier; elle fait de Charlemagne un souverain que Dieu guide par des songes[37]; mais elle n'insiste guère sur sa *pietas*: lorsque la prière de l'empereur a pour effet d'arrêter le cours du soleil, cette requête exorbitante est évoquée brièvement en trois vers qui décrivent l'orant prosterné, puis indiquent la demande[38]; il est vrai que les vers suivants révèlent la familiarité de Charles avec un ange qui lui dicte les ordres de Dieu[39]: Charles porte au moins en lui la *felicitas* de l'élu divin, et cette *felicitas* est particulièrement mise en oeuvre dans la laisse CCLXI, lorsque l'empereur est blessé par Baligant: ''Mais Deus ne volt qu'il seit mort ne vencut'' (v. 3609), et l'ange Gabriel descend l'exhorter: il porte alors le coup décisif et tranche la tête de l'émir (laisse CCLXII).

La *Chanson de Roland* est une ''chanson de Charlemagne'', et à cet égard, c'est sur la personne princière qu'elle concentre l'élection divine; mais elle est aussi une ''chanson des Francs'', c'est-à-dire l'épopée collective d'une nation. Le souverain y devient une sorte d'être mythique, incarnant le droit que la chrétienté porte en elle; mais il n'apparaît plus tout à fait comme une personne saisie comme Tancrède dans ses actions quotidiennes et, oserai-je le dire? dans son actualité. L'épopée transfère le pouvoir dans le domaine de l'utopie nostalgique; la chronique le décrit en termes de réalité légèrement déformée par l'hyperbole. Le passage de l'Histoire à la Légende ne s'est pas encore accompli dans les *Gesta Tancredi*, au contraire de ce qui se passe dans la *Chanson de Roland*, où l'Histoire est en quelque sorte occultée par la légendarisation.

C'est pourquoi le ''nationalisme'' de la *Chanson de Roland* est finalement plus utopique que celui des *Gesta Tancredi*. Malgré les strates anglo-normandes dont il faut bien constater l'existence dans le texte, la version d'Oxford fait prévaloir sur les particularismes régionaux un sens de l'unité nationale que l'on peut interpréter comme l'ébauche d'un patriotisme chevaleresque. Ce patriotisme est peut-être plus ''neustrien'' que Français au sens moderne de ce mot: la *Tere majur* commence au pied des Pyrénées, mais les Francs sont des hommes d'oïl. De cette communauté neustrienne, Raoul de Caen se souvient peut-être lorsqu'il évoque la solidarité des *Galli* et des *Normanni*, mais il est avant tout un homme de Normandie, au service d'un haut lignage normand. On peut donc parler chez lui d'une nation normande, d'ailleurs plus complexe qu'il n'y paraît d'abord.

Car Raoul a sans doute rompu ses attaches avec Caen; il s'est installé en Orient, il y fait carrière; il est dévoué aux Normands de Pouille et de Calabre; les textes que nous citions tout à l'heure glorifiaient ces "pieds noirs" avant la lettre établis définitivement en Méditerranée; la vieille Normandie du Nord, celle du comte Robert, est une terre d'injustice et de désordres; c'est la nouvelle Normandie, celle d'Italie et du Levant, qui devient le règne exemplaire de la *fortitudo*, de la *sapientia* et de la *pietas*.

Entre la *Chanson de Roland* et les *Gesta Tancredi*, les rapprochements ne sont pas fortuits et la comparaison n'est pas gratuite: même apologie de la chrétienté en armes contre l'Islam, et même conscience que dans ce combat, les meneurs d'hommes sont les chevaliers du Nord[40]. Mais chez Raoul de Caen, la prouesse n'est plus tant du côté des Francs que du côté des Normands de l'Italie méridionale, et le "nationalisme" normannique se teinte de racisme antiméditerranéen: à la haine du Sarrasin viennent s'ajouter la défiance à l'égard du Grec, le mépris du Lombard et même l'hostilité contre les gens des pays d'oc. Le Normand Roger II de Sicile sera certes beaucoup moins prévenu contre les cultures de l'Orient et du Midi lorsqu'il fera de Palerme un extraordinaire carrefour des civilisations; mais les *Gesta Tancredi* nous laissent entendre que cette tendance à l'assimilation a dû se heurter à bien des résistances. L'expérience française en Algérie a récemment mis en lumière les contradictions d'une implantation conquérante en territoire annexé de façon durable: on dénigre la population autochtone, on l'exploite, mais on collabore avec elle, et l'on finit par adopter partiellement ses manières de vivre. En même temps, le "pied noir" cultive un patriotisme qui le rattache, malgré la distance, à sa terre d'origine: de la même manière, les Normands expatriés gardaient une vive conscience de leur appartenance ethnique. Peut-être ont-ils rêvé d'une nouvelle Normandie, bastion de l'Occident contre le Grec et contre le Turc. Antioche à Boémond, et non à Raimond de Saint-Gilles, trop vite hellénisé, en Méditerranéen qu'il n'a jamais cessé d'être. La *Chanson de Roland*, malgré sa violence, échappe à de semblables exclusives. L'image qu'elle dessine de la France est plus conforme à la notion moderne de la patrie française: un pays propice à la coexistence harmonieuse des diverses provinces, dans le cadre d'une unité nationale supérieure à tous les particularismes locaux.

De toute façon, mon enquête m'a permis de souligner la relative modernité de deux grandes oeuvres, dont les accents souvent actuels n'ont rien perdu de leur fraîcheur.

Notes

[1] Voir *Guillaume de Pouille: La Geste de Robert Guiscard*, éd., trad., et commenté par Marguerite Mathieu, Istituto Siciliano di Studi Bizantini e Neoellenici, testi e documenti, 4 (Palermo, 1961). J'utiliserai l'édition de Gérard Moignet de la *Chanson de Roland* (Paris, 1969), et je renvoie aussi à Gerard J. Brault, *The Song of Roland: An Analytical Edition*, 2 vol. (University Park and London, 1978), dont l'édition dispose d'une excellente traduction anglaise en regard de l'édition, notes abondantes et bibliographie à jour. En ce qui concerne Raoul de Caen, j'utiliserai le tome III du *Recueil des Historiens des Croisades, publié par les soins de l'Académie Impériale des Inscriptions et Belles-Lettres, Historiens Occidentaux* (Paris, 1866), pp. 603-716, et la traduction de François Guizot, *Collection des mémoires relatifs à l'histoire de France, depuis la fondation de la monarchie française jusqu'au 13ᵉ siècle*, 23 (Paris, 1825), pp. 1-194. Sur l'idée de nation au moyen âge, je renvoie à Ferdinand Lot, "La naissance et le développement d'un sentiment national", dans *Recueil de travaux historiques*, 1 (Paris et Genève, 1968), pp. 312-21. Voir aussi Karl-Ferdinand Werner, "Les nations et le sentiment national dans l'Europe médiévale", *Revue historique* 244 (1970), 285-304, et Joachim Ehlers, "Karolingische Tradition und frühes Nationalbewusstsein in Frankreich", *Francia* 4 (1976), 213-35. Sur l'expansion normande et la conscience relative d'une "normannité" au début du XIIᵉ siècle, je citerai quelques travaux récents: David C. Douglas, *The Norman Fate* (Berkeley, 1976); Ralph H. C. Davis, *The Normans and their Myth* (Londres, 1976; sur le "mythe normand" chez Dudon de Saint-Quentin, Orderic Vital, etc.); John Le Patourel, *The Norman Empire* (Oxford, 1976); Jean Decarreaux, *Normands, papes et politique religieuse en Italie méridionale* (Paris, 1974).

[2] Voir mon article "Une légende épique en genèse: Les *Gesta Tancredi* de Raoul de Caen", in *La Chanson de geste et le mythe carolingien. Mélanges René Louis* (Saint-Père-sous-Vézelay, 1982), pp. 1051-62.

[3] Sur la définition de l'épopée comme glissement de l'Histoire à la légende, voir René Louis, *De l'Histoire à la Légende*, 2 vol. (Auxerre, 1947). Voir aussi l'excellent article de Jean-Marcel Paquette, "Épopée et roman: Continuité ou discontinuité", *Etudes littéraires* 4 (1971), 9-38.

[4] Cf. l'exhortation qu'adresse Turpin aux preux qui vont mourir (laisse LXXXIX) et plus particulièrement le v. 1129: "Chrestïentet aidez a sustenir!"

[5] Cf. le vers 1015 de la version d'Oxford: "Paien unt tort e chestïens unt dreit" et les vv. 8 et 9 de la laisse I (à propos de Marsile "ki Deu nen aimet", v. 7): "Mahumet sert e Apollin recleimet: / Nes poet guarder que mals ne l'i ateignet".

[6] Cf. la laisse ultime de la version d'Oxford (CCXCI) où saint Gabriel enjoint à l'empereur d'aller au secours du roi Vivien assiégé par les païens à Imphe.

[7] Les occurrences du mot *Franceis* se présentent surtout en début de vers, pour introduire un discours collectif (vv. 243, 278, 334, etc., formulation de type *Dient Franceis*).

[8]V. 3050. Le personnage est nommé dès le v. 171 parmi les conseillers de Charlemagne les plus proches du prince. Il est tué par Baligant v. 3470. Il porte le même surnom que Richard Ier, qui fut duc de Normandie de 943 à 996, et qui fut enterré à l'abbaye de Fécamp, "où un certain Turoldus fut moine avant de passer en Angleterre avec le Conquérant", écrit Gérard Moignet, *Chanson de Roland*, note de la p. 39. Sur la "normannité" de la *Chanson de Roland*, je renvoie à Ettore Li Gotti, *La "Chanson de Roland" e i Normanni*, Biblioteca del Leonardo, 40 (Florence, 1949) et à David C. Douglas, "The *Song of Roland* and the Norman Conquest of England", *French Studies* 14 (1960), 99-116. Sur la théorie des "strates" dans la *Chanson de Roland* (une strate anglo-normande se serait ajoutée à un original français), mes hypothèses ne sont pas contradictoires avec Robert A. Hall, "Linguistic Stratas in the *Chanson de Roland*", *Romance Philology* 13 (1959), 156-61.

[9]Laisses CCXXI à CCXXIV. Les vv. 3047-49 disent des Normands: "Armes unt beles e bons cevals curanz; / Ja pur murir cil n'erent recreanz. / Suz ciel n'ad gent ki plus poissent en camp". Les Bretons "chevalchent en guise de baron, / Peintes lur hanstes, fermez lur gunfanun" (vv. 3054-5); les Poitevins et Auvergnats "Chevals unt bons e les armes mult beles" (v. 3064); des Flamands et Frisons nous apprenons que "Ja devers els n'ert bataille guerpie" (v. 3071). Quant aux Lorrains et Bourguignons, leur éloge occupe quatre vers: "Helmes laciez e vestues lor bronies; / Espiez unt fort e les hanstes sunt curtes. / Si Arrabiz de venir ne demurent, / Cil les ferrunt, s'il a els s'abandunent" (vv. 3079-82). Ces quelques notations me semblent moins méliuratives que celles qui qualifient les Bavarois ("Suz cel n'ad gent que Carles ait plus chere, / Fors cels de France", vv. 3031-32) et les Allemands, qui comme les Normands "Ja por murir ne guerpirunt bataille" (v. 3041).

[10]Cf. les vers 371-73, où Blancandrin évoque devant Ganelon Charles "Ki cunquist Puille e trestute Calabre. / Vers Engletere passat il la mer salse, / Ad oes seint Perre en cunquist le chevage". Voir aussi la laisse CLXXII avec les plaintes de Roland sur Durendal, où le héros évoque ses conquêtes, dont l'Anjou, la Bretagne et le Maine (vv. 2322-24) - allusion aux campagnes du Conquérant avant Hastings? - et l'Angleterre et l'Écosse (vv. 2331-32) - mais que viennent faire ici la Pologne et l'Islande? Il faut faire sa part à la fantaisie du poète et rappeler d'autre part que la conquête de l'Italie du Sud par Charlemagne fait l'objet d'*Aspremont*, qui s'inspire sans doute d'un *Girard de Vienne* primitif. Reste que, dans ces passages, le souvenir de l'expansion normande n'est pas contestable, me semble-t-il, et j'y vois la marque propre de Turold.

[11]Moignet, *Chanson de Roland*, note p. 217.

[12]Eugène Ewig, "Xanten dans la *Chanson de Roland*", in *La Chanson de geste et le mythe carolingien*, pp. 481-90.

[13]René Louis, "La grande douleur pour la mort de Roland", *Cahiers de Civilisation Médiévale* 3 (1960), 62-67.

[14]Voir son index géographique, *Chanson de Roland*, p. 311, et son index des noms propres, p. 314.

[15]Vv. 372-73. Voir ci-dessus note 10, où ces vers sont cités.

[16]Voir ci-dessus note 8.

[17]Ibid.

[18]Voir l'introduction de l'édition citée ci-dessus note 1.

[19]P. 610: "Olim quippe ei milites Normannia, Longobardia pedites suggerebat: Normanni, qui vincerent, Longobardi, qui numerum augerent, in bella trahebantur. Horum populus alter belliger, alter venerat ministrator. (Ut autem ambo belligeri, tamen duo tantum, et de duobus pauci.) Ad haec conducti pretio, coacti edicto, non ultronei, non gloriae avidi militabant. Nunc contra gens totius Galliae excita, totam quoque Italiam veniens sociavit ... Omnes armati, omnes bellici, omnes laboriferi, quicumque Wiscardigenae castris famulantur. Adde Wiscardidas, Tancredum et fratres Willelmum Robertumque, Poenis leonibus audaciam similem, tam cognatione generis, quam belli studio Boamundi germanam".

[20]P. 621: "Quum igitur eo usque Normanni fugientibus institissent, densati cunei vires resumunt; et qui modo fugaverant, ipsi quoque in fugam sunt conversi. Interea Normanniae comes et Boamundus duas tantum, singuli suam, instruxerant acies; jamque gradatim alacres praelium inibant".

[21]P. 622: "Ibi denique regius sanguis Willelmides, quis, cujus stirpis, cui militet memor, verticem nudat, his increpat: "Eho, Boamunde, quorsum fuga? Longe Apulia, longe Hydrantum, longe spes omnis finium latinorum; hic standum, hic nos gloriosa manet aut poena victos, aut corona victores..."". Est-ce Guizot qui a inventé le cri de "Normandie"? (Je rappelle que les *Gesta Tancredi* ne nous ont été conservés que par un manuscrit unique.)

[22]P. 651: "Franci ad bella, Provinciales ad victualia".

[23]P. 676. La querelle affronte d'abord des gens de divers langages, et Raoul de Caen souligne cette opposition entre les chevaliers qui parlent français et ceux qui parlent occitan. La fin du texte que je cite d'après la traduction de François Guizot met aussi en lumière cet aspect linguistique du conflit. Voici l'original latin de ce texte: "Narbonenses, Arverni, Wascones, et hoc genus omne Provincialibus; Apulis vero relique Gallia, praesertim Normanni conspirabant; Britones, Suevos, Hunos, Rutenos et hujus modi linguae suae barbaries audita tuebatur. Et hoc quidem extra muros" (p. 676). Je note enfin l'expression *reliqua Gallia*, qui incorpore de fait le monde occitan (mais la Provence y est-elle comprise? Elle est alors terre d'Empire) à une communauté française qui coïncide avec la "Gaule chevelue" de César et avec l'ensemble des territoires qui doivent obédience à la monarchie capétienne. Et j'ajoute que ce texte semble exprimer la conscience d'une certaine "romanité": l'occitan, langue romane, est exclu de la *barbaries* propre au breton et aux langues germanique, hongroise et slave (si *Hunos* désigne les chevaliers de Hongrie et *Rutenos* ceux de Bohême et de Pologne).

[24]Les *Gesta Dei per Francos* figurent dans PL 156:679-838, et dans le t. III du *Recueil des Historiens des Croisades*, pp. 587-601 (juste avant les *Gesta Tancredi*); cf. la traduction de François Guizot, *Mémoires relatifs à l'histoire de France*, 9 (Paris, 1825), pp. 3-338. Voir Jacques Chaurand, "La conception de

l'Histoire de Guibert de Nogent'', *Cahiers de Civilisation Médiévalee* 8 (1965), 381-96.

[25]Voir Guillaume de Poitiers, *Gesta Guillelmi ducis*, éd. Raymonde Foreville (Paris, 1952), pp. 29, 65-69. Henri Ier a suscité contre Guillaume, vassal indiscipliné dont l'expansion l'inquiète, une coalition à laquelle participent les *principes universi . . . ex inimicis jam inimicissimi* à l'égard du duc normand. Et l'auteur ajoute (pp. 64-66): "Rex egerrime ferebat, et velut contumeliam suam diffiniebat quam maxime ulciscendam, cum imperatorem Romanum, quo majus potentiae sive dignitatis nomen in orbe terrarum aliud non est, amicum et socium haberet; provinciis multis praesideret potentibus, quarum domini aut rectores militiae suae essent administri; comitem Guillelmum suum nec amicum nec militem, sed hostem esse; Normanniam quae sub regibus Francorum egit ex antiquo, prope in regnum evectam; superiorum ejus comitum, quamquam ardua valuerint, nullum in haec ausa illatum''. Faut-il ajouter que Guillaume de Poitiers est probablement né à Lisieux et qu'il est l'intime du Conquérant comme Raoul de Caen est l'intime de Tancrède? On comprend d'autre part les motivations du roi: son vassal a conclu une alliance avec l'Empereur du Saint-Empire Henri III, et il cherche à transformer sa principauté territoriale en royaume!

[26]*Historia Ecclesiastica*, éd. Marjorie Chibnall, 3 (Oxford, 1972), p. 108. Robert Courteheuse s'est réfugié chez Philippe Ier, qui l'installe à Gerberoy près de Beauvais et lui donne des subsides. Mais c'est indirectement encourager le jeune prince dans sa rebellion et le corrompre par le fait que Gerberoy, lieu d'asile traditionnel, attire les *gregarii equites* qui sont souvent sans foi ni loi: "Hac igitur occasione multa mala pullularunt, et filii perditionis fraude vel vi contra inermes et innocuos prodierunt et innumeras iniquitates nequiter machinati sunt''. Est-ce alors que Robert commença à faire preuve de cette indulgence coupable à l'égard des malfaiteurs que Raoul de Caen flétrit dans un texte dont je citerai plus loin la teneur? (voir note 31).

[27]Par exemple le *Roman de la Rose*, où Guillaume de Lorris donne à Male Bouche une escorte de Normands (v. 3872 de l'éd. de Félix Lecoy, 3 vol., Paris, 1965-70), que Jean de Meun présente plus tard ivres (v. 21264). Guillaume de Digulleville - un Normand - s'en indigne dans son *Pèlerinage de la Vie Humaine* (texte dans Pierre-Yves Badel, *Le Roman de la Rose au XIVe siècle. Étude de la réception de l'oeuvre* [Genève, 1980], p. 369).

[28]Le plus récent article sur cette question est celui de Philip E. Bennett, ''Encore Turold dans la tapisserie de Bayeux'', *Annales de Normandie* 30 (1980), 3-13 (Turold serait bien le nain près du cheval, mais la cartouche peut aussi désigner le chevalier qui est à sa gauche). Quelle que soit l'identité de ce poète, je pense avec André Burger qu'il s'est montré assez respectueux de la tradition rolandienne avant le manuscrit d'Oxford; voir son livre *Turold, poète de la fidélité. Essai d'explication de la ''Chanson de Roland''* (Genève, 1977).

[29]Voir Ulrich Mölk, ''Die älteste lateinische Alexiusvita'', *Romanistisches Jahrbuch* 27 (1976), 273-315, et ''La *Chanson de saint Alexis* et le culte du saint en France aux XIe et XIIe siècles'', *Cahiers de Civilisation Médiévale* 21 (1978), 339-55. C'est dans ces régions qui vont du Soissonnais à la Wallonie que s'est

répandu le culte de saint Alexis avant qu'il n'atteigne les pays anglo-normands, où il a connu dans un deuxième temps un grand essor, expliquant peut-être les rédactions anglo-normandes de la *Chanson*.

[30]Cf. John F. Benton, "'Nostre Franceis n'unt talent de fuïr': The *Song of Roland* and the Enculturation of a Warrior Class", *Olifant* 6 (1978-79), 237-58. L'auteur y insiste (p. 245) sur le "nationalisme capétien" dans le poème et sur la "récupération" par la monarchie française de la nostalgie carolingienne.

[31]*Historiens Occidentaux*, chap. XV, p. 616: ". . . Genere, divitiis, facundia non secundus duci [sc. Guillaume le Conquérant], sed superior; par in his quae Caesaris sunt; quae Dei, minor: cujus pietas, largistasque valde fuissent mirabiles, sed quia in neutra modum tenuit, in utraque erravit". *Pietas* signifie ici, bien évidemment, 'pitié' et non 'piété'.

[32]Suite du texte cité dans la note précédente: "Siquidem misericordiam ejus immisericordem sensit Normannia, dum, eo consule, per impunitatem rapinarum, nec homini parceret, nec Deo licentia raptorum. Nam sicariis manibus, latronum gutturi, meochorum caudae salaci, eamdem quam suis se reverentiam debere consul arbitrabatur. Quapropter nullus ad eum vinctus in lacrymis trahebatur, quin solutus mutuas ab eo lacrymas continuo impetraret. Ideo, ut dixi, nullis sceleribus frenum, immo omnibus additum calcar ea tempestate Normannia quarebatur. Hujus autem pietatis soroculam eam fuisse patet largitatem, quae accipitrem sive canem argenti summa quantalibet comparabat; quum interim mensa consularis unicum haberet refugium rapina civium". La fin de ce passage, revenant sur les prodigalités du duc Robert, témoigne d'une injustice fiscale que Raoul de Caen connaît sans doute pour en avoir constaté le poids autour de lui quand il résidait encore dans sa ville natale.

[33]Le jugement initial de Raoul de Caen sur Raimond de Saint-Gilles tend cependant à rendre les Occitans responsables du fait que leur seigneur ne se soit pas plus distingué lors de la croisade: un bon prince desservi par un mauvais peuple, telle est la leçon de ce singuilier éloge (pp. 616-7): "Novissimus omnium Raimundus comes Sancti Aegidii emicat obsessor; novissimus, inquam, tempore, non divitiis, non potentia, non consilio, non militari multitudine; nam in his omnibus a primordio claruit inter primos, et mox aliorum quum effluxisset pecunia, hujus affluxerunt et praecelluerunt divitiae. Illa nominarum gens frugi, non prodiga, parcitati potius quam famae serviebat; exemploque territa alieno, non, ut Franci, in distrahendo, sed semper in augendo substantiam desudabat. Ergo suum comitem egere rerum sagax utilium, divinusque futuri populus non permisit: virum aequitatis cultorem, iniquitatis ultorem, virum ad timidos agnum, ad tumidos leonem". La dernière phrase manifeste le goût de Raoul de Caen pour l'antithèse et pour le calembour. Les aptitudes des Occitans à tirer des circonstances le plus grand profit économique possible ne sont pas vraiment condamnées ici, mais elles le seront un peu plus tard dans les *Gesta Tancredi* (voir ci-dessus note 21), et c'est à la lumière de ces développements ultérieurs qu'il faut, je pense, interpréter le présent énoncé.

[34]*Historiens Occidentaux*, p. 605: "Aduc adolescens juvenes agilitate armorum, morum gravitate senes transcendebat".

[35]Ibid. Voici ce texte: "Disputabat secum in dies animus prudens, eoque frequentior eum coquebat anxietas, quod militiae suae certamina praecepto videbat obviare dominico. Dominus quippe maxillam percussum et aliam jubet percussori praebere; militia vero saecularis, nec cognato sanguini parcere. Dominus tunicam auferenti dandam esse et penulam admonet; militiae necessitas ambobus spoliato reliqua quae supersunt esse auferenda urget. . . . At postquam Urbani papae sententia universis Christianorum gentilia expugnaturis peccatorum omnium remissionem ascripsit, tunc demum quasi sopiti prius experrecta est viri strenuitas, vires assumptae, oculi aperti, audacia geminata. Prius namque, ut praescriptum est, animus ejus in bivium secabatur, ambiguus utrius sequeretur vestigia, Evangelii, an mundi. Experientia vero armorum ad Christi obsequium revocata, super credibile virum accendit militandi duplicata occasio".

[36]Cf. l'éloge de Tancrède par le "peuple" (l'ensemble des chevaliers chrétiens) après son exploit sur le Bardal, où il a été le premier à traverser le fleuve sous les flèches des Grecs, puis le premier à le refranchir pour dégager l'arrière-garde attaquée par traîtrise (chap. 7, p. 610): "O ubi et quando et quis in filiis hominum per tibi, Tancredo? A quo tam remota segnities? Tam disjuncta quies? Tam aliena fortitudo? Tam elimata superbia? Tam elimata luxuria? Quis vocatus velocior, quis rogatus facilior, quis offensus placabilior? Felices tanto pignore atavi, tanto atavo posteri, tanto alumno Calabri, tanto sobole Normanni! Felices illi quibus tu contigisti gloria sua: at nos longe feliciores, quibus est pro muro audacia tua. Tua audacia adversus impugnatores nobis est clypeus, adversus expugnandos arcus et gladius. Si periculum antecedit, illuc praemitteris: item si sequitur, pone cedis. Benedictus Deus qui te reservavit praesidium plebi suae, et tu benedictus qui eam protegis in brachio virtutis tuae". Plus généralement, sur la *felicitas* du chef normand, voir Pierre Bouet, "La *felicitas* de Guillaume le Conquérant dans les *Gesta Guillelmi* de Guillaume de Poitiers", in *Proceedings of the Battle Conference on Anglo-Norman Studies* 4 (1981), pp. 37-52.

[37]Voir Herman Braet, *Le songe dans la chanson de geste au XIIe siècle*, Romanica Gandensia, 15 (Gand, 1975).

[38]Laisse CLXXIX, vv. 2449-51: "Culchet sei a tere, si priet Damnedeu / Que li soleilz facet pur lui arester, / La nuit targer et le jur demurer".

[39]Vv. 2454-57: "'Charle, chevalche, car tei ne falt clartet. / La flur de France as perdut, ço set Deus. / Venger te poez de la gent criminel.' / A icel mot est l'emperere muntet".

[40]Les rapprochements entre la *Chanson de Roland* et les *Gesta Tancredi* sont d'autant moins gratuits que Raoul de Caen connaît une version de la *Chanson de Roland* très proche de la version d'Oxford: André Burger, dans l'ouvrage signalé ci-dessus dans la note 28, cite (p. 59) ces deux vers de Raoul dans le chap. XXIX, lors de la bataille de Dorylée (il s'agit de Robert de Flandre et de Hugues de Vermandois): "Rollandum dicas Oliveriumque si comitum spectes hunc hasta hunc ense furentes". Burger rapproche ces deux vers du v. 1120 de la version d'Oxford: "Fier de ta lance et jo de Durendal!". Dans le même ouvrage, Burger rappelle (p. 60) d'autre part (ce qui souligne un peu plus l'aspect normanno-chrétien du ms. *O*) que le *chevage* de saint Pierre (v. 373, voir ci-dessus note 10)

avait été établi en Angleterre par Offa de Mercie en 787 et que Guillaume le Conquérant l'avait rétabli; il faisait sans doute l'objet d'un litige entre Rome et la monarchie anglo-normande autour de 1100. Enfin, en ce qui concerne la géographie du poème, Burger comprend (p. 70), comme déjà Hermann Suchier dans *Zeitschrift für romanische Philologie* 4 (1880), 583-84, *Seinz* (v. 1428, voir ci-dessus note 12) non comme la ville de Sens, mais comme *Ad Sanctos*, c'est-à-dire Xanten en Rhénanie, et il rappelle qu'Honorius d'Autun désigne encore, au début du XIIe siècle, dans son *De imagine mundi*, la Neustrie comme le pays compris entre Rhin et Loire. Voir aussi à ce sujet Eugène Ewig, ''Xanten dans la *Chanson de Roland*'', dans *La chanson de geste et le mythe carolingien. Mélanges René Louis*, s.e., 7 (Saint-Père-sous-Vézelay, 1982), pp. 481-90.

Forest and Voyage: Signs of *Sententia* in the *Entrée d'Espagne*

Nancy Bradley-Cromey

The *Entrée d'Espagne*, hybrid linguistically, hybrid in genre, is testimony to such phenomena as shifting aesthetic tastes, evolving ideals of heroism, and the enduring appeal of Rolandian *materia* in an early fourteenth-century North Italian setting. While it is often classified as a romance epic, little has been done to show how such a term actually works within the text, or to what extent the text extends, and escapes, definitive labelling. Our purpose here, in concentrating on two motifs in Part II, is to demonstrate how the poet's avowedly didactic intent is given form; then to reveal how the Paduan utilizes these and the hermit episode to complete the educative odyssey of his hero; and, finally, to suggest that his *sententia* involves a *correctio* of both epic and secular romance.[1]

The Paduan will conceal his identity, but is explicit regarding authorial intent. He opens with an eloquent dedication to the martyred Christ, whose death, he specifies, was meant to teach, and notes his concern with questions of doctrine (vv. 1-7).[2] Emphasizing that it is "la loy Deu" (v.23) that provides his theme, he means to demonstrate the societal and moral laws of faith which the Christian knight must obey to attain salvation. He adds: "Vos voil canter e dir por rime e por sentençe" (v. 9).

We shall need, briefly, to examine the term *sententia* in order to assess its applicability to the above statement. On the one hand, Priscian defined *sententia* as "oratio generalem pronuntiationem habens, hortans ad aliquam rem vel dehortans vel demonstrans qual sit aliquid."[3] Accordingly, Quintilian's *Grammaticus* included the composition of *sententiae* as an important step in the instruction of literary analysis. They were, typically, aphorisms, maxims, statements of popular wisdom with a claim to veracity. He suggest Aesop's fables as a model text.[4]

On the other hand, the term was extended in Antiquity to designate the "sense, meaning, signification, idea, notion" of a literary text, and was used in this way by Cicero and Lucretius.[5] It is this second, extended semantic field which appears in Hugh of St. Victor's three-part process of reading: one proceeds from *littera* through *sensus* to the *profundior intelligentia* of *sententia*, the deeper meaning accessible only via exposition and interpretation.[6] In an analysis to which we are indebted here, D. W. Robertson, Jr. traces the evolution of *sententia* and of *sentence*, noting that both imply an allegorical reading: "The result of allegorical interpretation might be either called *sens* or *sentence*" in the Middle Ages, with the latter term more prevalent in the fourteenth century when the *Entrée* was written. Further, while until the twelfth century *sentence* alluded exclusively to doctrinal content, its use was increasingly broadened and eventually it became a general term referring to the meaning or import of any text, whether sacred or profane.[7]

I hope to demonstrate here that the *Entrée*'s forest and voyage motifs are indeed signs of an intended *profundior intelligentia*. "Vos voil canter e dir ... por sentençe" undoubtedly anticipates the many maxims, proverbs, and rhetorical embellishments present in the text. We also believe that the poet intended a deeper reading which is twofold: the *Entrée*'s *sententia* involves not only the uses of heroism, but the uses of literature as well.

The Paduan perceives himself as recipient of one of a series of literary and military contracts, originating in dream-visions from Saint James. As originator of the first literary contract, the pilgrim saint appeared to Turpin, ordering him to write the account of the Spanish campaign; as originator of a military contract, the saint appeared to Charles, reminding him of an apparently forgotten promise to reconquer "paganized" Spain. Subsequently, Turpin appeared to the Paduan, with instructions to rewrite the Latin text of the campaign, accessible then only to "gient letree" (v. 49): he stipulates that the new text be in the form of an "estorie rimee" (v. 53), "A ce qe ele soit e leüe e cantée" (v. 56) before a broader public.

The present text, then, is both the product of a second literary contract (transmitted in the poet's vision of Turpin) and the narrative vehicle of its military counterpart (it tells the story of the campaign). The poet synthesizes his dual intention, stating that he has undertaken this task with Turpin's promise that "ma arme [my pen as my weapon in the quest for Christian victory] en seroit sempres secorue et aidee" (v. 54). We might note the *correctio* evident on the literary, as well as the military, axis: the extant *Entrée* corrects the difficult comprehensibility of the Latin model, while Charles is correcting his own procrastination in pursuing the reconquest of Spain.

In previous studies of the *Entrée*, the writer has examined the epic context of Part I: character presentation, themes, and episodes correspond generally to late medieval norms. For example, Roland is still the unconquered hero, though not unquestionably invincible: the three-day duel with Ferragu has rendered him aware of his human limitations. Charles has diminished dramatically in stature: the opening episodes depict him as defeatist, erratic, impulsive, even unethical. His authority is neither absolute nor unquestioned, as illustrated by the five initial conflicts/confrontations with Roland, in which Roland prevails, as well as in Naimon's chastizing "sermon" to him on the responsibilities of leadership. Part I culminates in Roland's unauthorized, independent conquest of Nobles, Charles's vindictive blow, and the hero's subsequent abandonment of the campaign for a seven-year sojourn in the Infidel Orient.[8]

Disorientation is perhaps the most fitting description of Roland's state as he rides away from Pamplona. Lost in a thick forest that will open and close Part II, Roland brings to mind both Arthurian and Dantean models. Like Chrétien's knights, his passage into the forest introduces a new phase of the hero's *aventures*. The forest is the border space of transition in the *Entrée*, marked by an absence of signs associated with epic or courtly society. It is also the transformational space for the hero himself, who must relinquish modes of behavior familiar to his epic functions and begin to learn the codes of this initially menacing new world. Just as the narrative is re-orienting itself from an epic to a romance plane, Roland's disorientation reflects the hero's hesitant transition from the known epic community to the yet unknown world before him. Having abandoned the world of the *chanson de geste*, Roland passes into a forest metaphorically representing the alienation, disorder, and despair which such loss arouses. The *planctus* he utters (vv. 11,145-71) stresses not the awareness of wrongdoing or readiness to repent, but, rather, loss of worldly, knightly status familiar to the *roman* in Béroul's Tristan, Chrétien's Yvain, and other *chevaliers errants*. "Or sui ci cum ermite" (v. 11, 461), Roland deplores, marking the hermit as a negative sign of exclusion from the collectivity of epic community. It will be with different resonance that the word recurs at the close of the *Entrée*. The initial situation thus complete, Roland must begin his voyage: "Seigne son vis, a Diex se commanda; . . . Mais vil se tient qe ne sa o il va" (vv. 11,494, 11,496).

That few voyages in medieval literature are gratuitous of meaning has been underscored by Jean Subrenat: "Mais du moins est-il incontestable que le voyage n'est jamais, dans une grande oeuvre littéraire du XIIᵉ ou du XIIIᵉ siècle, un événement purement fortuit ou gratuit. Il signifie toujours quelque chose; il a toujours ... un rôle à jouer, une valeur à révéler."⁹ The topoi of both act and agent share the Augustinian *homo viator* and Arthurian *chevalier errant* referents. Roland's main narrated voyages will take him from France to Spain, then to Mecca and Jerusalem, returning him finally to Spain. The voyages function literally and metaphorically to make and mark change: as an exciting force, displacement motivates the narration of the hero's *aventures*. Voyage is also education, the leading out and away, and it is progress toward destinations initially unknown ("Mais vil se tient qe ne sa o il va," v. 11,496), identification of which will externalize the voyage within. Thus from the familiar epic sites of Spain, Roland moves to two holy cities, the one pagan (Mecca), which will emerge from its own forest of darkness to conversion; the other, Jerusalem, the earthly city of God.

In order, then, to motivate a tropological reading in this shifting narrative axis, one must recast the Roland abandoning overlord and Christendom as indeed guilty of Charles's accusations of pride and treason. Accordingly, Roland will have violated Divine Order immanent in the lord-vassal bond: having fallen from grace, he is entering the dark pathless forests of spiritual perdition. The issue of *orgueil* in the *Chanson de Roland* has generated lengthy debate and numerous hypotheses; it may be that the multiplicity of interpretations itself, insofar as they are supported by the text, is evidence of intentional open-endedness. The *Entrée*'s *chanson de geste*, however, demonstrates, in an unequivocal manner where the epic ethic can lead if taken to its logical extremes. The Paduan avoids the possible ambiguity of his predecessors to show us that a vassal's heroic pride logically *will* come into conflict with overlord authority, and that the result will be a breakdown of the feudal relationship upon which the epic world order itself depends.

The *Entrée*'s Roland, rejected by the epic world (Charles vows to kill him, v. 11,116) and, in turn, rejecting it ("Mielz veul morir qe je ni li ensaigne / Se je riens li valloie en la gere d'Espagne," vv. 11,151-52), now sees that world as a *ficta disciplina*. His present task is to correct *his* vision, just as the narrative will correct its own. Thus we see Roland beginning his voyage with a prayer relating the fall of God's angels for their *superbia*, and a reminder that God gave explicit orders to Adam on the perils of violating the hierarchy of creature/Creator. This prayer, one of several marking the increased religious orientation of Part II, concludes with Roland's hope that "cest çamin me faites en tal gise fornir / Que mielz me soit a l'arme par le vos loi emplir" (vv. 11,761-2). Roland now becomes a pilgrim expiating mankind's first and most universal sin: in a

Christian context, the "heroism" which set him against Charles is no less grave than Ganelon's treason in the *Roland*, since both stand ultimately guilty of defiance of Divine Order. Jean Charles Payen, commenting on vassal revolt, states: "Quiconque en effet s'insurge, même à bon droit, contre un mauvais souverain, s'attaque moins à un homme indigne qu'à une fonction sainte."[10]

Roland now refers to the discourse of his epic behavior as "parole vaine" (v. 11,455). We find it pertinent (if also topical) that the "new" Roland of Part II will be a linguistic marvel, able to speak the language of whatever peoples he encounters in the East. The language of *superbia-orgueil* is no longer viable. What he must learn now is the new language of "la loy Deu," which the text will forge by means of an ordered process of *correctio*. The Paduan shows us that epic language and ethics, on the level of Christian morality, may be misused. While within a secular context they provided an acceptable system of discourse, they are now reviewed, recast, and their valorization radically altered. Augustine stipulated that things used as signs of other things may suggest a good or evil sense: thus, according to context, they may contain diverse, even contradictory meanings. "Thus one thing signifies another and still another in such a way that the second thing signified is contrary to the first, or entirely different."[11] The epic, then, is the old language, the old world: according to the Augustinian principle of contraries, Roland's actions throughout Part I are in need of correction.

Part I, culminating in the collapse of the community crusade mission and in the hero's pseudo-death as he is bloodied by Charles's blow, serves to demonstrate the faults and limitations of the genre and the values it represents. To the ethical *correctio*, we may add a metatextual one: the poet has written a *chanson de geste about* the genre as literary production, the correction of which will form the basis of Part II.

The next phase, then, is for Roland to move into the world of romance, the ethical and literary successor of the epic. In v. 367, the poet had already pronounced his negative judgment on Arthurian narrative, dismissed as "flabes d'Artu" as opposed to his own "gloriose cançons" (v. 366). We are thus aware that Roland's *entrée*, or sojourn, into the world of secular romance can only be part of a longer journey. His presence amidst amorous princesses and luxurious courts is doubly educational in intent: the hero, like the reader, must enter this world in order to appraise its flaws. Both must experience in order to judge. Thus, just as he did in Part I, the Paduan composes a *roman* in order to show the limitations of the genre: he integrates a Roland therein who will use this context to correct previous failings, but once having *become* the ideal hero appropriate to the genre, must reject it, too, as incomplete and unfulfilled.

Progress in the internal voyage is evident in the first major episode of Part II when Roland offers to defend the Princess Dionés in her resistance to be a matrimonial pawn. Roland declares, demonstrating the new language he is learning: "Home qi veult parlant estre honoré / Dou poi, dou trop doit estre amesuré" (vv. 12,282-83). Subsequently, commenting on his victory over the late would-be husband: "Ce senefie que ceschuns fait infance / Que contre droit montre orgoil ne bubance" (vv. 13,173-74). Progress is likewise evident in Roland's refusal of rewards in the opulent oriental courts, insisting that he must avoid the Icarus error, as well as criticism from "li saiges de gramaire" (v. 13,463). Once again, language is an issue: accepting reward would be to revert to the "parole vaine" of pride, now corrected both by laws of language and morality. Another character can now remark of Roland that he combines "Proesce et sens et nature atenpree" (v. 13,477). He has corrected, re-channelled his epic energies to recognize their origin and end, so that he now reinterprets his own conquest of Nobles from Charles's point of view and can attribute his victory and power to "L'aute Vertu qui li avoit donee" (v. 13,504).

The culmination of Roland's pilgrimage of expiation and reorientation, and the final shift of narrative axis, is in the hermit episode. As in most texts, the hermit has a didactic function: he is an ancient holy man named Sanson, easily suggesting a model of Christian militant asceticism. Jean-Pierre Perrot notes that the hermit functions as a presence on the knight's voyage, to stop the fallacious quest or adventure and to aid the knight to see truth.[12] The *Entrée*'s hermit fulfills each of these functions: further, a curious typological relationship with Roland is suggested by the "adventures" that led Sanson to forsake the world. Should we miss this, Roland asks him to narrate his tale, for "Le uns poroit de l'autre aucune profit traire" (v. 14,698). As a prideful youth, Sanson had abused paternal benevolence, and in a violent confrontation, murdered his father (Charles will claim that Roland's departure nearly caused his own death). Sanson retreated in shame into the forest, where for many years he has combined the strictest Christian asceticism with crusader zeal, vigorously slaying the many Saracen giants in the neighborhood. The pilgrim Roland, too, has refused most secular pleasures in the East, and while fighting within "pagan" armies, has never felled another Christian. A close bond is established between the two from the moment when Roland is able to take into his hands the hermit's reliquary cross, a sign of his own sanctity.[13] The two share at this point the solitary existence of the self-named exile, both seeking a perfection greater than the secular world, the world of epic and romance, can offer. The episode concludes with Sanson's revelation— and realization—of his own death and an angelic prophecy of Roland's destiny. The hero is told that he will embody the ideals of Christian chivalry for another seven years, then to die a martyr, betrayed by someone he trusts.

The voyage-forest motifs recur, with different resonance, at the end of the *Entrée*. Disembarking on the return voyage on an unrecognized shore in Spain, Roland encourages his companions not to fear, for "Je sai bien ou je sui venus et arivés" (v. 14,423)—a measure of how far his journey has brought him since the "Mais vil se tient qe ne sa ou il va." Thus the ideal knight possesses a double text in his own mind: he voyages, on the *sensus* level, to seemingly gratuitous places, undergoing apparently gratuitous adventures. Yet without specifically knowing where he is going, he possesses a *profundior intelligentia* of his own experience: he possesses his own *sententia*. The text signs this in the path which now opens miraculously before Roland in the forest. In a short while he is re-united with the French in great joy.

It is the hermit episode which completes Roland's heroic evolution. When he describes himself as "Ecce servus Domini" (v. 15,164), his new language, that of the Church, informs us how to interpret his remaining acts. This *servus Domini* at last identifies himself by his true name, after several false identifications in the East, all of which shared one element, which was to render him an enemy of Charles. He can now abolish those erroneous definitions of self: they have been corrected.

The hermit's didactic role concludes with the admonition: "Mais qi a Deu ne sert n'est saje ni prodon" (v. 14,784). This verse is interesting as an echo of the Oxford's "Rollant est proz e Oliver est sage." Taking up the two epithets, the Paduan demonstrates that neither, alone, is sufficient to define the hero of his corrected text. The admonishing "Mais qi a Deu ne sert" invalidates the secular semantic field of both: the implication is clear that both *sagesse* and *prouesse* must be interpreted and enacted in a religious sense as components of the chivalric *servus Domini*.

The *Entrée* recognizes the Church's warning about the particular dangers of heroic pride, that other sins find their vent in the accomplishment of evil deeds, but pride lies in wait for the good deeds, to destroy them. If John of Salisbury had been justified in complaining of the potential dangers of the new literature about Arthur and Tristan[14] and Thomas Aquinas was willing to tolerate *jongleur* art only as a necessary manifestation of man's need for *ludus* and *solatium* (although with a warning to respect moderation),[15] the *Entrée* does indeed offer a *correctio* of the pleasures of the text.

The Roland who returns to Pamplona will continue the fight, following the hermit's instructions that he put into action what he has learned. He will fulfill what Guillaume de Conches specified as the *raison d'être* of creature and Creator: Roland's sanctity, like God's, demonstrates that "all good radiates with greater beauty when it is shared and spread throughout a community of men."[16] If the *Entrée*'s Roland has undergone a mystical experience in the final episode, he will not retreat to a hermit's hut. His will be the *via positiva*, reunion and re-integration within the secular community.

I would like to emphasize that although divided into two major parts, the *Entrée* discloses distinct structural and episodic parallels between its parts, unifying the whole and enriching the *sententia* level. The *compagnonnage* motif, Roland with Olivier in Part I and with Prince Sanson in II: the initial close Charles-Roland bond in I and the similar Sultan-Roland bond in II: the subsequent conflict between Charles and Roland in I, and between the Sultan and his nephew in II bear witness to structural symmetries. Finally, Roland's major battle of I, in which the "epic" hero is delineated and depicted by his desire for autonomy at Nobles, anticipates the Malquidant combat of II, where Roland's humble acceptance of military control of Persia signals a decisive change in the pattern of parallels and thus marks more strongly his evolution away from the postures of pride.[17]

The *Entrée* thus re-examines the dialectic between feudal vs. religious heroism and carries on the debate of definition of the hero. Topical invention has combined elements of form and intent to construct what the poet terms his "gloriose cançons" (v. 366). In accordance with Aquinas's thesis that art is based on principles of spiritual activity and its goal is to produce perfect forms, the Paduan had endeavored to demonstrate the processes that create perfected form.[18]

Still more interesting is the poem's realization of an heroic ideal evolved in three phases within one text, within one character. Roland is not prepared to profit from his encounter with the hermit until he has experienced and corrected the failings of his epic and romance manifestations. Likewise, the poet does not offer the ideal, definitive, tropologically functional text until he has created, and put into question, two imperfect forms-as-texts. It is here, I believe, that we may situate the Paduan's claim to originality in the prologue to Part II: conforming to rhetorical and Thomistic prescriptions, he has composed his work with an inner conception or sense of the processes (voyage) necessary to its perfect realization, to the specific contingencies of literary form and the tastes of his public. The *idea* of its final perfection governs each aspect of the constructive process. Thus, just as the Roland of forest and voyage is engaged in a quest, the text, too, proceeds with a sense of order in search of its own perfect form.

Notes

[1]*L'Entrée d'Espagne, chanson de geste franco-italienne*, ed. Antoine Thomas, SATF, 2 vols. (Paris, 1913). For purposes of narrative logic, I have divided the text at v. 11,137, immediately following Charles's blow. With the Nobles episode as the culmination of Part I, Roland's abandonment of the French at Pamplona and departure for the East open Part II, with a second protasis anticipating it (vv. 10,939-96).

[2]See Alfred Adler, "Didactic Concerns in *L'Entrée d'Espagne*," *L'Esprit Créateur* 2 (1962-63), 107-09. He points out that the Roland-Ferragu debate "ever so modestly reflects certain rather sophisticated concerns; a readiness to demonstrate mysteries of the Christian faith in accordance with *nature* and *reson*," p. 107.

[3]Priscian, *De pre-exercitamentis rhetoricis*, ed. Keil (Leipzig, 1860), p. 553f. Cited in Heinrich Lausberg, *Handbuch der literarischen Rhetorik: Eine Grundlegung der Literaturwissenschaft*, 2 vols. (Munich, 1960), 2:270.

[4]*The Institutio oratoria of Quintilian*, trans. Harold E. Butler, Loeb Classical Library, 4 vols. (Cambridge, 1963), 1:156-58. "Sententiae quoque et chriae et ethologiae subiectis dictorum rationibus apud grammaticos scribantur, quia initium ex lectione ducunt; . . . quia sententia universalis est vox. . . ."

[5]"Sententia," *A Latin Dictionary*, ed. Charlton T. Lewis and Charles Short (1879; rpt. Oxford, 1966).

[6]*The Didascalicon of Hugh of St. Victor: A Medieval Guide to the Arts*, trans. Jerome Taylor (New York, 1961), 6. 8. 147.

[7]D[urant] W. Robertson, Jr., *A Preface to Chaucer: Studies in Medieval Perspectives* (Princeton, 1962), pp. 315-16. It should be noted that OF *sentence* retained its definition of "parole qui renferme un grand sens, pensée morale; jugement; proverbe" (Littré, *FEW*, *Grand Larousse*). It is also included in the *Poetria nova* of Geoffrey of Vinsauf under *ornatus facilis*; see Edmond Faral, *Les arts poétiques du XII*[e] *et du XIII*[e] *siècle* (1924; rpt. Paris, 1962), pp. 231-32.

[8]"Roland as Baron Révolté: The Problem of Authority and Autonomy in *L'Entrée d'Espagne*," *Olifant* 5 (1977-78), 285-97; "Further Explorations of Nobles: Its Foundations" (paper read at the Fifteenth International Congress on Medieval Studies, Kalamazoo, Michigan, May, 1980); and "*L'Entrée d'Espagne*: Elements of Content and Composition, Diss., Univ. of Wisconsin, 1974. For a thorough summary and analysis of the Nobles episode and its relationship to earlier versions of the *Entrée*, see André de Mandach, *Chronique dite Saintongeaise, Texte franco-occitan inédit 'Lee': à la découverte d'une chronique gasconne du XIII*[e] *siècle et de sa poitevinisation*, Beihefte zur Zeitschrift für romanische Philologie, 120 (Tübingen, 1970), pp. 127-40. For analogies in compositional stratification between the *Entrée*, Cid, and *Chanson de Roland*, see Erich von Richthofen, "Théorie de la genèse du *Roland* confirmée par l'analogie de celle du *Cid*," *La Chanson de geste et le mythe carolingien, Mélanges René Louis, publiés par ses collègues et ses élèves à l'occasion de son 75*[e] *anniversaire*, ed.

André Moisan, Bibliothèque du Musée Archéologique Régional, 2 vols. (Saint-Père-sous-Vézelay, 1982), 1:382-87.

⁹Jean Subrenat, "L'attitude des hommes en face du voyage d'après quelques textes littéraires," *Voyage, quête, pèlerinage dans la littérature et la civilisation médiévales,* Cahiers du CUER MA, Sénéfiance 2 (Paris, 1976), p. 409.

¹⁰Jean Charles Payen, *Le motif du repentir dans la littérature française médiévale (des origines à 1230),* Publications romanes et françaises, 98 (Geneva, 1967), p. 165.

¹¹Augustine, *De Doctrina christiana,* ed. M. Amelia Klenke (Washington, D.C., 1943) 3:25. 36-37.

¹²Jean-Pierre Perrot, "Le sens de l'errance dans la plus ancienne version française de *La Vie de saint Julien l'Hospitalier,*" in *Voyage, quête, pèlerinage,* p. 487.

¹³In a fragmentary manuscript of the *Entrée, Mss. vari* E. 181 of the Reggio Emilia Municipal Library; the second of two folios introduces a character unknown to Marciana XXI (= 257). Candidus, cited by Roland as first to welcome him upon his arrival in Persia, is presented in the company of Prince Sanson and participates in a ceremonial group immersion and clothing exchange immediately before Roland confers knighthood on them. René Specht, "Cavalleria francese alla corte di Persia: l'episodio dell'Entrée *d'Espagne* ritrovato nel frammento reggiano," *Atti dell'Istituto Veneto di scienze, lettere ed arti* 135 (1976/77), pp. 496, 498, situates the fragment within the long lacuna at v. 13,992. He also notes "una certa tendenza moralizzante, e mi domando se il bagno che secondo l'uso medievale precede l'addobbo, non trasfiguri, qui, persino un battesimo segreto, di cui solo Rolando conosce il significato e l'importanza." Suggestion of sacerdotal functions here reinforces the present thesis of Roland's spiritual evolution.

¹⁴John of Salisbury, *Policraticus: The Statesman's Book,* trans. Murray F. Markland (New York, 1979), p. 12 and passim.

¹⁵Thomas Aquinas, *Summa Theologica,* IIᵃ, IIˢᵉ, q. 168, a. 3, ad 3ᵐ: "Ludus est necessarius ad conversationem humanae vitae et ideo etiam officium histrionum quod ordinatur ad solatium hominibus exhibendum non est secundum se illicitum." Cited in Edgar De Bruyne, *Études d'esthétique médiévale* (1946; rpt. Geneva, 1975), 3: 340.

¹⁶Guillaume de Conches, *Comment sur la Consolation de Boèce, et Gloses sur le Timée,* ed. J. M. Parent (Paris, 1938), p. 128. My translation.

¹⁷In the Malquidant episode (vv. 13,233-991), the Sultan invests the kneeling Roland with the *baston* and *verge* of his new position as "baillis ... de tote Perse," concluding: "'Lieve,'" dist il, "'que l'autisme Mahon / A governer bien ma tere toi don.'" (see vv. 13,494-522). André de Mandach comments that Roland "conquiert la Perse au nom d'une synthèse oecuménique islamo-chrétienne," *Chronique dite Saintongeaise,* Beihefte fur Zeitschrift für Romanische Philologie, 120 (Tübingen, 1970), p. 138.

¹⁸Thomas Aquinas, *Summa Theologica* Iᵃ, IIˢᵉ, q. 57, a. 4, cited in De Bruyne, *Études,* 3:318, who comments: "En tant que participant de la vie

spirituelle, l'homme manifeste trois activités principales, celles du savoir, de l'agir et du faire. Le savoir est réglé de la manière la plus apparente par la science, l'agir par la prudence, le faire par l'art. Il s'ensuit que la création artistique est avant tout un phénomène de l'esprit au même titre que l'action morale ou la recherche scientifique,'' and in *Études*, 3:326-27: ''L'art pour saint Thomas n'est donc pas l'ensemble des créations artistiques, il est un principe d'activité spirituelle.... L'art a pour but non point de réaliser la perfection de l'artiste mais celle de l'oeuvre: 'Bonum artis consideratur non in ipso artifice sed magis in ipso artificatio. Factio enim in exteriorem materiam transiens non est perfectio facientis sed facti, sicut motus est actus mobilis.'''

Reconstructing the Lost *Chanson de Basin*: Was it a *Couronnement de Charlemagne*?

Constance B. Hieatt

In 1978, I suggested that "perhaps it is time to reconsider exactly what the lost *Chanson de Basin* was likely to have contained," and advanced some eleven points as a likely "scenario."[1] While these points are still defensible, some now need qualification, and the whole picture can now be substantially enlarged in light of further evidence which has emerged since 1978 or which I had not yet examined at that time.[2]

In the same year, Joseph J. Duggan re-affirmed the existence of a now lost *chanson* in his paper for the Eighth Congress of the Société Internationale Rencesvals entitled "The Thief Basin and the Legend of Charlemagne: was there a *Chanson de Couronnement de Charlemagne*?" His main arguments were that the council scene in the Old Norse *Karlamagnús saga* sequence involving Basin conforms to a pattern found in similar scenes in French epic literature and that the relics said in this part of the saga to be in the pommel of the sword Durendal provide evidence that the source was not only French but an assonanced *chanson de geste*. Duggan believed this evidence called into doubt the existence of the prior compilation which was the subject of the late Paul Aebischer's conjectures in several books and articles.[3] But echoes of an assonanced French original do not disprove the possibility of an intermediary version: most

103

students of the saga agree that Part I, of which the Basin chapters constitute the beginning, was based on a pre-existing compilation of *chansons de
geste* translated into Norwegian in the thirteenth century, as was suggested
by Gustav Storm a century before Aebischer's time.[4]

More important, and more controv rsial, questions arise in connection with the discrepancies of names and other details of the tale between
French references, the saga, and Dutch and German versions. As Duggan
correctly reports, the saga agrees with French accounts against the Dutch
and German, and even the Danish *Karl Magnus Krónike*, in calling the
thief Basin rather than Elegast (Danish Alegast); and, on the other hand,
the saga is unique in naming the conspirator Renfrei, as against the Gerin /
Garin of French sources and the Eggheric / Eckerich of Dutch and German
versions.[5] Duggan, remarking that all extant versions of the tale are
derivative and none stems directly from any one other, suggests we should
not concern ourselves with its "origin" other than to note that it has a
venerable ancestry in folktale analogues going back to the time of Herodotus, and he makes the conjecture that "Gerin and Renfrei were
probably rival names in the French tradition: this would account for the
hesitancy of the *Restor du paon*, which simply calls the conspirator 'un
rice traïtour,' pointedly avoiding greater precision."[6]

But the saga's Renfrei is one of a pair of brothers, unlike any other
conspirator in the various versions of this tale: his brother is called Heldri,
which makes it certain that these two are the villainous Rainfroi and
Heudri of the equally apocryphal tale known as *Mainet*. All scholars who
have recently considered the saga's Basin chapters in relation to *Mainet*
have agreed, however, that there is no real relationship between the two
stories, and that the use of these names in the saga must be the result of a
confusion between two originally independent tales.[7] The question is,
then, whether the saga (or its source) was alone in this confusion, or
whether the problem may have arisen from a variation in the French
tradition of the kind Duggan sees in the *Restor du Paon*, or in a multiplicity of variants arising from a distant original version underlying both
the French (and in the case of the saga, French-derived) versions and those
preserved in Germany and the Netherlands.

That there was indeed a common, written original preceding these
divergent versions has been the conclusion of recent thorough assessments
of the situation. The earliest to put a convincing case for this conclusion
was, as far as I know, Eckhard L. Wilke, whose dissertation *Der mitteldeutsche Karl und Elegast* considered two large bodies of material, the
references in (mostly) French sources to the thief Basin and a conspiracy
against Charlemagne, and the three extant independent but parallel full
accounts of what is basically the same story: the Old Norse saga, the Dutch

Karel ende Elegast, and the German *Karl und Elegast*.[8] Wilke's admirable demonstration of the artistic superiority of the Dutch poem over the German and his comparison of other accounts to what is said in the latter lead to a strong presumption that the German poem is the version most faithful to an ultimate original source from which all literary variants descend. Its pedestrian quality appears to reflect the fact that it was *not* carefully re-worked, as was the Dutch poem. In many important ways, *Karl und Elegast* seems to reflect the implications of the scattered references in French sources rather than the idiosyncratic traits of the Dutch poem with which it shares many names and details.

Wilke's findings are bolstered by an article in Dutch by M. C. A. Brongers entitled *"Karel ende Elegast* en de Oudnoorse *Karlamagnús saga."*[9] This discusses many close correspondences between the saga and the Dutch poem, with some reference to the German, including ten passages which show such striking verbal similarities that they probably represent verses in a common written source, which Brongers, as Wilke, assumes to have been French. Such was also the assumption of Kerstin Schlyter in her article investigating the bases of the names of various key personages in the Basin tale, which argues that *Eggheric* is simply the expectable Dutch translation of *Gerin*. A more recent, and yet more thorough, Dutch investigation, however, aims to prove that the ultimate "original" was not French at all, but Middle Dutch.

This is the second volume of A. M. Duinhoven's monumental study, *Bijdragen tot reconstructie van de "Karel ende Elegast."*[10] Duinhoven argues, among other things, that *Basin* must be derived from *Elegast* and *Gerin* from *Eggeric* rather than vice versa, and that the Dutch and German setting of Ingelheim is the original location rather than the saga's Ardennes. His reasons are partly historical and partly philological. I have neither the space nor the knowledge of Dutch philology to assess the weight of his evidence here, except to remark that I find all of it interesting, much of it convincing, and some of it in line with conclusions I had already reached.[11] It is clear, however, that there is sufficient evidence for his case to make it dangerous to assume a French "original" as underlying all extant versions, and it should be understood that in advancing an outline of what must have been the contents of the *Chanson de Basin* I am not necessarily outlining the "original" except insofar as the original had features to be found in French versions, including the source of the saga.[12]

Of course, on the other hand, the versions which are not "French" in provenance provide a good deal of necessary evidence to confirm what was or was not in the saga's source, and, in general, I assume that features to be found in any analogue, French or otherwise, and also in the saga, or in both French and non-French analogues even if not in the saga, may be assumed to have been in the *Chanson de Basin*. The outline which follows gives such facts as can be thus ascertained, along with some conclusions and some informed conjectures.

1. *An angel addressed Charlemagne three times, directing him to get up from his bed and steal or lose his life. Charlemagne was reluctant, but obeyed after the third command.* Sources reporting the angelic warning and command are the chronicle of Alberic des Trois-Fontaines (c. 1240),[13] *Renaus de Montauban* (c. 1200),[14] *Le Restor du Paon* (c. 1325),[15] *Karlamagnús saga* (c. 1240),[16] *Karel ende Elegast* (c. 1350),[17] and *Karl und Elegast* (c. 1300).[18] In the three full accounts, the angel's command is threefold. In the Dutch and German versions, it is essentially the same command repeated—although with more variation in the Dutch— and the king shows marked reluctance the first two times. In the saga, the message is delivered in two installments; first, the king is told to flee to friends because his life is in danger, a command he obeys at once, and on the next night the angel gives a two-part command to get up and steal, which, after initial puzzlement, the king obeys when the angel adds the second part (Chapter 1). It is worth noting that while the saga indirectly summarizes speeches quoted directly in the other two sources, there are obvious resemblances between the three versions.[19] That hesitation or reluctance on the king's part figured in the source is also suggested by *Renaus de Montauban*'s statement that he did not dare to refuse.

2. *Charlemagne was accompanied on this errand by a thief named Basin.* It is unlikely that this name was specified by the angel, since the saga version is alone in this detail, but the name Basin persists in all French versions.[20]

3. *Basin was a nobleman in disgrace who had committed an offence against the royal household and turned to thieving; no common thief, he was well-known to Charlemagne.* An obvious difference between the saga and the Dutch and German versions is that the angel specifically names "Basin the thief" to the saga's Karl, telling him to take him along, while in the other two Elegast is an exiled duke whom Charlemagne recognizes when they happen to meet. But Karl must have known Basin, since he knows how to summon him to come. Further, when Basin answers Karl's summons he is initially fearful—as anyone known to be a thief might well be when summoned into the royal presence—but he makes a dignified submission suitable to a vassal of high rank. He is hereafter treated as an equal among Karl's barons.

This situation may be clarified by various references elsewhere. One in *Jehan de Lanson*[21] suggests a former enmity between Charles and Basin; the chronicle of Philippe Mouskes suggests that Basin had formerly injured the king.[22] *Karl und Elegast* specifies that Elegast had formerly stolen a great deal from the king,[23] and even *Karel ende Elegast*, in which Karel says he exiled Elegast for little cause, has Elegast remark later that the king is angry at him for stealing valuables, including two horses (ll. 1080-86): although he has indignantly rejected the suggestion of his companion that they go and rob the king! Note also that Basin's high standing in Charlemagne's retinue after these events is witnessed by *Jehan de Lanson*, where he is found among the Twelve Peers (e.g., l. 1914) and helps Charlemagne win the day by making use of the same sort of tricks he is said to use in the Basin story proper.

4. *Charles assumed a cognomen of a kind which described his nature in a veiled way so that his real name would not come to the wrong ears during the stealing expedition.* In the Dutch and German versions he does so to disguise his identity from the thief, calling himself Adelbrecht—a fitting description of his kingly nature—in the Dutch version; the German version apparently echoes this with the form Olbrecht. The French version lying behind the Magnus of the saga may have had something like Mainet, and indeed this is another connection between the saga version and *Mainet*: the motive in both for the adoption of the cognomen later to become added to the king's given name is to protect him from his enemies, not to conceal his identity from the companions among whom he agrees to use a pseudonym—which companions include, in the saga (ch. 2), the thief. No other source confirms the saga's version in this respect.

5. *The raid was made by night.* This is stated in the three full accounts, the *Restor du Paon*, and the chronicle of Alberic des Trois-Fontaines. A nocturnal raid is not only more suitable for stealing, but makes possible the overhearing of the chief conspirator's confidential report to his wife of the details of the conspiracy, given the widespread agreement that they were in bed at the time.

6. *Charlemagne's journey to steal started in a location in the Ardenne and was accomplished in one night's journey or less to a location in the Liège-Tongres vicinity.* The saga's Tung (Tongres) is near *Karel ende Elegast*'s Eggermonde (Aigremont, near Liège); both would be reachable in a day or night's ride from the Ardennes, where Karl and Basin start in the saga. Wilke thought the Dutch poet substituted Ingelheim, a city near Mainz which is impossibly distant from Aigremont, because of the presence of the angel; the German poet gives the starting point as Urlous, wherever that may be.

Duinhoven, however, gives some interesting facts which indicate that the ultimate original may have given Ingelheim, and that what is confused in *Karel ende Elegast* is Eggermonde; if he is right, a redactor writing in French—presumably in the Walloon area, where all the place names in this part of the saga are located—accepted Aigremont and changed the starting

107

point to one at a more reasonable distance. As Duinhoven points out, the historical basis of the *Basin / Elegast* story is most certainly a Thuringian rebellion under the leadership of Hardradus in the year 785. However, Sigebertus of Gembloux, whose chronicle (c. 1100) was a source of Alberic's (among others), placed this event in the year 788, when Charlemagne was staying at Ingelheim, and called the leader Hardericus, the name Alberic gives for the "conspirator" who caused the angel's warning and command to steal.[24] The account Sigebertus gives of the year 788 begins with a more sensational conspiracy which was indeed exposed and foiled at Ingelheim in that year, one led by Charlemagne's first cousin, Tassilo of Bavaria. Duinhoven argues that these two conspiracies, assigned erroneously to the same year, must have been confused, and he explains Eggermonde as a misreading of *tegermanie* 'of Germany,' which he interprets as *teggermonde* 'of Aigremont.' Hardradus, of course, came from Germany, across the Rhine from Ingelheim, as did Tassilo.

7. *The traitor's name was alternatively known as Gerin or Hardré.* Alberic's Hardericus appears to lie behind both forms. Duinhoven believes that *Eggeric* is derived from Middle Dutch forms *Herderic / Erderic*, probably falling under the influence of the place name *Eggermonde*; and that from this in turn is derived the French *Gerin* (*Eggerin), rather than vice-versa, as suggested by Schlyter. He remarks that *Hardré* would have been the form to be expected in French as a derivative of *Hardericus* (or, alternatively, *Herdri*), but this does not occur in French versions. However, *Hardré* did persist in French as the name of a traitor: it is used for another conspirator thwarted by the same Basin in *Jehan de Lanson*. And a form such as *Herdri* must lie behind the saga's Heldri. The confusion of Hardré / Herdri with *Mainet*'s Heudri would not be surprising, given the parallels between the two stories; and thus, inevitably, we get the saga's Renfrei.[25]

Presuming this is the case, yet a third historical conspiracy (or rebellion) enters the background, for Heudri and Rainfroi get their names from Chilperic and Raginfrid, who revolted against Charles Martel, the grandfather of Charlemagne, about seventy years before the rebellion of Hardradus. And, as it happens, they were overcome in the Ardenne, where the saga locates Charlemagne at the time of the conspiracy of Renfrei and Heldri.[26]

8. *Basin used charms or spells of some sort—probably an herb which induced sleep—in the course of the raid.* While the saga is not as forthright about this as other sources,[27] there are traces of the spells there, too—one of which was unfortunately obscured in my translation as published, which, in turn, misled Duinhoven, to whom my apologies are due.[28]

9. *Basin was the only one to actually break in, while Charles waited outside; on his second foray, he overheard the traitor's confidences to his wife, which he subsequently reported to the king.* Only in the saga is the king present in a second foray, so that he can overhear the plot details himself.[29]

10. *Basin first took some miscellaneous treasure, then a horse, a saddle, and a sword.*[30] Probably the horse was omitted in the Dutch version and the sword in the German because no significant use was made of either, the saddle being the primary evidence that the witness had been in the traitor's hall. The horse is produced in the saga and also, albeit secondarily, in the German version. No version makes real use of the sword, which may owe its existence to an original reading or 'arms' rather than 'saddle' for the principal evidence, according to Duinhoven.[31]

11. *The traitor expected his wife to keep his secret.* This is stated in similar wording in the five main accounts.[32]

12. *The conspiracy was to be carried out at either Christmas or Pentecost. Renaus de Montauban* gives Christmas, the *Restor du Paon* Pentecost; in the saga it is planned for Christmas but actually foiled at Pentecost. Interestingly, Charlemagne's stay at Ingelheim in 788 was from Christmas until the Easter season; during this period, the conspiracy of Tassilo was put down on the occasion of a council of state.

13. *There were twelve conspirators in all.* This is noted in the saga, *Karl und Elegast,* and *Renaus de Montauban.* While *Karel ende Elegast* is vague about all the details of the conspiracy, it says that sixty men were posted to disarm the conspirators and their retinue; if twelve conspirators each had four companions, that would make sixty.

14. *The knives to be used were distinctive and sharp, and were to be concealed in the conspirator's sleeves.* There are some close parallels in wording here.[33]

15. *The traitor's wife was Charlemagne's sister.* This is stated in the Dutch and German versions and in one of the manuscripts of the *Restor du Paon,* although the preferred variant of that line of the poem indicates that she is a cousin rather than a sister.[34] The poet of the *Restor du Paon,* Jean de Brisebare, may have been exercising caution in hesitating to commit himself to calling her a sister, as he appears to have been in withholding the name of the traitor (see above). No kinship is mentioned in the saga, but there the traitor is Renfrei: presumably the translator or compiler recognized this as the name of a half-brother, who could not have married Charlemagne's sister.

Duinhoven points to Tassilo's kinship to Charlemagne as explaining this detail. Tassilo was the son of Charlemagne's father's sister, but a word or phrase describing him as related "through a sister" could have been misunderstood and thought to apply to a sister of Charlemagne himself.[35]

16. *The traitor's wife lamented for Charles and said her husband deserved to be hanged, and/or threatened exposure.* Neither the saga nor the Dutch poem preserves the full reaction, but *Karl und Elegast* (11. 748-60) combines the different words reported in the saga and in *Karel ende Elegast*, and the *Restor du Paon* gives a parallel version.

17. *Angered by her response, the traitor struck his wife and caused blood to flow from her nose, which Basin, under or beside the bed, caught in his right glove.*[36] Only the German version substitutes a silk cloth for the glove.

18. *Charlemagne consulted his counselors on how to avert the conspiracy; among them was the Duke of Bavaria.* This title in the Dutch poem probably means Naimes. While in the saga his father, Videlun, still holds that title, Namlun (Naimes) plays the more prominent part in the council scene. Basin, as Duggan suggests, was no doubt also present. I do not recognize Naimes among the advisors mentioned in the German version (11. 1310-410), but that is a pretty strange group, apparently including the king's father, Pipin. Note that Duinhoven reports that the conspiracy of Tassilo was exposed with the help of certain loyal Bavarian leaders.

19. *As the conspirators entered, each was disarmed by a different member of Charlemagne's retinue.* Only *Karel ende Elegast* is (characteristically) vague about this point.

20. *The chief conspirator denied his guilt even when confronted with evidence.* The Dutch poem is again eccentric, no doubt because Elegast is to be kept the center of attention.

21. *The king condemned the traitors to be hanged.* That he commuted the sentence to beheading with a sword in the saga and that the hangings were preceded by duels in the Dutch and German versions does not change this fact.

22. *Basin was rewarded with the hand of the traitor's wife and his lands and goods.* While the latter are not mentioned in the Dutch and German versions, the German says that the lands originally confiscated from Elegast had been given to Eckerich (11. 239-253); it follows that they would now be returned to their original owner. Note that this reward is another indication of the high status of Basin in the saga: it would surely have been quite excessive for a common thief, whether or not the wife concerned was the king's sister.

23. *The conspiracy took place at the time of Charlemagne's coronation or very shortly afterwards. Renaus de Montauban*'s version may reflect the Christmas / Pentecost confusion of the saga: it seems likely that

the *Chanson de Basin* had the coronation on Christmas and the conspiracy scheduled for the following Pentecost, as the saga's shift seems to suggest. Note, in this connection, that *Renaus de Montauban* mentions the punishment of Renfrei and Heudri, who must be the chief *sers* of line 10110, but does not mention their names. This may indicate that the poet, who calls the chief conspirator Gerin, knew that he was also called by a name easily confused with Heudri.

This, then, is as far as it is safe to go in reconstructing the contents of the lost *Chanson de Basin*, which surely was the basis of the opening of *Karlamagnús saga* and the various references and brief accounts in extant French sources. Those more adept in Old French than I am may enjoy reconstructing assonanced verses based on the parallel passages which seem to echo a common wording, but they should bear in mind the possibility that the ultimate original may not have been French. And it is questionable whether the *chanson* can be referred to as a *Couronnement de Charlemagne*, when only the saga makes the conspiracy and the coronation coincide exactly and when, as those who have read this evidence will have gathered, the saga, or its source, was an adaptation which was certainly not always faithful to the *chanson* version.

Notes

[1] Review article on Eduard Rombauts, "Le *Karel ende Elegast* néerlandais et la *Chanson de Basin*," *Études Germaniques* 31 (1976), 369-91, in *Olifant* 5 (1978), 299-306.

[2] My further research in this area owes a considerable debt to the expertise in Middle and Modern Dutch of my husband, A. Kent Hieatt.

[3] Most fully and finally in Aebischer's *Textes norrois et littérature française du Moyen Age* (Geneva, 1972). Duggan's article is in *VII Congreso de la Société Rencesvals, Pamplona, Santiago de Compostela, 15 a 25 agosto de 1978* (Pamplona, 1981), pp. 107-15. Professor Duggan was unable to correct his typescript in time to prevent the printing of the erroneous statement that Aebischer believed the source of *Karlamagnús saga I* to have been Latin; in agreement with other scholars, Aebischer thought it must have been Anglo-Norman.

[4] Gustav Storm, *Sagnkredsene om Karl den Store og Didrik af Bern hos de nordiske folk* (Christiania, 1874). On the question of the saga's sources and Aebischer's theories, see Povl Skårup's introduction in *Karlamagnús saga, branches I, III, VII et IX*, ed. Agnete Loth, trans. Annette Patron-Godefroit (Copenhagen, 1980), pp. 333-55.

[5] *Karl Magnus Krónike*, ed. Povl Lindegard Hjorth (Copenhagen, 1960) follows the saga version faithfully in all other respects (aside from oddly spelled names, omissions, etc.) and is thus of no value as an independent witness to the content of the Basin story; similarly, the German *Karl Meinet* (ed. Adelbert T.

Keller, Stuttgart, 1858; see also the text ed. Duinhoven cited in n. 16 below) is not discussed here because it is derived from the Dutch version, although it is earlier than the extant Dutch texts.

[6]In *VIII Congreso de la Société Rencesvals, Pamplona - Santiago de Compostela (15 a 25 agosto de 1978)* (Pamplona, 1981), p. 108.

[7]See Jacques Horrent, *Les versions françaises et étrangères des Enfances de Charlemagne* (Brussels, 1979), and Kerstin Schlyter, "Reinfrei, Heldri et Basin dans la Première branche de la Karlamagnus Saga," in *Travaux de Linguistique et de Littérature* 18/1 (Hommage à la mémoire de Gérard Moignet; Centre de Philologie et de Littératures Romanes de l'Université de Strasbourg, 1980), pp. 401-12.

[8]Eckhard L. Wilke, *Der Mitteldeutsche Karl und Elegast*, Marburger Beiträge zur Germanistik, 27 (Marburg, 1969).

[9]M. C. A. Brongers, "*Karel ende Elegast en de Oudnoorse Karlamagnús saga*," *De nieuwe taalgids* 65 (1972), 161-80.

[10]A. M. Duinhoven, *Bijdragen tot reconstructie van de "Karel ende Elegast"* (Groningen, 1981), vol. 1, Assen, 1975.

[11]While I have not yet seen any full reviews of this recently published book, remarks in correspondence received from scholars in the area (and in one case, a report of remarks made at a conference) suggest Duinhoven's work may generate some controversy. A letter from Professor Willem P. Gerritson of the Middle Dutch Institute at Utrecht suggests his entire agreement with Duinhoven's findings; on the other hand, one from Dr. Rombauts (ems. Prof., Leuven) expresses extreme skepticism. Both wrote in 1981.

[12]An outline of the "original" is suggested in my article "The *Karlamagnús saga* Version of the *Chanson de Basin*," in *Les sagas de chevaliers (Riddarasögur), Actes de la Ve Conférence Internationale sur les sagas (Toulon, July 1982)*, ed. Régis Boyer (= *Civilisation* 10, 1985), pp. 235-47.

[13]"Conjuratio valida facta est ab Austrasiis contra Karolum regem auctore Harderico ... et, ut in cantilena dicitur, ad istam conspirationem congnoscendam Karlus magnus monitu angeli ivit de nocte furari." Quoted in *Karlamagnús saga ok kappa hans*, ed. Carl R. Unger (Christiania, 1859), p. xiii.

[14]These are the pertinent lines:
> Je ving en dolce France o mon riche barné,
> Et si pris tos les sers qui furent el regné.
> Je les fis tos ardoir et la poudre venter.
> Adonc me fis en France, merci Deu, coroner,
> Galiene m'amie à grant joie espouser.
> Quant je cuidai avoir tot mon regne aquité,
> Dont juerent ma mort trestot li .xii. per;
> Si me durent mordrir par .i. jor de Noël.
> Dex me menda par l'angle que je alasse embler;
> Voirement i alai, ne l'ossai refuser.
> Je n'oi clef ne sosclave por tresor esfondrer;

Dex me tramist à moi .i. fort larron prové;
Basins avoit à nom, mena me en la ferté,
Et si entra dedans por l'avoir assembler.
Illuec oï Gerin le conseil demonstrer,
Qui le dist à sa fame coiemen, à celé.
Basins le me conta, quant il fu retornés.
Je atendi le terme et si les pris provés,
Les coutiaus ens es manches, tranchans et afilés.
Je en fis tel justisse, comme vos bien savés,
Pendre, ardoir et destruire et les membres coper.

Lines 10109-29 in the edition of *La Chanson des Quatre Fils Aymon*, ed. Ferdinand Castets (1909; rpt. Geneva, 1974); in the older Michelant edition, pp. 266-67.

[15]The pertinent lines are the following:
Ne trouvons nous que Diex par son angle manda
Au fort roy Charlemainne et si li conmanda
Que il alast embler? Et li roys y ala
A Basin l'enchanteur, par nuit s'acompaingna,
Qui par enchantement en la maison entra
D'un rice traïtour, s'oï et escouta
Que li leres disoit. "Ma dame, entendés cha:
Je vuel que secrés soit ce que vous orés ja."
Et la dame a celer errant li otria.
"Dame, dis li traïstres, Karles murdris sera
A ceste Pentecouste que plus ne vivera.
Bien le sai, car je fui ou l'en le devisa."
Quant la dame l'oÿ d'angoisse tressua,
Car c'estoit ses cousins et si le maria.
"Certes, ce dist la dame, li bons roys le sara."
Quant li traytres l'ot si grant cop li donna
Parmi le neis que tout son vis ensanglenta.
Basins passsa avant et si s'agenoulla
Si retint en son gant le sanc qu'ele sainna
Et puis vint a.Charlon et le fait li conta.
Et Charles s'en retraist et Dieu en mercia
Et bien contre ce fait puissedi se garda.

Lines 609-30 in the edition of Richard J. Cary (Geneva, 1966). An important variant given here for 1. 622 (wrongly given as 621 in the note) is, "Car son frere fu Charles...."

[16]See editions cited in notes 4 and 12; my English translation is in *Karlamagnús Saga: the Saga of Charlemagne and His Heroes*, 1 (Toronto, 1975), pp. 54-102.

[17]The editions I have primarily used are those ed. A. M. Duinhoven (Zwolle, 1969, and The Hague, 1982); the former also prints a *Karlmeinet* text in parallel columns, and the latter contains a useful introduction summarizing the author's

findings in *Bijdragen tot reconstructie. . . .* There is also a Modern Dutch edition by Eduard Rombauts (Culemborg, 1973).

[18]*Karl und Elegast*, ed. Josef Quint (Bonn, 1927).

[19]See Brongers, pp. 167-68; Wilke, p. 21.

[20]To others that have been cited can be added, e.g., a reference in *Auberi le Bourguignon* quoted in Gaston Paris, *Histoire poétique de Charlemagne*, 2d ed. (1905; rpt. Geneva, 1974), p. 318; Paris, of course, also included—in whole or in part—many of the other passages here cited.

[21]*Jehan de Lanson*, ed. John Vernon Meyers (Chapel Hill, n.d. [1966?]), ll. 2986-87.

[22]See Paris, p. 318, and Wilke, p. 53.

[23]Lines 257-64.

[24]Sigebert's account is in PL 160:150.

[25]There is nothing unusual about such a confusion of names, given the vagaries of manuscript (and oral) transmission of the like. Consider, e.g., the remarkable variants in the *Mainet* story documented by Horrent: three such versions do not attribute the problems of the young Charlemagne to half-brothers at all; those which do give these brothers names in many forms, ranging from Hainfroi and Heudri through Landris and Lanfroi to the unrecognizable Manfre and Eldois (p. 42).

[26]This coincidence of location and the probable relationship of the names Rainfroi and Heudri to Raginfrid and Chilperic are noted by Aebischer (pp. 40-45), Schlyter (p. 404), and Duinhoven (1982, p. 25).

[27]E.g., *Karel ende Elegast*, ll. 804 ff., 881-83; *Karl und Elegast*, ll. 626-628; *Restor du Paon*, l. 613; *Elie de Saint Gille*, ed. Gaston Raynaud (Paris, 1869), ll. 1979-86.

[28]"Basin . . . was able to tell, in his shrewdness, that everyone in the hall was asleep" (p. 60) should read "Basin . . . brought it about, through his wiles, that. . . ." I fear I was misled by others who had claimed that there was no trace of "enchantment" in the saga's Basin and thus took an alternate, but wrong, interpretation of the phrase. The use of a charm or spell is confirmed by a later reference: see p. 66 of my translation.

[29]Aside from the German and Dutch versions, this is reported in *Renaus de Montauban* and the *Restor du Paon*.

[30]See chap. 2 of the saga and *Karl und Elegast*, ll. 789-809.

[31]See *Karel ende Elegast* (1982), p. 52.

[32]That is, including *Renaus de Montauban* and the *Restor du Paon*.

[33]See Wilke, pp. 57-58.

[34]See n. 15; there is a striking similarity in wording between *Restor du Paon*, l. 622, and *Karl und Elegast*, l. 761.

[35]See *Karel ende Elegast* (1982), pp. 40-44.

[36]See Wilke, pp. 59-60.

In Search of the Lost Epics of
the Lower Rhône Valley

Alice M. Colby-Hall

Did the medieval inhabitants of Orange take the slightest interest in the epic hero that we call Guillaume d'Orange? In theory, I should not be asking this question; for it should be self-evident that the local population, and especially the rulers of Orange, would have felt strong admiration for the warrior who was said to have delivered the city from the hands of the Saracens and become its first governor. My question should be completely ridiculous—and I certainly wish it were. But what concrete evidence do we have that local writers produced any literature praising Guillaume and recounting his exploits or that natives of Orange appreciated such literature, whether it was of local origin or not?

The twelfth-century Latin biography of Guillaume describes the taking of Orange, and the description appears to be derived from a *chanson de geste*, but the biography itself was composed at Guillaume's own monastery of Gellone, now called Saint-Guilhem-le-Désert. In other words, it came from the region around Montpellier and may, or may not, have close ties with the local traditions of Orange. Inasmuch as all the surviving William cycle epics that deal with Orange are written in French rather than Occitan, scholars have been hard put to demonstrate the southern origin of this material and, by and large, have considered that these epics originated in the north and were aimed at a northern audience.

Does the sheer lack of objective evidence force us to accept this widely held view? I think not; for such evidence is, in fact, available and has long been accessible to medievalists. For one reason or another, it has simply gone unnoticed. On October 18, 1112, Pope Paschal II sent a letter to Béranger, the bishop of Orange, confirming the total separation of the diocese of Orange from that of Saint-Paul-Trois-Châteaux. The beginning of the document is lost; and the remaining portion, which has survived in a twelfth-century copy now preserved at the Bibliothèque du Musée Calvet in Avignon (MS 1830, fol. 5^r), begins with a tantalizing adverbial clause that deserves to be quoted in full: "[... Aura]sice siquidem civitatis populus aliquando ita exaltatus est, ut illius civitatis nomen vulgaribus passim carminibus celebretur; alquando ita depressus, ut ejus ecclesia civitatis alterius ecclesiçe vel subdita sit vel unita."[1] This explanatory clause can be translated as follows: "... since indeed the people of the city of Orange have been so exalted that the name of that city is celebrated everywhere in vernacular songs and, at the same time, have been so abased that its church has either been made subject to, or joined to, the church of another city." As Paschal II goes on to demonstrate the legality of the procedures already used to appoint a bishop of Orange, it becomes clear to the reader that the Pope finds it disgraceful and humiliating for a city as famous as this one to be deprived of ecclesiastical independence. And what is the source of that fame? The city is praised *carminibus vulgaribus* "in vernacular songs"; and it receives this praise *passim*, that is to say, "far and wide."

This letter was first published in 1715 in Volume 1 of the *Gallia Christiana* (Instr., p. 132), with errors and omissions that do not affect the passage under discussion, and was reprinted in 1870 in the second edition of this volume. In 1896, the document was carefully re-edited by Léopold Duhamel and published in the *Mémoires de l'Académie de Vaucluse* 15, 395-96; and, in 1916, a third edition, which differs only slightly from that of Duhamel, was incorporated into the *Gallia Christiana novissima* (*GCNN*). Despite the existence of these three editions, no scholar, to the best of my knowledge, paid any attention to the literary implications of Pope Paschal's letter until 1956, when the historian and archivist Jacques de Font-Réaulx identified the Pope's *carmina vulgaria* as epic poems concerning Guillaume d'Orange. This interpretation is hidden away in the introduction to Font-Réaulx's edition of the will of Tiburge d'Orange, which appeared in a relatively inaccessible *Festschrift* honoring Raoul Busquet.[2]

Font-Réaulx translates the expression *carminibus vulgaribus* with the phrase "par des chants vulgaires" and equates these *chants* with *chansons de geste*. In this context, the adjective *vulgaris* does not mean "popular," but rather "vernacular," as in the title of Dante's *De vulgari eloquentia*. We are dealing with *chants en langue vulgaire*. But are these *chansons de geste*? In all probability, yes; but shorter poems may also be involved.

What is their narrative content? Why have they brought fame to Orange? Font-Réaulx is certainly right in assuming that only one body of epic material could have produced this effect, namely, the tales linking Guillaume, count of Toulouse, with the history of Orange. However, because he is thinking exclusively of the surviving Old French poems, he fails to perceive the linguistic issue raised by the word *vulgaribus*. Since the songs were being sung *passim*, the Pope was not necessarily referring to a single non-Latin language. In fact, it is far more likely that he had at least two vernaculars in mind, that he was alluding to languages such as French, Italian, Occitan, Franco-Italian, and Franco-Provençal—to name only the most obvious possibilities. Whatever languages were involved, it seems abundantly clear that the Pope's reasoning would make little sense if none of the poems alluded to were composed for the entertainment of the residents of Orange and in a language they could readily comprehend.

In all probability, Paschal II's argument is borrowed from the reasoning of the local leaders who sought his support. To justify this contention, we need to look into the bishopric controversy. In a letter written some time between 1061 and 1070 (GCNN, no. 51), Pope Alexander II threatened the temporal ruler of Orange, Bertrand-Raimbaud, with excommunication, should the latter persist in his efforts to remove the church of Orange from the diocese of Saint-Paul-Trois-Châteaux. Around 1086, the clergy of Orange elected a bishop named Guillaume; and this election had the approval of Pope Victor III (*GCNN*, col. 30). In 1095, Pope Urban II decreed that the two bishoprics should be reunited upon the death of Guillaume (*GCNN*, no. 58). The latter died in 1098 (*GCNN*, no. 59), and in 1100, Pope Paschal II reprimanded the people and the clergy of Orange for their obstinate refusal to obey the bishop of Saint-Paul-Trois-Châteaux (*GCNN*, no. 63). The local clergy eventually persuaded the Pope that the conditions which had originally determined the union of the two bishoprics no longer obtained. Consequently, they were given the right to choose their own leader; and, in 1107, Béranger was elected bishop of Orange with the full consent of the clergy, the assembled populace, and the reigning prince of Orange, Giraud Adhémar (*GCNN*, no. 66).

If we accept the line of descent proposed by Font-Réaulx ("Testament," pp. 48-49), Giraud Adhémar was the first husband of the Tiburge d'Orange who made her will about 1150. The modern form of this princess' name conceals the fact that during her own lifetime she would have been called Tiborc, that her real name could even be regarded as a nickname for Guiborc, the Occitan equivalent of Witburgh. Four children are mentioned in the will of Tiborc: Guillaume, Tiburge, Tiburgette, and Raimbaut. Tiborc's second husband was Guillaume d'Omelas, but Font-Réaulx assigns the children called Guillaume and Tiborc to her first marriage ("Testament," pp. 50-51). If these two children were not simply named after their parents, what motivated the choice of names? And, furthermore, why did they each call two of their own children Guillaume and Tiborc?[3] One strongly suspects that an epic tradition lies behind the popularity of these names in the ruling family and that Giraud Adhémar and his wife Tiborc were well aware of their city's glorious past.

Is it surprising then that Paschal II alludes to that past when confirming the ecclesiastical independence of Orange after the legality of Béranger's election was challenged in 1112 by the bishop of Saint-Paul-Trois-Châteaux (*GCNN*, nos. 70-71)? It seems only too likely that if the Pope had had no personal acquaintance with the *carmina vulgaria*, the clergy, backed by Giraud Adhémar, would have dispelled his ignorance. Furthermore, there is solid evidence that the rulers of Orange in the eleventh and twelfth centuries were eager to control the local church for their own purposes.[4] One can safely assume that the real reasons for the bishopric controversy were decidedly secular.

Guillaume, the son of Tiborc's daughter Tiborc and Bertrand de Baux, became prince of Orange about 1181;[5] and, in 1184, he officially took the church of Orange under his paternalistic protection.[6] Attached to the document placed in the hands of the clergy was a pendant seal showing, on one side, a large horn, and on the other, the prince, armed and on horseback, carrying a sword in one hand and, in the other, a shield decorated with a horn.[7] This horn still appears on the escutcheon of the city of Orange and on that of the house of Orange-Nassau. According to what seems to be a local tradition, the horn originally belonged to the armorial bearings of the epic hero Guillaume d'Orange, who, on that account, was called Guillaume au Cornet.[8] Was Guillaume de Baux initiating a tradition or merely inheriting one from his mother's family? The latter is more probable.[9]

I realize that the epithets *al corb nés* and *al cort nés* are sufficiently confusing without the added complication of *al cornet*, but the time has come to take the *cornet* seriously and not brush it aside or pass over it in silence as scholars have done since the nineteenth century.

On what grounds has the *cornet* been considered irrelevant in discussions of the legendary Guillaume d'Orange? Let me quote the statement made in 1898 by Hermann Suchier, in the introduction to his edition of the *Narbonnais*: "On sait que par un malentendu des chroniqueurs le *cort nes* de Guillaume a été pris pour un *cornet*."[10] Since Suchier's "on sait" relieves him of any obligation to give the source of this information, we remain unenlightened as to the identity of the *chroniqueurs* and the exact nature of the misunderstanding. In all probability, he is thinking of early modern historians such as Joseph de la Pise and Honoré Bouche, whose views, in fact, still deserve the attention of researchers. Wilhelm Cloëtta, in his edition of the *Moniage Guillaume*, alludes to the "malentendu bien connu" and refers the reader to Suchier's treatment of the *cornet* problem.[11] Scholars who have worked extensively on the William cycle in more recent times make no mention whatsoever of the *cornet*, probably, in large measure, because this object does not appear in any of the surviving French versions of the William stories.

Why, then, did Suchier and Cloëtta decide to deal with this topic? Because the *cornet* does play a rôle in the *Nerbonesi*, a prose compilation made about 1410 by Andrea da Barberino, the author of the still popular *Reali di Francia*. In Andrea's Italian version of the *Prise d'Orange*, Orable and Thibaud can recognize Guillaume by the coat of arms on his shield: a golden horn on an azure field.[12] One would expect to find an azure horn on a golden field, given the arrangement of the tinctures on the modern escutcheon. In any case, whether Andrea has made a slight mistake or is portraying an earlier stage in the evolution of these armorial bearings, his inclusion of the horn should not be dismissed as an anachronism based on his personal knowledge of local heraldry; for the horn forms part of a larger pattern that seems to reveal the broad outlines of a local epic tradition.

Bédier calls Andrea's heroine Guibourc,[13] but Andrea does not actually use this name. For him, the converted Orable is not Guibourc or even Ghiborga, as one would expect in an Italian paraphrase of the story, but rather, Tiborga, a natural Italianization of the name Tiborc. The man who governs Orange in the absence of Orable's husband Thibaud is called Dragonetto, which probably reflects a local tradition connected with Mondragon, a fortified town just to the north of Orange; for, in the twelfth century, three lords of Mondragon received the name Dragonet.[14]

These details would be far less significant if Andrea were merely recounting the plot of the *Prise d'Orange* as we know it from North French manuscripts; but, unlike the author of the North French *Prise*, he cannot be accused of creating a work of imagination that has little connection with a real place. As I have shown in a recent article,[15] he does not distort local topography by placing Orange so close to the Rhône that one can escape from the palace of Gloriette by means of an underground tunnel and reach the river in fifteen or twenty minutes—to achieve that, one has to place Orange to the east of the Camargue and take advantage of the old Roman *cloaca maxima* of Arles.[16] No, Andrea does not need to borrow a tunnel from downstream, since Guillaume and his accomplice, Gui, enter Orange by disguising themselves as Christian pilgrims to Jerusalem who are bringing a message from Thibaud to Orable on their way back from the Holy Land. When they return to Nîmes in order to obtain forces with

119

which they can take Thibaud's city, they leave through an ordinary gate rather than a secret tunnel, since the Saracens in Orange have no reason to regard them as enemies. When Thibaud returns to attack Orange after Guillaume and his army gain possession of it, Andrea gives us a full account of the ensuing siege. Although this episode is necessary to the plot and is mentioned specifically in an Occitan epic, the *Chanson de la Croisade albigeoise*,[17] no authentic version of it has survived in the various manuscripts of the North French *Prise*.

Andrea is not alone in providing us with a non-tunnel version of the *Prise*. The same situation occurs in the prose *Guillaume d'Orange*, compiled soon after 1450 according to the calculations of François Suard in his recent book on this epic.[18] The pilgrim disguise is also used in this version; but here Guillaume is accompanied by four allies, they go to Orange seeking a safe-conduct to Jerusalem, and they perform the service of telling Orable how Guillaume conquered Nîmes with his unusual wagon train. Like his predecessors, Johannes Weiske[19] and Carl Weber,[20] Suard (pp. 55-56) comments on the wide divergences between the versified *Prise* and the prose redaction and is unable to find a precise source for these divergences in the cyclical manuscripts. Given the importance of geographic accuracy for a local audience, one suspects that the absence of the tunnel motif is a sign of indigenous origin and that the relatively simple pilgrim disguise which makes a tunnel escape less necessary is an essential part of the local epic tradition.

Andrea claims to have based his treatment of the *Prise* on the work of Herbert le Duc, de Danmartin, whose *Foucon de Candie* he uses extensively.[21] Herbert's *Prise*, if it ever existed, has not survived; and it is entirely possible that Andrea is deliberately misleading us. However, Schultz-Gora, in the introduction to his edition of *Foucon de Candie*, cites the occurrence of Occitan words and Occitanisms as proof that Herbert had direct contact with the culture of southern France.[22] This poet may very well have acquainted Andrea with the Orangeois tradition, if the latter did not have access to a local Occitan source, thanks to the presence of many Italians in fourteenth-century Orange[23] and Avignon.

One final bit of evidence points to local interest in Guillaume d'Orange and also to the existence of an Occitan *Prise d'Orange* before the northern *Prise* was composed. When the poetess Azalaïs de Porcairagues laments the passing of the troubadour Raimbaut d'Orange soon after his death in 1173,[24] she says with great affection: "I commend to God Belesgar / And, in addition, the city of Orange / And Gloriette and the castle / And the Lord of Provence / And all those who wish me well there / And the arch where the combats are portrayed. / I have lost the one who possesses my life, / And I will forever be sad on account of it!"[25] It is safe

to conclude, I think, that this visitor to Orange had been told the significance of Gloriette, the palace of the Saracen queen Orable who was
destined to marry Guillaume. Since Azalaïs treats Gloriette, the castle, and
the arch as separate entities, this passage should be taken into consideration by anyone attempting to identify the buildings mentioned in medieval
stories about Orange. Henri Grégoire once supposed that the name Gloriette designated the famous Arch of Triumph after its transformation into a
castle,[26] but this was obviously not the information supplied to Raimbaut's
guests. It should also be noted that, according to Azalaïs, Gloriette is not
synonymous with the castle. In other words, we are dealing with the two
buildings which Claude Régnier posits for the archetype of the North
French *Prise* on the basis of the manuscript tradition.[27] Since it is likely
that the original poem was revised under the influence of the epic known as
Aliscans, the revision now referred to as the archetype probably dates
from the very end of the twelfth century.[28]

What was the language of the original poem, Régnier's "rédaction
archaïque"?[29] Thus far, most scholars have tacitly assumed that the extant
versions of the *Prise* are all derived from a French source; but this
assumption rests on another, namely, that the citizens of medieval Orange
felt little or no enthusiasm for a hero who, rightfully or wrongfully, had
acquired a connection with their town.

But Raimbaut d'Orange was certainly acquainted with Gloriette; and
his nephew, Guillaume de Baux, had a horn on his escutcheon; and
Guillaume's mother and grandmother were both named Tiborc. Furthermore, even the Pope himself had to admit, in the year 1112, that a city so
famous in song was, in fact, humiliated by not having its own bishop.
Inasmuch as Guillaume and Tiborga are the hero and heroine of a *Prise*
story more appropriate to Orange than the surviving French epic, everything points to the existence of a poem, a *chanson de geste* in all probability, that deserves to be called the **Presa d'Aurenga*. Chaytor would
have it that the residents of southern France preferred epics written in
French because this language was regarded as more suitable for the
chanson de geste than Occitan.[30] It seems far more plausible, however,
that the original *Prise d'Orange* and, for that matter, any local versions of
other epics concerning the Midi, were written either in Occitan or in
Franco-Occitan; and by this I mean an artificial literary language that was
comprehensible to a wide audience in both northern and southern
France.[31]

In my view, therefore, the presence of so-called French forms in the
Occitan epic known as the *Roman d'Arles* does not necessarily indicate
that the poem is based, directly or indirectly, on a northern source.[32] In
this partially prosified *chanson de geste*, the William and Charlemagne

cycles meet; but Charlemagne and the heroes of Roncevaux are also connected with Arles through material preserved in such texts as the *Pseudo-Turpin* and the *Kaiserchronik*. In a recent article concerning the graves of these heroes, André Moisan justifiably concludes that the Arlesian episodes related or mentioned in the extant texts presuppose the existence of local stories dealing with Charles' return from Spain and the burial of some of his men in the cemetery of the Alyscamps.[33]

We may never know what form these stories took, whether they were oral or written, whether they were in poetry or in prose; but I can safely predict that new insights and unsettling changes of perspective lie in store for anyone who goes hunting for lost epics in the lower Rhône valley.[34]

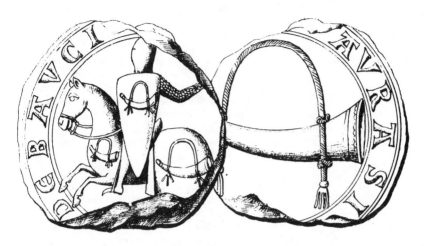

Figure 1
Seal of Guillaume de Baux, June 1193

Figure 2
Seal of Hugues de Baux, August 1214

Notes

¹*Gallia Christiana novissima*, ed. J.-H. Albanès and Ulysse Chevalier, 6, *Orange* (Valence, 1916), no. 72, col. 40; hereafter cited as *GCNN*. Since the last two syllables of the first word of this text are preserved in the manuscript and the scribe consistently calls the city *Aurasica* rather than *Arausica*, I have corrected the reading [... *Arausi*]*çe* given in the *GCNN* edition. It is clear from the remainder of the letter that Orange is the city referred to in this passage.

²Jacques de Font-Réaulx, "Le Testament de Tiburge d'Orange et la cristallisation de la Principauté," in *Mélanges Busquet: Questions d'histoire de Provence (XIᵉ-XIXᵉ siècles)* (*Provence Historique*, fasc. hors série, Dec., 1956), pp. 41-58. The interpretation under discussion occurs on pp. 41-42.

³Convenient genealogical charts showing all the family relationships mentioned in this paper can be found in Édouard Baratier, Georges Duby, and Ernest Hildesheim, *Atlas historique: Provence, Comtat, Orange, Nice, Monaco* (Paris, 1969), pp. 123-24.

⁴Font-Réaulx, "Testament," pp. 42-45, and Jean-Pierre Poly, *La Provence et la société féodale (879-1166)* (Paris, 1976), pp. 269-79.

⁵Louis Barthélemy, *Inventaire chronologique et analytique des chartes de la maison de Baux* (Marseilles, 1882), nos. 76, 79.

⁶*GCNN*, no. 97. As Font-Réaulx has pointed out ("Testament," p. 43 n. 8, and "Le Trésor des chartes des Baux," *Provence Historique* 4 [1954], 145), a better copy of this document, but without the names of the witnesses, is to be found in the *Mémoires* of Jacques de la Pise (Orange, Archives municipales, Série II, Fiche de dépouillement 15, fols. 15ᵛ-16ʳ), father of the historian Joseph de la Pise. I am happy to report that I have located a second copy, identical to this one except for minor spelling variations and containing the witnesses' names, in Jacques de la Pise's *Mémoyres du chapitre d'Orange* (Avignon, Bibl. du Musée Calvet, MS 2912, fols. 182ʳ-182ᵛ) and also a somewhat faulty *vidimus* attesting to the presence of the original document in the ecclesiastical archives of Orange in 1651 (Avignon, Bibl. du Musée Calvet, MS 2912, fols. 781ʳ, 786ʳ-787ᵛ). Both of these copies are preserved among the materials assembled by Gaspard de la Pise with a view to preparing a revised edition of his father Joseph's well-known *Tableau de l'histoire des princes et principauté d'Orange* (The Hague, 1640).

⁷After reproducing the document in his *Mémoires*, Jacques de la Pise describes the seal in the following terms: "Le seel est pendant en cire, auquel d'un costé est le prince à cheval, armé, l'espée à une main, de l'autre, l'escu couvert d'un cornet, et de l'autre costé est un grand cornet" (fol. 16ʳ). The copy in Avignon (see n. 6) is followed by a similar description: "En un repli du parchemin est le seel, pendant à double queue de chevrotin, en cire, d'un costé le prince à cheval, l'espée à une main, son escu en l'autre, un cornet dessus, et de l'autre costé un grand cornet" (fol. 182ᵛ). According to the expense account of Jacques and Joseph de la Pise (Avignon, Bibl. du Musée Calvet, MS 2913, fols. 548ʳ, 551ᵛ, 553ʳ), the former had access to this act of protection in the archives of the diocese

of Orange and must have completed his *Mémoires* some time between 1602 and 1607.

Prior to my discovery of this depiction of Guillaume's seal, the earliest known example of a seal adorned with the *cornet* was the one that this same prince attached to a document in June, 1193 (Marseilles, Archives départementales des Bouches-du-Rhône, B 294). It is an equestrian seal, very similar and quite possibly identical to the one examined by La Pise. See Laugier's drawings of the seal in Louis Blancard, *Iconographie des sceaux et bulles conservés dans la partie anté-rieure à 1790 des Archives départementales des Bouches-du-Rhône* (Marseilles, 1860), fol. ed.: pl. 26, no. 4; 4º ed.: pl. 19, no. 1 (mislabeled as the seal of Bertrand de Baux); and Barthélemy, *Inv.*, pl. VIII, no. 24 (see fig. 1). Since the upper edge of the seal is partially broken off, the sword that Guillaume must have been holding in his right hand is no longer visible. Cf. the position of the arm and sword of his brother Hugues in Blancard, fol. ed.: pl. 25, no. 3, 4º ed.: pl. 19, no. 4; and Barthélemy, pl. I, no. 1 (see fig. 2). When examining Guillaume's seal in Marseilles, I noticed that the horn on his shield is the most prominent of the three that decorate the equestrian side. The other two are, in fact, difficult to perceive; and this may, or may not, be due solely to deterioration of the seal. The additional horns, if present on the seal of 1184, were perhaps too inconspicuous to attract the attention of La Pise.

[8]See especially Joseph de la Pise, *Tableau*, p. 51, and Joseph Bastet, *Histoire de la ville et de la principauté d'Orange* (1856; rpt. Marseilles, 1977), pp. 23-28. A complete history of the *cornet*, with many illustrations, can be found in Elisabeth C. M. Leemans-Prins, "De Hoorn van Oranje," *Holland: Regionaal-historisch tijdschrift* 11, no. 2 (1979), 94-103.

[9]Judging by the evidence that has been brought to light thus far, Guillaume was the first member of the Baux family to adopt this heraldic device. Thereafter, its use by anyone belonging to this family is always an indication of close ties with the principality of Orange. The standard symbol for the house of Baux is a sixteen-pointed star (see fig. 2). For copious documentation, see Blancard, *Iconographie*, fol. and 4º ed., pp. 48-55, and Barthélemy, *Inv.*, pp. 549-64.

[10]Hermann Suchier, *Les Narbonnais*, 2 (Paris, 1898), p. xxxv.

[11]Wilhelm Cloëtta, *Les deux rédactions en vers du Moniage Guillaume*, 2 (Paris, 1911), 171-72.

[12]*Le Storie Nerbonesi*, ed. Ippolito G. Isola, Collezione di Opere Inedite o Rare dei Primi Tre Secoli della Lingua, 47, 1 (Bologna, 1877), 410-11, 435.

[13]Joseph Bédier, *Les légendes épiques*, 3d ed., 1 (Paris, 1926), p. 322.

[14]See the genealogical chart in Étienne de Smet, *Mondragon de Provence des origines à 1536* (Avignon, 1977), pp. 166-67.

[15]Alice M. Colby-Hall, "Orange et Arles: Un royaume pour deux Guillaumes," *Bulletin des Amis d'Orange* 22, 1ᵉʳ trim. (1981), 13-19.

[16]I defend this hypothesis at some length in "Le substrat arlésien de la *Prise d'Orange*," in *Actas del VII Congreso de la Société Rencesvals* (Pamplona, 1981), pp. 83-86. My principal arguments are also set forth in "Orange et Arles."

ALICE M. COLBY-HALL

[17]*Chanson de la Croisade albigeoise*, ed. and trans. Eugène Martin-Chabot, Classiques de l'Histoire de France au Moyen Age, 24 (Paris, 1957), laisse 159, vv. 49-50.

[18]François Suard, *Guillaume d'Orange: Étude du roman en prose*, Bibliothèque du quinzième siècle 44 (Paris, 1979), pp. 98-108.

[19]Johannes Weiske, *Die Quellen des altfranzösischen Prosaromans von Guillaume d'Orange* (Halle, 1898), p. 41.

[20]*Die Prosafassungen des "Couronnement de Louis," des "Charroi de Nîmes" und der "Prise d'Orange,"* ed. Carl Weber (Halle, 1912), p. 39.

[21]Andrea refers to Herbert as *Uberto, duca di San Marino* (1, 366).

[22]Herbert le Duc, de Danmartin, *Folque de Candie*, ed. Oscar Schultz-Gora, 4, *Einleitung*, ed. Ulrich Mölk, Beihefte zur Zeitschrift für romanische Philologie, 111 (Tübingen, 1966), p. 25.

[23]Françoise Gasparri, "Les Italiens à Orange au XIVe siècle," *Provence Historique* 29 (1979), 47-67.

[24]Aimo Sakari, "Azalais de Porcairagues, le Joglar de Raimbaut d'Orange," *Neuphilologische Mitteilungen* 50 (1949), 24-25, 180-81.

[25]Vv. 41-48 of "Ar em al freg temps vengut," ed. Sakari, in "Azalais," pp. 184-86. The Occitan text of this stanza (p. 185) runs as follows:

A Dieu coman Belesgar
E.*n* plus la ciutat d'Aurenga
E Glorïet, e.l caslar -
E lo seignor de Proenza
E tot can vol mon ben lai -
E l'arc on son fag l'assai.
Celui perdiei c'a ma vida
E.n serai toz jornz marrida!

[26]Henri Grégoire, "Les monuments inspirateurs: Comment Guillaume de Toulouse devint Guillaume d'Orange," *Provence Historique* 1 (1950-51), 32-44.

[27]*Les rédactions en vers de la "Prise d'Orange,"* ed. Claude Régnier (Paris, 1966), p. 361.

[28]*La Prise d'Orange*, ed. Claude Régnier, 5th ed., Bibliothèque française et romane, série B: Éditions critiques de textes, 5 (Paris, 1977), p. 35.

[29]Ibid., p. 34.

[30]Henry J. Chaytor, *The Provençal Chanson de Geste* (Oxford, 1946), pp. 23-24.

[31]In his *Cultura e lingua francese delle origini nella "Passion" di Clermont-Ferrand* ([Milan, 1962], pp. 58-60), D'Arco Silvio Avalle uses the term "Franco-Occitan" to designate a literary blend of Occitan and Poitevin. I see no reason not to extend its use to all artificial mixtures of French and Occitan, since these are much in need of a label without dialectal implications. For example, however one defines the ingredients that make up the hybrid language of the Oxford *Girart de Roussillon*, this important koiné can appropriately be called Franco-Occitan.

126

[32]I thus concur with Mario Roques' criticism of the linguistic conclusions reached by the poem's editor, Camille Chabaneau, "Le *Roman d'Arles*," *Revue des Langues Romanes* 32 (1888), 479. In Roques' opinion ("Le *Roman d'Arles*," *Histoire Littéraire de la France*, 38 [1949], 639 n. 1), Chabaneau's French forms are in all probability "francismes littéraires."

[33]André Moisan, "Les sépultures des Français morts à Roncevaux," *Cahiers de Civilisation Médiévale* 24 (1981), 139-41.

[34]This paper was previously published in *Olifant* 8/4 (summer 1981).

127

The Evolution of
the Matter of Fierabras:
Present State of Research

André de Mandach

In an irony of fate, the story of Fierabras was the first *chanson de geste* ever to be edited by a philologist (Immanuel Bekker, 1829), yet it was so completely overshadowed by the *Chanson de Roland* discovered a few years later that it became the most neglected French epic. More than 150 years have elapsed since the milestone of this first publication; yet, the incredible riddle of the versions of the epos, in verse and in prose—in French, Latin, Spanish, Portuguese, Italian, German, Dutch, Irish, and English—has not been solved. Due to the "Cinderella" status of the matter of Fierabras, most of the versions remained unpublished until recently. A large number of printed texts were simply not taken into account because they were written in Middle English, Spanish, Portuguese, or medieval Italian and thus seemed insignificant to the predominantly French historians of French literature, the majority of whom were unable to read these works; consequently, these versions remained hermetically sealed documents.

Let us recall that the matter of Fierabras forms a literary diptych, its two panels containing the following:
A. *The Destruction of Rome*. After the invasion of Italy and the sack of Rome, the Saracens abscond to Muslim Spain with the relics of the Passion of Jesus Christ. Charlemagne pursues them.

B. *The Song of Fierabras*. After prolonged hostilities, Charlemagne and his troups vanquish the Saracens in Spain. The Christians' itinerary has started at Morimonde, where they have disembarked, and ended at the bridge of Mautrible on the river Flagot and at the nearby fortress of Aigremore, where the Saracens have led captive a few Christians. The Emir Balan's daughter, the beautiful Princess Floripas, pities the Christians imprisoned by her father and sets them free because she has already fallen in love with one of them—Guy of Burgundy—during the siege of Rome by the Saracens; they subsequently become engaged. Together with her brother Fierabras she accepts baptism, then marries her lover, the new king of Spain. The holy relics of Christ are retrieved and brought to Saint-Denis, where they attract thousands of pilgrims, reinforcing the belief that France is God's own country and that the French king is the defender of faith.

Some manuscripts combine the two panels of the literary diptych, while others relate only one or the other. Most scholars have limited their research to only four texts, whereas I have taken into account no fewer than 130 texts; moreover, I have bibliography of manuscripts and incunabula which contains 105 items for Europe alone. These figures bring into perspective the tremendous progress made lately.

Four texts formed the main base of scholarly research in the past:

1. *P*. The Provençal version of the early thirteenth century published by Bekker in 1829, thanks to a preserved transcription by Lachmann; it includes the final third of the *Destruction of Rome* and the full *Song of Fierabras*. The first printing of 1829 was followed in June 1830 by a second printing, still bearing the date of 1829 and with a list of a large number of errata. Later, Hoffmann and Baist, as well as Fischer, compiled new lists of errors; nevertheless, a large number of erroneous readings or misprints can still be found. According to Pierre Bec and Max Pfister, the elaboration of a new publication of this literarily and linguistically relevant text has discouraged scholars to date.[1]

2. *Mousket*. Around 1245, Bishop Philippe Mousket of Tournai composed a summary of the *Destruction of Rome*. It was published in 1836-38 by the Baron de Reiffenberg, with several errors.[2]

3. *A*. A poor edition of the *Song of Fierabras* in French verse was published in 1860 by Kroeber and Servois. In the main it is simply a transcription of the MS. Bibl. Nat., f. fr. 12603 of Paris, dating back to the thirteenth century, with occasional corrections based on one fragmentary Vatican manuscript of the fourteenth century, MS. Bibl. Vat. Regina 16 16 B, anno 1317, and two fifteenth-century manuscripts of London and Paris, MSS Brit. Lib., Royal 15 E VI and Bibl. Nat., f. fr. 1499. A

number of lines were simply omitted by the editors, and several mistakes were committed.[3]

4. *Hanover*. In 1873 Gustav Gröber published an Anglo-Norman *Destruction de Rome* based on the thirteenth-century manuscript of Hanover, Provinzialbibliothek, IV 578. However, he did not edit the text as it was, but rather fancied to turn it into an artificial Picardian scripta as he imagined existed at that time; as a result, this edition is not trustworthy.[4]

The material used by scholars such as Gaston Paris, Joseph Bédier, Gustav Gröber, Heinrich Jarník, Mario Roques, and Philippe Lauer represents a very tiny base, and much importance cannot be ascribed to it. I originally planned to expose their various theories on the evolution of the matter of Fierabras, following a summary of the late Hamilton M. Smyser, but soon realized that this device would have taken much space and have been of little interest.

1) *The new research tools in the matter of Fierabras*

To infuse new blood into the matter, I took a number of steps. In 1981 I completed an edition of the *Song of Fierabras* based on the Hanover manuscript of the fourteenth century, bearing the variants of the other texts in French verse, an edition that had been established by Alfons Hilka and his team at the University of Göttingen in the thirties. Among the variants included were those of the MS E of the Escorial, dating back to the thirteenth century, one of the very best; those of the MS D (Didot-Louvain) have to be especially noted. The latter is a thirteenth-century Anglo-Norman text, in places the most archaic—even the most archaic of all. Unfortunately, it was destroyed during a German bombing of Louvain in 1940. It was believed to be completely lost except for the excerpts of a few lines published by Léon Gautier. Fortunately, I discovered that two passages of an unidentified transcription by the Hilka team belonged to the Didot-Louvain manuscript; I have edited and published these passages in my *Naissance et développement de la chanson de geste en Europe*, V, *La geste de Fierabras. Le jeu du réel et de l'invraisemblable Avec des textes inédits* (Geneva, 1987), Appendix III.

In this volume I produce a detailed analysis of the evolution of the matter of Fierabras and expose a full bibliography listing the 105 texts for Europe alone previously mentioned. Also included is a new edition of Mousket's verse summary based on the unique manuscript of Paris, and a new edition of the Geneva fragments of the end of the thirteenth century.[5]

In addition, I have had the good fortune to discover and publish the fragments of a mainly Walloon, partially Lorrain *Fierabras* belonging to the group of amplified texts of the Meuse-Moselle basin, known at this time through diverse fragmentary writings of Strasbourg, Metz, and Mons and the fifteenth-century anonymous prose published by Maria Carla Marinoni (Milan, 1979) and a few years later by Jean Miquet (Ottawa, 1983). Following the kind suggestion of Louis Remacle, I asked Martine Thiry-Stassin of the University of Liège to provide a collateral linguistic study of its scripta. Moreover, Marc Le Person of the University of Lyons III is preparing a critical edition of *Fierabras* for his doctorat at the Sorbonne under the guidance of Professor Roger Lathullière. Le Person bases his publication on the Escorial manuscript and includes a complete catalogue of the non-orthographical variants of all other texts in French verse—including the Didot-Louvain and the newly discovered fragments.

2) *The new research tools in the matter of the "Destruction of Rome"*

In 1973 I discovered a good handwritten edition of the Hanover *Destruction of Rome* with textual, linguistic, and literary line commentaries by the late Albert Stimming of the University of Göttingen. I turned it over to Heinrich Speich, who planned a new diplomatic edition on this basis for his doctoral dissertation at the University of Zurich under the direction of Marc-René Jung. Under these circumstances, the topic was not supposed to be released to the public until Speich had defended his thesis. However, Luciano Formisano independently published the Hanover manuscript in his critical edition (Florence, 1981), in which he attempts to re-establish the Picardian model of this Anglo-Norman text.

Volume five of my *Naissance et développement de la chanson de geste en Europe* contains a new edition of the Geneva text, these arcaic fragments of the *Destruction of Rome* discovered in 1915 by Ernest Muret and published in *Romania* 44 (1915-17), 215-20. The technique of this version with its ill forebodings and favorable predictions is strikingly reminiscent of that of the *Chanson d'Antioche*. Together with Mousket's verse summary and the hybrid *Fierabraccia ed Ulivieri*,[6] the Geneva text affords a good idea of the most archaic version of the literary diptych of the *Geste de Fierabras* (the WHITE VERSION). The transition between the *Destruction of Rome* and the *Song of Fierabras* that reports the massing of the Saracens' troops is only to be found in this version and the *Sowdone of Babylon*. This link has never been acknowledged to date, as Romance scholars familiar with medieval Italian have ignored the existence of a relevant Middle English text, while on the other side Anglicists occupied with the *Sowdone* have never thought of referring to an Italian text in this connection.

3) *The new perspectives*

In sum, what is still lacking is the European prospect. From the point of view of the whole matter of Fierabras, the combined European-Latin

American outlook is nonexistent. If being aware of the nature of the language or knowing the country where a certain text was composed does not seem particularly thrilling, on the other hand I ascribe much importance to which stage of development of the Fierabras matter this writing belongs and whether it pertains to oral, written, or mixed chains of communication. For Romance and English scholars of the United States, it is particularly fascinating to observe how oral transmission works in the new world among the old farmers of the sierras of Puerto Rico, who are still singing the *décimas* of Fierabras, Floripas, and Guy of Burgundy.

By scrutinizing the nomenclature of the Fierabras songs in Chile, northern Colombia, Panama, Cuba, Brazil, and Puerto Rico, then by drawing a parallel to the naming of the European texts, I was able to discover what can be termed the *Ur-Fierabras* (in French, the *Fierabras primitif*). The *décima* of Panama, e.g., is a hybrid, a combination of this *Ur-Fierabras* and the series of six ballads composed by one *aficionado* of Compostela, Juan José López of the beginning of the eighteenth century, studied by Hans-Erich Keller.[7] These *romances* were inspired by Nicolás de Piamonte's Spanish adaptation of Jehan Bagnyon's *Fierabras* of the end of the fifteenth century.

Until recently, these pieces were only known through printed fly sheets (*pliegos sueltos*) of the eighteenth century, published a century later by Agustín Durán in his *Romancero*. However, a second version exists, producing several archaic lines, which is close to the model of Juan José López. This version was sung by the reciter David Sandoval in 1951 in Patagonia (650 km south of Santiago de Chile, between Valdivia and La Unión) to the folklore scholar Yolanda Pino Saavedra.

The Spanish and Portuguese colonists transmitted those songs to Latin America, then these themes passed on either in the form of books or of fly sheets or through oral transmission from generation to generation. In 1536, at the Rio de la Plata in Argentina, a soldier under the sentence of death was singing ballads called *Los Doce Pares de Francia*, a title equally reminiscent of the Spanish prose of Piamonte and the ballads of Juan José López called *Romances de Carlo-Magno y de los Doce Pares de Francia*.[8]

4) *Claude Fauriel's theory*

In the *Histoire littéraire de la France*,[9] Claude Fauriel ventured a hypothesis as to the origin of the Fierabras story, basing his arguments mainly upon the only published edition at the time, the Provençal version. According to him, the story dates back to the Reconquista of Portugal in the late eleventh century, i.e., to the times of Raymond and Henry of Burgundy, the founders of the Burgundian dynasties in Spain and Portugal.

A close study of the Provençal version has allowed the writer to ascertain that in fact Henry of Burgundy, "el Bergonho Anris," is quoted as a member of Charlemagne's army fighting the Saracens in western Spain. In the *Cantar de mio Cid* (twelfth cent.), Henry is called *Don Anrrich*. The chief enemy of the French under the Saracen Sowdone is Sortimbrand of *Conimbre*; now, *Conimbria*, *Conimbre* are the old names of *Coimbra* on the Mondego, Raymond's and Henry of Burgundy's first capital of their new realm. Historically, the French took up their quarters in Coimbra and Montemor, a city thirty kilometers down the Mondego from Coimbra. In *Fierabras*, the French headquarters is not *Monte-mor* but *Mori-monde*, a humorous nickname: indeed, before the fortress was seized by the Christians it was the 'world of the Moors'; furthermore, in view of my later observations on the river name *Flagot*, it is noteworthy to observe that *Morimonde* is the loose reversal of *Montemor*. Proceeding on their triumphant way, the French reached a large river, presumably the Tajo or Tejo, Latin FLUMEN TAGO, abbreviated on the maps as FL. TAGO. The obvious question to formulate next is what kind of French-sounding name might have been fabricated from this appellation. The *Song of Fierabras* calls the large stream Flagot, a designation which indeed sounds quite French: is it an anagram of *Fl-agot*? Numerous other place and proper names of *Fierabras* are given code appellations; my recent book offers solutions to some of these riddles. These mere samples demonstrate that Fauriel's hypothesis is not to be taken lightly.

Just as Gaston Paris and Joseph Bédier suggested a century ago, thanks to their prodigious insight, the *Destruction of Rome* appears to have been conceived of as a prelude to the *Song of Fierabras*. Its actual events stem from the history and topography of Rome in the sixth to the eleventh centuries, in particular the middle sixth century. Together, the *Destruction of Rome* and *Fierabras* were combined into a literary diptych which the writer terms the WHITE VERSION. As mentioned above, we know it through Philippe Mousket, the Geneva fragments and *Fierabraccia ed Ulivieri*. As was the case with my edition of the *Chanson d'Aspremont*, the matter is so intricate that the creation of a stemma of the whole evolution is beset with difficulties. We can, however, distinguish between more archaic and more evolved versions. The more archaic a version, the lighter the color I have attributed to its name.[10]

5) *The White, Yellow, Rose and Blue Versions*
In the course of the twelfth century, the WHITE VERSION was subjected to a re-adjustment: the YELLOW VERSION. It is preserved in the Hanover *Destruction* and the hybrid Provençal version, as well as in its derivates, the ROSE and BLUE VERSIONS. In these texts, the French

134

troops arrive before Rome after the sack of the Eternal City and the Saracens' escape to Morimonde in Spain. Originally, the duel between Fierabras and Oliver took place in or near Rome, and Oliver threw the flasks of Christ's holy balsam into the Tiber. In the YELLOW VERSION, this brilliantly narrated episode is transferred to Morimonde in Spain, where it picturesquely inaugurates the second part of the literary diptych, the *Song of Fierabras*.

The ROSE VERSION is a dramatized adaptation of the full YELLOW VERSION, including both the *Destruction* and *Fierabras*. Composed in England, it was adapted to the taste of the English audience for action and drama. Psychological interpretations and lengthy conversations are reduced, and humour abounds. We are aware of it through an Anglo-Norman text of the mid-fourteenth century, the Egerton manuscript of the British Library, published by Louis Brandin as late as 1938,[11] and through an English slapstick comedy adaptation of the fifteenth century, the *Sowdone of Babylon*, a text which has just been republished by Stephen F. Lappert.[12] It is also known to us through the first 3420 lines of the hybrid Ashmole *Firumbras*, a combination of the ROSE VERSION and the first BLUE VERSION. The ROSE VERSION offers the most systematic structure of all, and often the most archaic arrangement of episodes. Unfortunately, it has been neglected by the French and German scholars who have dealt with the matter of Fierabras, in part because the Anglo-Norman Egerton text did not become available before World War II, partly because these scholars did not understand Middle English. My recent book contains a ''Table of Concordances'' between the YELLOW, ROSE, and BLUE VERSIONS which should facilitate comparison. This concordance reveals that several important episodes were omitted from the Hanover manuscript of the *Destruction of Rome*, whereas they are included in the ROSE VERSION. As a result, the true worth of the ROSE VERSION, and especially that of the Middle English texts, can now fully be acknowledged.

The BLUE VERSION itself is a hybrid. To a large extent it derives from the YELLOW VERSION, but it includes reminiscences of the *Destruction of Rome* relating to the fight of the French inside of Rome, i.e., an episode borrowed from the WHITE VERSION. Some texts, especially MSS Paris, Bibl. Nat., f. fr. 12603, and Madrid, Escurial, M-III-21,[13] involve literary fossils of the WHITE VERSION: Fierabras and Oliver measure swords near Morimonde on the Spanish coast, but Oliver throws the flasks of Christ's holy balsam into the lower Tiber, the *Far de Rome*. Here the whole *Song of Fierabras* swells from an approximate 3000 lines to more than 6200 lines!

In my check-list of *Fierabras* texts, I counted all versions during a period of more than four centuries, including two manuscripts, the Editio Princeps of 1478, the numerous reprintings of Geneva, Lyon, Paris, Troyes, etc., the reworking for the Bibliothèque Bleue in Troyes, and so on, arriving—as previously stated—at 105 items, of which 91 refer to the BLUE VERSION. This schedule affords proof as to how wide the diffusion of *Fierabras* has been in Europe alone: no doubt it was the best-seller of all medieval French epics.[14]

6) *Jehan Bagnyon*

Bagnyon's French prose adaptation is principally preserved through three works: the two manuscripts of Geneva and Cologny-Geneva, and the Edition Princeps of 1478 printed in Geneva. Bagnyon's work is not a mere translation, but a skillful adaptation of the twelfth century text to the era of the first dawnings of Humanism and Renaissance. Bagnyon also possessed a great deal of managerial skill: at his suggestion, three communities were consolidated into the city of Lausanne, and he became its first mayor in 1481. As an apt organizer, he stressed the figure of Fierabras in the structure of his book; moreover, he tried to explore the psychological and moral background of the deeds of the protagonists—a must on the shores of the Lake of Geneva!

Bagnyon's text as revealed in the two manuscripts had its definite flaws. Its orthography was sometimes very provincial. Fortunately, Adam Steinschaber of Römhild (near Schweinfurt), a former student at the University of Erfurt, applied all his German punctiliousness to Bagnyon's manuscript and published it in an admirable printed form, the Editio Princeps of 1478; this achievement has never been recognized to date. In his time, however, the work was crowned with success, to the point that six years after its first printing, William Caxton adopted it for his English translation of *Fierabras* and published it in London. *Fierabras* was the second book ever printed in Geneva and the fourth ever put to press in London by Caxton, a fact that underlines its relevance in the eyes of the public of that time. Caxton's *History and Lyf of the Noble and Crysten Prince Charles the Grete* (1484) left its mark on the history of English prose.

In 1498, Pedro Hagenbach published in Toledo Nicolás de Piamonte's translation of Bagnyon's work into Spanish; this translation knew inordinate success in Spain, in the French Pyrenees, in Portugal, and Latin America. Castet (near Arudy, dep. Gers) and a nearby Basque village in the dep. Pyrénées-Atlantiques saw in the eighteenth and nineteenth centuries the performances of French and Basque plays on the Twelve Peers of

France, Fierabras and the Battle of Roncesvalles, all dependent on Ba-gnyon-Piamonte.[15]

In Portugal, Jeronimo Moreyra de Carvalho published in 1728 a translation of Piamonte's Spanish version, the *Historia do Emperador Carlos Magno, e dos doze Pares de França*; two centuries later, a play or *auto sagramental* entitled *Auto de Floripes* is acted: its text was published in 1954 in Lisbon, and a film was subsequently produced, as mentioned, by Camâra Cascudo, who also alludes to plays on the theme of Fierabras in the interior of Brazil.[16] During the feasts of St. Nicholas and of the Virgin of Guadalupe, on December 6 and 12 in Acatlán (Near Izucar de Matamoros, close to Puebla), in Puebla itself, and in Tlaxcala (Mexico), *Danzas de Moros y Cristianos* are performed with re-enactments of epi-sodes of *Fierabras*.[17] Thus, Jehan Bagnyon scored the greatest success of any medieval French author in France, England, Germany, Spain, Portu-gal, and Latin America; yet, to reiterate, he is practically unknown today.

To sum up: Born during the Reconquista of Portugal, the matter of Fierabras was enriched by a lengthy prelude set in Rome, the papal seat and the capital of the Christian world on the eve of the twelfth century, as an incentive for the crusades into the Occident and Orient. Organized as a literary diptych, with a refined interlaced technique, it has passed through a number of stages to become a best-seller in Western Europe and Latin America.

Even though this field has been spurned in the past, new tools of research are now brought into being. For scholars throughout the world, it raises the promise of new discoveries.

Notes

[1]*Der Roman von Fierabras, provenzalisch*, ed. Immanuel Bekker, Ab-handlungen der Preussischen Akademie der Wissenschaften, historisch-phi-lologische Klasse 10 (Berlin, 1829). Both editions, the small and the large, have the same title and date. Pierre Bec has informed me that Michael A. Pountney and a colleague will probably publish a new edition on the basis of the former's *Thèse de IIIᵉ Cycle*, entitled *Fierabras d'Alichandre. Chanson de geste occitane du XIIIᵉ siècle, éditée d'après l'unique manuscrit* (Diss., Poitiers, 1980).

[2]Philippe Mouskès, *Chronique rimée*, ed. Frédéric de Reiffenberg, 1 (Brussels, 1836), vv. 4664-717.

[3]*Fierabras. Parise la Duchesse*, ed. Auguste Kroeber and Gustave Servois, Anciens Poëtes de la France 4 (Paris, 1860).

[4]Gustav Gröber, ''La *Destruction de Rome*, première branche de la chanson de geste *Fierabras*,'' *Romania* 2 (1873), 1-48.

[5]André de Mandach, *Naissance et développement de la chanson de geste en Europe*, V, *La geste de Fierabras*. *Le jeu du réel et de l'invraisemblable*. *Avec des textes inédits* (Geneva, 1987), Appendix I, sections *a* and *b*.

[6]Elio Melli of the University of Bologna, who is preparing a new edition of this work, includes several manuscripts and incunabula not available to Edmund Stengel's edition *Il cantare di Fierabraccia ed Ulivieri*. *Italienische Bearbeitung der Chanson de geste Fierabras*, Ausgaben und Abhandlungen aus dem Gebiete der romanischen Philologie, 2 (Marburg, 1881); separately, he has recently published MS 6208 of the Guarnacci Library of Volterra: *I Cantari de Fiorabraccia e Ulivieri*, Biblioteca di Filologia Romanza della Facoltà di Lettere e Filosofia di Bologna 3 (Bologna, 1984).

[7]Hans-Erich Keller, "Un autre legs de la légende poétique de Charlemagne en Espagne," in *Essor et fortune de la chanson de geste dans l'Europe et l'Orient latin*, Actes du IXᵉ Congrès International de la Société Internationale Rencesvals pour l'Étude des Épopées Romanes, Padoue-Venise, 29 août - 4 septembre 1982 (Modena, 1984), pp. 321-31.

[8]See Irving A. Leonard, *Romances of chivalry in the Spanish Indies. With some registros of books to the Spanish colonies* (Berkeley, 1933); *Los libros del conquistador* (Mexico and Buenos Aires, 1953), pp. 60, 228, 376; Yolanda Pino Saavedra, "La *Historia de Carlomagno y de los Doce Pares de Francia* en Chile. A la memoria de Vicente T. Mendoza," *Folklore Americas* [Havana] 26, fasc. 2 (1966), 1-29, esp. pp. 2-3. See also Francisco Rodriguez Marín, *El Quijote y Don Quijote en América* (Madrid, 1911), p. 32; Luis da Câmara Cascudo, *Literatura oral* (Rio de Janeiro, 1952), p. 203.

[9]Claude Fauriel, "Ferabras," in *Histoire littéraire de la France*, 22 (1852), p. 208. See also, for certain facts, G. A. Knott, "The Historical Sources of Fierabras," *The Modern Language Review* 52 (1957), 504-09.

[10]Mandach, *Naissance et développement*, V, Appendix IV, chap. 5.

[11]Louis Brandin, "La *Destruction de Rome* et *Fierabras*. Ms. Egerton 3028, Musée Britannique, Londres," *Romania* 64 (1938), 18-100.

[12]Stephen F. Lappert, *The Romaunce of "The Sowdon of Babylone"*: *A Critical Edition*, Dissertation Abstracts International 36 (Feb. 1976), 319.

[13]See Hermann Knust, "Ein Beitrag zur Kenntniss der Escorialbibliothek. Französische Literatur: *Le chevalier de la Charrette*. *Fierabras*," *Jahrbuch für romanische und englische Literatur* 9 (1868), 43-72.

[14]Mandach, *Naissance et dévoloppement*, V, Appendix 5, chap. 6.

[15]See Hans-Erich Keller, "La *Pastorale de Roland*: A Basque Theatrical Interpretation of the Battle of Roncevaux," *Olifant* 5 (1977-78), 29-41; and "Une histoire de Charlemagne en Suisse Romande," in *Mélanges d'études romanes du Moyen Age et de la Renaissance* (Strasbourg, 1978), pp. 259-69 (about Jehan Bagnyon and his work).

[16]Luis da Câmara Cascudo, "Roland au Brésil," *Marche Romane* 12 (1962), no. 3, 69-76; Jean-Marie D'Heur, "Note additionnelle," *Marche Romane* 13 (1963), no. 3, 85-95; Teófilo Braga, "Os livros populares portuguezes (folhas-

volantes ou literatura de cordel)," *Era Nova* 1 ([Lisbon,] 1880-81), 3-19, 193-203; Luis da Câmara Cascudo, *Cinco livros de povo* (Rio de Janeiro, 1953), p. 443.

[17]Arturo Warman Grij, *La danza de Moros y Cristianos* (Mexico, 1972); Mandach, *Naissance et développement*, V, Appendix IV, chap. 6.

Le développement de la *Geste de Montauban* en France jusqu'à la fin du moyen âge

François Suard

La geste de *Renaut de Montauban* a connu, depuis son apparition au début du treizième siècle et jusqu'à la fin du moyen âge, un développement extraordinaire. Non seulement en effet la chanson a été traduite ou adaptée en néerlandais, en allemand, en italien et en langue norroise, mais d'innombrables suites ou remaniements, en vers ou en prose, ont cherché à exploiter l'intérêt et l'émotion suscités par la légende[1].

Ce succès, que l'on pourrait comparer par exemple au manque relatif d'audience du *Cycle de Guillaume d'Orange*[2] à la fin du moyen âge, fait question: qu'est-ce qui, dans les thèmes développés par la chanson, dans les personnages qu'elle met en scène, dans sa structure même, peut expliquer un tel bonheur? Impossible, peut-être, d'apporter ici des réponses assurées; c'est pourtant de ce type de problème que dépend, à notre avis, la compréhension des voies dans lesquelles s'est engagée la geste au cours des étapes qui ont marqué son extension.

Notre enquête débutera donc par un examen de la chanson du treizième siècle, que nous scruterons en nous demandant quels sont les éléments qui portent le germe des développements ultérieurs. Nous étudierons ensuite ces développements dans le domaine français, nous efforçant de les situer les uns par rapport aux autres, de façon à proposer, dans le cadre du *Renaut*, une problématique de la création littéraire épique et post-épique.

141

La chanson de Renaut de Montauban[3]
à *la charnière de l'épopée et du récit*

La lecture de *RM* fait apparaître une fresque dramatique très serrée, d'où se dégagent des scènes puissantes, de tonalité diverse. Le pathétique est fréquent et résulte de plusieurs types de situation: scènes de bataille ou de meurtre (mort de Lohier, vv. 605-703; mort de Beuves d'Aigremont, vv. 1610-25; combat de la roche Mabon, vv. 7241-511), construction rigoureuse d'un suspens (guet-apens de Vaucouleurs, vv. 5999-6683; préparatifs pour l'exécution de Richard, vv. 10396-530), face à face tragique (rencontre d'Aimon et de ses fils devant Montessor, vv. 2385-2401; vaines propositions de paix faites par Renaud lorsque Charles est captif à Montauban, vv. 12791-914) ou réconciliations émouvantes (les frères de Renaud se repentant de l'avoir accusé de trahison, vv. 6753-88; Aimon faisant parvenir de la nourriture à ses enfants, vv. 13499-591). Le comique, pourtant, n'est pas absent: il est lié aux tours de Maugis, véritables gabs dont l'empereur fait les frais. On se souvient, notamment, du séjour incognito du larron sous la tente de Charlemagne, lorsqu'il parvient non seulement à se faire servir par le roi, mais à contraindre Charles à lui mettre le morceau dans la bouche:

> Maugis oeuvre la geule a guisse de grifon
> Et Charles li mist ens le morsel a bandon.
> (vv. 9654-55)

Il faut noter aussi la place importante faite au merveilleux. Celui-ci accompagne généralement les tours de Maugis, mais n'est pas toujours destiné à faire rire; à Montauban, par exemple, il a d'abord une fonction stratégique, lorsque Maugis endort ceux qui pourraient l'empêcher de porter secours à ses cousins (vv. 7603-08). Le merveilleux chrétien est présent lui aussi, soit lorsqu'une nuée, envoyée par Dieu, interrompt le combat entre Roland et Renaud (vv. 12271-84), soit lorsque des miracles désignent la dépouille de Renaud comme un corps saint (vv. 18236-395). À côte du pathétique, du comique et du merveilleux, il convient donc de noter l'esprit religieux de certaines scènes, notamment dans la dernière partie du poème qui se présente, on le sait, comme une légende hagiographique.

Mais si le lecteur assimile sans difficulté ces tonalités diverses, s'il peut se représenter la chanson comme une fresque bigarrée[4], c'est que le texte possède, dès le début, une double caractéristique: d'une part une aptitude à construire des scènes de nature variée mais fortement individualisées, d'autre part un dynamisme, un mouvement qui évite toute rupture entre les différentes scènes, grâce aux relations établies entre elles. Or la première caractéristique nous paraît relever de procédés épiques, tandis que la seconde résulte de procédés narratifs. Sans doute n'y a-t-il pas, dans le principe de cette complémentarité, quelque chose qui distingue a priori *RM* des autres chansons, qui sont elles aussi épiques et narratives; l'histoire de Renaud et de ses frères nous paraît cependant avoir à cet égard une place à part, comme à la charnière de l'épique et du narratif, et c'est dans la nature et le dosage des procédés employés que réside probablement l'originalité du poème.

Renaut de Montauban et la confrontation épique

La chanson se caractérise tout d'abord par la présence de situations relationnelles paroxystiques, c'est-à-dire de tensions violentes dues aux relations qu'entretiennent les protagonistes. Ces tensions résultent le plus souvent des oppositions qui se produisent au sein de la communauté féodale ou de la communauté familiale.

Les conflits de type féodal sont particulièrement décisifs pour notre texte, puisqu'ils sont au point de départ du poème, avec les reproches adressés par Charlemagne à Beuves (vv. 28-73); on peut dire également qu'ils structurent l'ensemble de l'oeuvre, qui peut se lire comme un conflit de pouvoir entre un souverain - Charlemagne - et des vassaux, les quatre frères et leur cousin. D'autres personnages que les fils Aimon peuvent au reste être concernés par ce type de conflit, ainsi les pairs de France lorsqu'ils doivent s'opposer aux volontés injustes de leur seigneur (jugement de Richard, le frère de Renaud, vv. 9950-10258; départ des pairs lorsque Charlemagne refuse de sauver Richard de Normandie, vv. 15053-115).

Étroitement liés aux conflits de type féodal, les conflits de type familial accentuent le caractère tragique de la situation du héros épique dans *RM*. La fidélité d'Aimon à Charles l'oblige à devenir l'ennemi de ses propres enfants:

> Karles apele Aymon si l'a mis a raison;
> La jura li dux Aymes sor les seins abandon,
> Et forsjura ses filz sor le cors seint Simon,
> Jamais n'auront del suen vaillant .i. esperon,
> Nen es recetera a plain ne a maison[5].

Ogier, à l'inverse, refuse constamment de trahir les obligations de la parenté, qu'il tend même à privilégier par rapport au devoir vassalique: on se souvient de ses manoeuvres retardatrices pour sauver ses cousins à

Vaucouleurs (vv. 7318-539). Quant au roi Yon, terrorisé par les menaces de Charles, il viole à la fois ses devoirs de seigneur - "Renaus est mes hom liges, si com vos le savés" (v. 5830) - et les obligations familiales:

> Et si a ma seror a moillier et a per
> Renaus en a .ii. fils qui sunt de bel aé.
>
> (vv. 5832-33)

Des combinaisons innombrables peuvent être obtenues à partir des deux modèles relationnels que proposent la féodalité et la parenté; non seulement en effet un conflit peut privilégier l'un des deux types, ou au contraire les imbriquer l'un dans l'autre, mais il peut être soit médiatisé, soit rester sans solution et conduire à la destruction des protagonistes; enfin le rôle joué par un des partenaires peut être modifié (Aimon se réconcilie avec ses enfants; Yon devient leur ennemi), alors qu'un autre peut persister dans sa relation antérieure (Renaud reste fidèle à Yon).

On voit donc la richesse potentielle de ces situations relationnelles, et l'on comprend pourquoi, dans l'imaginaire du lecteur, le poème, comme le ferait un film, organise autour de scènes d'une grande intensité le déroulement du récit. Cette richesse ne suffit pourtant pas à expliquer le mouvement qui anime de telles scènes et les relie également entre elles; pour expliquer les qualités narratives de la chanson il convient aussi, semble-t-il, de faire intervenir la notion de déplacement.

Le "déplacement", pilier de la construction narrative

Tout, dans *RM*, est mouvement, et les scènes autour desquelles se structure le récit, loin d'apparaître comme figées, sont elles-mêmes le résultat de déplacements dans des domaines divers.

Déplacements dans l'espace tout d'abord. Le théâtre du drame se modifie constamment: Dordonne, Paris, la forêt des Ardennes, Montessor, Dordonne, Bordeaux, Montauban, la plaine de Vaucouleurs, Montauban, Trémoigne, Constantinople, Jérusalem, Palerme, Cologne, sont les lieux successifs de l'action. Sans doute, comme le suggère Jacques Thomas, cette errance peut-elle avoir le sens d'un pèlerinage symbolique se terminant par la passion; mais elle est d'abord mouvement propre du récit, qui entraîne le lecteur dans un espace imaginaire en perpétuelle mutation.

Déplacement dans le temps ensuite. Le récit n'explore pas seulement une période donnée de l'existence du héros; il se veut biographie de celui-ci, puisqu'il raconte ses enfances (adoubement, transgression qui le contraint à l'exil, mariage, mort), et circule même à travers plusieurs générations: le prologue est consacré à l'oncle de Renaud, tandis qu'à la fin du récit, un épisode important raconte les premiers exploits de ses fils, Yvon et Aymon (vv. 16602-7823).

Déplacement enfin au niveau du personnage épique lui-même. D'une part, avec le groupe que forment les quatre frères et leur cousin, le héros, tout en gardant sa cohérence, devient pluriel[6] et Renaud, qui est capable d'exprimer à lui seul toutes les virtualités du personnage épique, apparaît aussi comme le chef de file d'un groupe où s'attribuent et s'échangent les rôles possibles. Alard, le plus souvent, se présente comme conseiller, mais Maugis peut avoir la même fonction (vv. 3689-94); Richard est le plus souvent un guerrier impétueux, mais c'est Renaud qui tue Bertolai et qui veut, devant Montessor, faire périr Charlemagne[7]. Cette structure de groupe est donc essentiellement dynamique, puisqu'elle se prête à de continuels échanges entre personnages. Mais avec Maugis un autre type de déplacement s'ajoute au précédent et s'opère à l'intérieur du personnage. Maugis, larron et enchanteur, est aussi chevalier[8]; il peut être à la fois l'un et l'autre, comme lorsqu'il vient en aide à ses cousins dans les combats de Vaucouleurs, mais aussi tantôt l'un (chevalier, il affronte Olivier, 11180-208), tantôt l'autre (enchanteur, il vole la couronne de Charles et les épées des pairs, vv. 11611-50).

Grâce à ces divers procédés, *RM* acquiert une mobilité qui se donne comme la compétence narrative propre de la chanson. Les épisodes s'enchaînent les uns aux autres sans jamais lasser le lecteur, et les additions successives qui ont sans doute constitué le poème (prologue, rébellions vassaliques, légende pieuse) se fondent harmonieusement dans une cohérence dynamique.

Mais une telle efficacité narrative ne peut être dissociée de la force épique analysée plus haut. C'est dans la conjonction de ces deux propriétés que réside, à notre avis, le secret du développement, au cours du moyen âge, de la geste de Montauban, dont nous allons suivre maintenant les principaux aspects.

Un développement aux formes multiples

L'histoire de la légende n'est pas seulement caractérisée, comme pour beaucoup de textes épiques, par le phénomène de la mise en prose; elle combine au contraire les procédés les plus variés. La chanson du treizième siècle possède une tradition manuscrite fournie et témoignant de relectures nombreuses; elle se dote de plusieurs continuations, est mise en prose au quinzième siècle et se trouve ainsi à l'origine d'innombrables éditions. Avant la fin du quatorzième siècle un remaniement en vers, mis en prose au quinzième, et dont certaines parties seront imprimées, amplifie et modifie les données de la geste.

Une tradition manuscrite fournie, témoin d'un texte en perpétuelle évolution

La tradition manuscrite de *RM* est abondante[9], puisqu'elle ne compte pas moins de dix manuscrits: c'est beaucoup plus que les autres chansons de barons rebelles[10], et, du reste, que la plupart des textes épiques. Mais surtout l'examen des manuscrits, tel qu'a pu le faire Jacques Thomas pour l'épisode ardennais, fait apparaître un constant travail de réfection, qui va notamment dans le sens de l'amplification narrative. Ainsi, lorsque les quatre frères s'enfuient de Paris, après le meurtre de Bertolai, le manuscrit le plus ancien (D, Oxford, Bodléienne, 121, milieu du treizième siècle) conte l'affaire avec célérité. Les fugitifs réussissent à quitter la cour, mais à Senlis leurs chevaux faiblissent; Renaud désarçonne un adversaire, prend son cheval et le donne à Alard, tandis que Guichard et Richard montent en croupe sur Bayard[11]. Dans le MS O (Oxford, Bodléienne, Laud. misc. 637, a. 1333), seul Renaud parvient à éviter la capture, mais Maugis, qui accompagne Alard, Guichard et Richard, use de magie et délivre tout le monde:

> Parmi l'uis de la chartre a .i. soufle jeté,
> Que cil qui sunt dehors furent tuit enchanté,
> Li us de la chartre ovre si est laïs volé[12].

Avec le MS V (Venise, Saint-Marc, fr. XVI, 1390-1400), une péripétie nouvelle apparaît; une fois délivrés, les frères de Renaud et Maugis s'emparent de Charlemagne et l'emprisonnent à leur place:

> Maugis li mist el poins un brand d'acier letré,
> E dist: "Or guetera trestot estre son gré
> Karllemaine sa chartre ou tant a oscurté[13].

Naturellement, tous les manuscrits ne modifient pas leur modèle dans le même sens, mais nous pouvons déjà noter dans la tradition un courant qui tend à exploiter et à développer les éléments narratifs du texte.

Une nouvelle utilisation du personnage d'enchanteur: *Maugis d'Aigremont*

A une date relativement précoce (première moitié du treizième siècle), une nouvelle chanson, *Maugis d'Aigremont*[14], réutilise le déplace-

ment créé à l'intérieur du personnage épique traditionnel par la figure de
Maugis. Non seulement les traits caractéristiques de ce dernier sont accen-
tués - familiarité plus grande avec le merveilleux, apparition d'épisodes
amoureux -, mais la structure même du texte bascule du côté du roman
d'aventures, avec le schéma habituel au récit d'enfances[15].

A partir d'une séparation initiale, le récit déploie en effet une straté-
gie d'entrelacement des aventures qui a pour but ultime de réunir tout le
monde. Maugis et Vivien, fils de Beuves d'Aigremont et de la duchesse,
sont arrachés à leurs parents dès leur naissance, tandis qu'Ysane, soeur de
la duchesse et fille d'Hernault de Moncler, est emmenée en captivité chez
les païens. Vivien est conduit à Montbrant, tandis que Maugis, enlevé par
une esclave, est recueilli par la fée Oriande et qu'Ysane devient l'époux du
Sarrasin Aquillant de Mayogre, qui lui donne un fils, Brandoine. On
assiste donc au début de l'histoire à une sorte de dislocation de l'espace,
ainsi qu'à une multiplication des personnages: il conviendra, au fil des
péripéties, de revenir au théâtre initial de l'action et de réunir, non
seulement les personnages qui ont été autrefois séparés, mais tous ceux qui
sont petit à petit entrés en scène et se rattachent, d'une manière ou d'une
autre, au lignage d'Aigremont.

Maugis *d'Aigremont* fait donc un pas décisif en direction du roman
d'aventures et se trouve beaucoup plus différent de *RM* que certains textes
postérieurs, qui ont gardé une structure proche de l'épopée.

Poèmes épisodiques: *Vivien de Monbranc* et fin postiche de *Renaut de
Montauban*

Cette proximité relative à l'égard de la chanson traditionnelle est
notamment le fait de deux petites continuations qui se rattachent, l'une à
Maugis, l'autre à *RM*. Le *Vivien de Monbranc*, petit texte de 1099 vers
qui n'est contenu que dans le MS M (Montpellier, Faculté de Médecine, H
247)[16], prolonge en effet de façon assez directe le récit des aventures de
Maugis et de Vivien son frère, lequel devient le héros d'une nouvelle
guerre menée contre les païens; mais ce texte constitue également un
nouveau type d'introduction à *RM*: on assiste en effet aux enfances de
Renaud qui, en compagnie d'Alard, fait ses premières armes avec un
bâton, puisqu'il n'a pas encore été adoubé; d'autre part le conflit entre
Charlemagne et Beuves est rendu prévisible par le refus qu'oppose l'empereur à une demande d'aide militaire présentée par Beuves ainsi que par
la violence de Lohier. Il s'agit là, sans doute, d'une querelle différente de
celle qui est évoquée au début de *RM*, mais ce trait ne suffit pas, à notre
avis, à faire de *Vivien de Monbranc* autre chose qu'une continuation, sans

doute assez tardive de *Maugis*, dans laquelle un remanieur réélabore librement les données des textes antérieurs[17].

Le petit poème de 1244 vers qui prend place, dans le MS N (Paris, Bibl. Nat. fr. 766), après le texte de *RM*, doit être interprété comme une continuation de cette chanson, et non de *Maugis*. Le texte de liaison indique en effet que l'auteur veut compléter la chanson sur un point précis:

> Si diron de Maugis, le bon larron prové,
> Comme il ot puis sa pes a Charle le doté[18];

mais il va en fait plus loin et se donne pour tâche de raconter les circonstances de la mort des frères de Renaud et de ses fils, enfumés par les Sarrasins dans une grotte. Le titre donné au passage depuis Castets, *La mort de Maugis*, n'est donc pas très satisfaisant, car le remaniement ne modifie pas sur ce point les données de la chanson[19]; il laisse d'autre part entendre que le texte est une continuation du *Maugis*, ce qui est très inexact. Sans doute, la place faite au merveilleux est assez remarquable et peut traduire l'influence du récit d'enfances, mais l'élément religieux est, lui aussi, très important, et nous renvoie à *RM*[20].

Le remaniement en vers (fin du quatorzième siècle?)

Deux manuscrits des environs de 1440[21] nous ont transmis, l'un un texte très développé, l'autre deux fragments, procédant à coup sûr d'un remaniement antérieur, comme le montre un extrait des comptes de Louis, duc d'Orléans, en mai 1396, qui mentionne une tapisserie racontant ''l'istoire des enfans Regnault de Montauban et des enfants de Riseus de Ripemont''[22], épisode caractéristique du texte conservé. Dans la chanson primitive, en effet, Yvon et Aymon affrontent à la cour de Charles les fils de Fouques de Morillon, tué par Renaut à Vaucouleurs, alors que dans le remaniement ils sont en butte à la calomnie des quatre fils de Ripeu de Ribemont.

Outre l'extension considérable apportée au texte - le manuscrit développé compte environ vingt-neuf mille vers -, la caractéristique essentielle du remaniement est la modification apportée à l'équilibre du récit: sur 218 fols., seuls les 70 premiers sont consacrés à la guerre contre Charlemagne, soit un peu plus de 9000 vers, contre 13.400 dans l'édition Castets. C'est dire que la partie capitale du poème traditionnel est fortement abrégée, étant donné par ailleurs que le passage en question comporte des éléments nouveaux, comme une tentative de Ganelon pour faire périr Charlemagne.

Le plus important, pour l'auteur de la nouvelle rédaction, est donc ce qui suit la conclusion de la paix, et plus précisément le voyage de Renaud outre-mer ainsi que les aventures de ses enfants. Ce qui, dans la chanson du treizième siècle, tenait en 2700 vers environ, occupe ici près de 20.000 vers: il s'agit donc bien d'un remaniement, c'est-à-dire d'un rééquilibrage complet du texte.

Ce dernier s'opère dans un sens qui rejoint, au moins en partie, *Maugis d'Aigremont*. Le voyage outre-mer devient, en effet, dans l'amplification dont il est l'objet, une suite de péripéties qui s'enchaînent les unes aux autres, en se rapprochant de la technique romanesque de l'entrelacement des aventures[23]. Les épisodes amoureux tiennent une place importante, avec les amours des fils de Renaud ou les frasques de Berfuné, et le merveilleux est développé. De la sorte l'esprit épique cède parfois la place, comme dans *Maugis*, à un esprit héroï-comique. De même que le cousin de Renaud, dans le texte du treizième siècle, nous est présenté comme un séducteur - il est l'amant heureux, mais éphémère, de l'épouse de Marsile -, Berfuné, nain protégé par les fées, tente de conquérir Sinamonde. Revêtu d'un manteau qui confère l'invisibilité, il se glisse dans le lit de la jeune fille; celle-ci appelle au secours, et Renaud se précipite, mais il est aussitôt attaqué par Berfuné, qu'il ne voit pas, et doit combattre à l'aveuglette:

> Entour li escremist par grans aïremens,
> A .ii. mains quanque il pot, ainsi com pour faire renc.

Attiré par le bruit, Richier d'Acre vient à son tour, et croit que Renaut est devenu fou:

> ''Ayeue Dieu, dit il, sire sains Juliens,
> Qu'est il avenu Regnault, qui est li miens parens?
> Rendez li sa memoire, vrai peres sapiens!''

Mais il est lui-même attaqué par Berfuné et doit riposter, de la même façon que Renaud; de sorte que Baptamir, arrivant à son tour dans la chambre, pense que Renaud et Richier sont en train de se battre pour l'amour de Sinamonde, et leur fait aussitôt la morale:

> ''Laissiez le guerre ensamble, aux aultres combatés!
> C'est tout pour Sinamonde qu'estes aussi grevez:
> C'est tout contre raison, car nul droit n'y avez,
> Car en vostre contree estes vous mariés''[24].

149

Ainsi, en dépit des objectifs épiques affirmés de cette partie - Renaud veut conquérir Jérusalem, Angorie et les reliques de la Passion qui s'y trouvent -, la tonalité générale est de type romanesque.

On notera également que la place faite à Yvon et Aymon, les enfants de Renaud, s'accroît: à peine Angorie est-elle conquise que les païens, profitant du départ de Renaud pour la France, se rebellent; une nouvelle expédition outre-mer a lieu, dont les jeunes gens sont les héros. Le remaniement développe donc aussi une suite généalogique.

Reste la question de l'extension totale du poème. Le manuscrit le plus développé s'arrête à la mort de Renaud; il connaît pourtant les circonstances de la mort des trois frères du héros ainsi que de Maugis, puisqu'il raconte brièvement ces événements dans l'avant-dernier folio[25]. Nous trouvons le même récit, mais beaucoup plus développé, à la fin de l'autre manuscrit, qui nous propose en outre les aventures de Maugis devenu pape. Le manuscrit développé résume aussi une histoire de Marbrien, fils d'Yvon et petit-fils de Renaud, que seules les proses ont conservé en entier: l'enfant est enlevé par les païens et devient le pire ennemi de son lignage:

> Mes Sarrasins l'emblerent des qu'il fu enffanchon,
> A l'amiral Barré depuis le bailla on,
> Qui le fit dotriner a le loy de Mahon.
> . . . .
> Tant guerroia sen pere et le sien oncle Aymon,
> Que le sien pere fist vidier le region,
> Et le roynne aussi, Englentine au crin blon;
> En Franche s'en alerent le nobille royon.
> Marbrien si occhist le sien oncle Aymon,
> Mais il n'en savoit riens, pour vray le vous dizon.
> Mais puis sot il de vray qu'il estoit fieux Yvon,
> De quoy il se retraist a le loy de Jhezum...[26]

Or, comme les détails donnés ici correspondent parfaitement à la prose, qui revendique du reste un original en vers[27], il est probable qu'un récit en vers de l'histoire de Mabrien a existé. Le remaniement de la fin du quatorzième siècle serait donc beaucoup plus long encore que celui qui nous est parvenu, et raconterait l'histoire des Aymonides jusqu'à la génération des arrière-petits-enfants[28].

Mise en prose de la chanson primitive

Alors que le remaniement en vers multiplie, tout en conservant la forme initiale, les indices narratifs et transforme nettement le contenu du récit, la mise en prose de la chanson du treizième siècle se limite presque à l'abandon de la laisse et du vers. Les modifications existent, sans doute[29], mais le lecteur, en comparant les textes, reconnaît dans la prose la construction générale du poème.

Cette constatation permet de confirmer les observations que nous faisions plus haut sur l'originalité de *RM*: la chanson comporte, dès le début, des éléments significatifs de type narratif; pour passer du texte épico-narratif au récit romanesque, il suffit d'abandonner la forme versifiée et d'adopter la prose, dans laquelle nous pouvons reconnaître deux branches.

D'un côté une version isolée, représentée par un seul manuscrit (Londres, Brit. Mus., Sloane 960)[30], s'inspire de la version rimée la plus ancienne, celle du MS D; de l'autre six manuscrits utilisent des versions plus récentes et se divisent en deux sous-groupes, dans la mesure où la plupart (cinq sur six) commencent avec l'expédition de Charles contre les quatre frères réfugiés dans la forêt d'Ardenne, tandis que le MS Paris, Arsenal 3151 raconte d'abord l'ambassade de Lohier, la mort de Beuves et la querelle des échecs.

Les proses manuscrites présentent donc une pluralité de points de vue sur la légende: une version archaïsante se détache du lot, prenant pour support un modèle ancien; les autres textes recourent à des modèles plus récents, mais interprètent leur sujet de façon différente: pour la plupart, la guerre entre Charles et les fils Aimon n'a pas à être expliquée, soit parce qu'elle l'est dans d'autres récits, soit parce que le destin en décide seul; pour le rédacteur du manuscrit de l'Arsenal, au contraire, cette lutte inexpiable a une origine précise, qui doit être contée.

C'est la version de l'Arsenal qui est à l'origine des versions imprimées, qui paraissent tout d'abord sur les presses lyonnaises dans les années 1482-1485, chez Guillaume Le Roy, De Vingle, Nourry, puis à Paris chez la Veuve Michel Le Noir, chez Lotrian, Janot et Bonfons. Avec vingt-sept éditions, elles constituent le roman épique le plus connu jusqu'à la fin du seizième siècle[31]; sous le titre des *Quatre fils Aimon* - à partir de 1506 - l'ouvrage ne s'en tient évidemment pas là: il passe au dix-septième siècle dans la bibliothèque de colportage, fait les beaux jours de la Bibliothèque Bleue et est repris à la fin du dix-neuvième siècle par le catalogue de Pellerin à Epinal[32], où il demeure le seul témoin, à côté de *Huon de Bordeaux* et de *Valentin et Orson*, de la tradition épique. Encore faut-il remarquer que les *Quatre fils*, malgré les déformations inévitables apportées par les éditions successives, nous mettent plus directement en contact avec l'esprit épique que les deux autres romans: *Huon*[33] y figure en effet avec ses suites fantastiques, et *Valentin et Orson* est un véritable roman d'aventures[34].

Mise en prose de la chanson remaniée

Trois manuscrits, dont deux exemplaires de luxe, nous ont transmis la mise en prose amplifiée effectuée à partir du remaniement de la fin du quatorzième siècle[35]. Ce texte, daté de 1462, complète sur certains points les deux manuscrits qui nous ont légué la version versifiée: au delà de la mort de Maugis et des frères de Renaud, il raconte l'histoire de Mabrien, dans laquelle nous pouvons reconnaître la double influence de *Maugis d'Aigremont* et des continuations de *Huon de Bordeaux*. Comme Maugis, en effet, Mabrien est ravi à ses parents dès sa naissance, est élevé par les païens; il va même jusqu'à combattre contre les chrétiens, alors que Maugis se contentait d'opposer les païens entre eux. Quant à la suite de *Huon*, elle a fourni le séjour à l'île d'aimant, la rencontre du roi Arthur, des fées et de Caïn[36].

Dans la mesure où il est plus complet que son modèle en vers, le texte en prose, généralement fidèle à son modèle, quoique plus développé, nous permet de mieux saisir les perspectives du remaniement. Celui-ci a tout d'abord un esprit cyclique très affirmé: il s'agit de présenter l'histoire d'une geste à travers plusieurs générations, depuis Aimon, le père des quatre frères, jusqu'à un autre Aimon, fils de Regnaudin, petit-fils de Mabrien, arrière-petit-fils de Renaud de Montauban. A cette coupe généalogique, la prose ajoute même le *Maugis*, qui ne faisait probablement pas partie du remaniement en vers.

Cette volonté cyclique se traduit également par la volonté de rattacher le récit à d'autres traditions épiques. Il s'agit, bien sûr, de la *Chanson de Roland*, déjà très présente dans *RM*, mais qui se trouve ici constamment préfigurée, soit par le durcissement presque caricatural du personnage de Ganelon[37], soit par les annonces de la bataille: Marsile a en effet l'embarras du choix pour trouver des raisons de se venger des Français, puisque Maugis, dans la prose comme dans la chanson du treizième siècle, séduit sa femme, et puisque Roland lui coupe le poing devant Angorie[38]; quant au désastre lui-même, il est le résultat de la faiblesse de Charlemagne, qui a prêté l'oreille aux calomnies de Ganelon et lui a livré les Aymonides.

Il s'agit aussi, on l'a vu, de *Huon de Bordeaux* dans la version amplifiée, et de *Jourdain de Blaives* puisque, lorsque Mabrien s'attaque aux chrétiens, donc à ses parents, ces derniers trouvent un refuge auprès de Gérard de Blaives[39]. Dans ces conditions, on peut considérer que le remaniement se présente, aux quatorzième et quinzième siècles, comme une somme épique.

Éditions en rapport avec la prose amplifiée et épigones

Le remaniement en prose est resté inédit pour toute la partie qui correspond à la chanson primitive, c'est-à-dire depuis la présentation des fils Aimon à Charlemagne jusqu'à la mort de Renaud. Nous connaissons en revanche un *Maugis* et un *Mabrian* imprimés.

Le *Maugis* imprimé[40], édité pour la première fois en 1518 par Lenoir, qui l'associe à *Garin de Monglane*, est proche de la rédaction en prose, mais traduit une conception différente de la fonction du texte. En effet, alors que l'édition correspond à la prose manuscrite jusqu'à la fin de celle-ci - baptême de Vivien et d'Esclarmonde, mort d'Espiet, don de Bayard et de Floberge à Renaud -, l'imprimé ajoute une double continuation. En sept chapitres, il reprend le *Vivien de Monbranc* en le reliant directement à *Maugis*: les païens attaquent Monbranc, Vivien est capturé puis délivré, Othon d'Espolice trouve la mort; contrairement à la continuation du manuscrit de Montpellier toutefois, ce n'est pas le soudan de Babylone qui conduit l'expédition, mais Marsile et Baligant, et Marsile, au cours de la bataille finale, reproche à Maugis d'avoir fait de lui un mari trompé: "Par toy suis a villennie, mais tantost sera vengé le dueil de ma femme, laquelle tu deshonnoras par ta luxure, et par toy en ay eu mainte angoisse"[41].

Par ailleurs l'imprimé entend introduire à *RM*, mais il le fait d'une manière très particulière; en huit chapitres, en effet, il reprend l'histoire de Beuves d'Aigremont, en lecteur de *Maugis* et de *RM* en vers plutôt que de la vulgate en prose. Chez lui, deux ambassades successives sont envoyées à Beuves, comme dans la chanson, et non une seule, comme dans la prose; d'autre part Vivien est tué par Charlemagne au cours de la guerre qui suit le meurtre de Lohier.

Le *Maugis* imprimé est donc l'oeuvre d'un remanieur habile qui, utilisant des éléments déjà constitués - la rédaction manuscrite de *Maugis* ou la chanson, *Vivien de Monbranc*, le *Beuves d'Aigremont* en vers - fait de son oeuvre un texte autonome et par conséquent très différent, dans ses objectifs, de la prose manuscrite, dans laquelle *Maugis* n'est qu'un prologue. Plusieurs fois édité au seizième siècle[42], le roman est passé dans la bibliothèque de colportage et a été imprimé à Rouen, à Lyon et à Troyes.

La version imprimée de *Mabrian*, publiée pour la première fois chez Nyverd en 1525, a probablement pour modèle la dernière partie de la rédaction amplifiée en prose. Le titre de la première édition montre bien en effet que le texte, qui aurait très bien pu commencer avec l'enlèvement du fils d'Yvon, croit devoir apporter d'abord une conclusion à l'histoire de Renaud; or celle-ci ne s'explique que dans une perspective globale - celle du manuscrit -, et non dans le cadre limité d'une histoire de Mabrian. On lit en effet:

> Histoire singuliere et fort recreative, contenant le reste des faiz et gestes des quatre filz Aymon, Regnault, Allard, Guichard et le petit Richard, et de leur cousin le subtil Maugis, lequel fut pape de Romme. Semblablement la cronicque et hystoire du chevalereux, preux et redoubté prince Mabrian...

L'objectif propre à l'imprimé sera rétabli dans le titre - sinon dans le texte - de la seconde édition:

> La cronicque et hystoire singuliere et fort recreative des conquestes et faictz bellicqueux du preux, vaillant et le nompareil chevalier Mabrian, lequel par ses prouesses fut roy de Hierusalem, d'Angorie et de Inde la Majour...[43]

Dans le même temps, l'imprimé se présente comme la réécriture de la prose manuscrite. S'il utilise le plus souvent en effet une expression rapide, visant à l'efficacité narrative et présentant une tendance à l'abrègement, il recourt de temps à autre à un style savant, orné de latinismes, qui traduit le désir de conférer au texte de nouvelles lettres de noblesse. Ainsi, à propos de l'esclave perfide qui cherche un stratagème pour enlever le fils d'Yvon, le manuscrit nous dit: "Elle se advisa ung jour qu'elle iroit au pallais veoir la noble royne et controuveroit quelque bourde par quoy elle trouveroit maniere d'embler son enffant"[44]; cela devient dans l'imprimé: "Et ne dura gueres qu'elle n'eust trouvee astuxe et grande malice, si comme le sexe muliebre fait de legier; et ce fait s'en va, apres pourpensee cautelle, au palais..."[45].

Rien d'étonnant par conséquent à ce que ce travail de réécriture soit revendiqué par des auteurs, lettrés - Guy Bounay "licencié es loix, lieutenant du baillif de Chastelroux" - ou même nobles - Jehan le Cueur "escuyer, seigneur de Mailly en Puisaye, estant a Paris pour les affaires de ... Regné d'Anjou, en son vivant chevalier, seigneur de Mezieres..."[46].

Ces auteurs connaissent parfaitement les diverses traditions de RM. Ils renvoient dans leur prologue à la calomnie des fils de Fouques de Morillon, Constans et Rohart: ils ont donc lu la vulgate en prose, sinon la chanson primitive; ils évoquent la *Conqueste de Trebizonde*, dont nous parlerons plus loin, et la situent immédiatement après le triomphe des fils de Renaud[47]; mais ils connaissent également le remaniement dans son ensemble, puisqu'ils font allusion à diverses circonstances de l'expédition de Renaud outre-mer[48].

Le *Mabrian* imprimé est donc intéressant à plus d'un titre. Il manifeste la notoriété au seizième siècle de la tradition reinaldienne et l'attrait qu'elle exerce sur des écrivains; il montre également le succès dont peut bénéficier un projet de réécriture s'inscrivant dans une telle tradition: *Mabrian* eut un grand nombre d'éditions au seizième siècle, à Lyon et dans la Bibliothèque Bleue de Troyes[49].

Le cas de la *Conqueste de Trebizonde* est plus curieux. Antérieure à *Mabrian* - la première édition, due à Yvon Gallois, date de 1517[50] - ce texte ne se rattache pas à un événement caractéristique de l'histoire des Aymonides: tout au plus savons-nous, par exemple, que Renaud est déjà marié, puisque Clarice est "au travail et peine d'enfant"[51]; ce n'est donc pas une suite, à la manière de *Mabrian*, mais plutôt, pour reprendre un terme connu, une "incidence", qui se présente à la fois comme une allégorie politique et comme une fable mythologique.

Allégorie politique, le texte fait écho à l'alliance entre la Bretagne et la France, ainsi qu'aux expéditions d'Italie sous Charles VIII et Louis XII. Se donnant pour but de célébrer "le noble et triumphant lys et la treschaste hermine", il rend grâce à "la divine clemence protectrice et conservatrice" d'avoir défendu le lys contre les assauts de ses ennemis, et aussi pour lui avoir permis de se joindre à l'hermine[52]. On peut reconnaître ici le souvenir des deux mariages successifs d'Anne de Bretagne - la "treschaste hermine" - avec le "noble et triumphant lys", Charles VIII (1491) et Louis XII (1498). Par ailleurs le roman fait la plus large place à des exploits chevaleresques ayant l'Italie pour théâtre et consonne fréquemment avec tel ou tel événement des expéditions françaises.

On notera par exemple une splendide entrée des Français, commandés par Renaud, dans la ville pontificale, qui rappelle l'entrée solennelle de Charles VIII le 31 décembre 1494, ou l'épisode du soulèvement de Gênes, bientôt réprimé, qui correspond assez exactement aux événements de 1507. Quant à la conquête de Trebizonde, elle n'occupe que quelques pages à la fin du volume mais pourrait être comprise comme une transposition du rêve byzantin de Charles VIII[53].

La *Conqueste* emporte donc le lecteur dans l'univers chevaleresque brillant dans lequel se déroulent les guerres d'Italie; mais elle se propose également d'associer à la culture épique traditionnelle la culture savante de la Renaissance, et notamment la mythologie. Usant d'une langue ornée de tours savants, elle pare les héros de la geste, et surtout Maugis, des couleurs de la fable: celui-ci devient un rival de Mercure et connaît bien sa mythologie. Ecoutons-le maudire avec fougue l'aurore, qui l'arrache aux embrassements de Déiphile:

> O faschee femme du vieil Triton! Quel haste as tu de esmouvoir Apollo a illuminer les terres? Certes, tu te reposes envis entre les bras de ton mary, comme celle qui les baisiers de Cephalus . . . plus ayme. O envieuse! Pourquoy nous contrains tu nous separer, et que ne nous donnes tu telle nuit que jadis a Jupiter octroyas, lors que il coucha avec la belle Alcmene, mere du preux Hercules, quant de trois jours et trois nuictz ne te monstras? Certes, je croy que lors tu estois entre les bras d'iceluy Cephalus, et par ce ne te vouloys lever. Helas! Retarde ung peu, et toy, Titon, retire ton chariot jusques a ce que encore dix mille fois je baise m'amye[54].

On sait que Léon Gautier, qui a analysé le roman, ne l'appréciait guère[55]; pour notre part, nous sommes porté à un jugement plus indulgent. L'oeuvre ne manque pas d'esprit et n'est pas restée sans lendemain; elle a connu six éditions au seizième siècle, a certainement, en ce qui concerne le style, exercé une influence sur *Mabrian*, et manifeste à nouveau l'incroyable prestige dont jouit à l'époque la geste de Montauban: c'est en Renaud, et non en Ogier ou en Huon, que s'expriment les rêves chevaleresques et conquérants qui saisissent les rois de France à la fin du quinzième siècle et dans les premières années du seizième[56].

L'étude de la postérité de *Renaut de Montauban* jusqu'au début du seizième siècle nous a donc montré un texte, ou plutôt un ensemble de récits, en perpétuelle évolution. Pourvue d'une tradition manuscrite fournie, la chanson initiale ne cesse d'être revue et agrémentée d'épisodes nouveaux, comme l'histoire de la mort des frères de Renaud. Très tôt, un récit d'enfances, avec sa structure narrative caractéristique et le recours au merveilleux, vient raconter les origines de Maugis, le personnage le plus étrange de la geste; une petite suite, le *Vivien de Monbranc*, complétera encore l'histoire. Le quinzième siècle fixe un terme à l'évolution du poème primitif, qui est mis en prose, imprimé et devient un best-seller: le texte, malgré toutes les transformations, conserve jusqu'à la fin du dix-neuvième siècle une relative stabilité. Mais l'histoire de la geste ne s'arrête pas là: à la fin du quatorzième siècle s'élabore un remaniement en vers, qui sera mis en prose au début de la seconde moitié du quinzième; le début et la fin de cet immense récit ont un sort particulier, puisque *Maugis* et *Mabrian* sont imprimés au début du seizième siècle. Enfin, avec la *Conqueste de Trebizonde*, le rêve chevaleresque qui lance les Français à la conquête de l'Italie trouve encore ses héros dans les Aymonides.

156

Il serait sans doute présomptueux de prétendre déterminer avec certitude les raisons pour lesquelles la geste de Montauban s'est trouvée promue à une telle destinée, car ces raisons peuvent varier selon les pays où le récit a été diffusé: il faut rappeler que, dans les pays scandinaves, c'est Maugis qui a le premier rôle (Mágus saga), tandis que s'impose en Italie Rinaldo, brillant défenseur de la justice contre l'arbitraire ou la faiblesse du roi.

On peut croire toutefois, comme nous avons tenté de le démontrer, que l'équilibre tenu au départ entre données épiques et données narratives, ainsi que la variété de situations dramatiques créées par le personnage pluriel, ont constitué un véritable trésor narratif, dans lequel les siècles ultérieurs allaient puiser.

Notes

[1]La *Bibliographie* récemment constituée par Philippe Verelst dans *Romanica Gandensia* 18 (1981), 199-234, donne une idée précise de ce succès.

[2]Voir notre thèse *Guillaume d'Orange: Étude du roman en prose*, Bibliothèque du quinzième siècle 44 (Paris, 1979), 529-91.

[3]La seule édition complète disponible est encore aujourd'hui celle de Ferdinand Castets, *La Chanson des Quatre Fils Aymon*, Publications de la Société pour l'étude des langues romanes, 23 (Montpellier, 1909), à laquelle nous renverrons sans autre indication. Pour la partie du texte comprise entre l'adoubement des fils Aimon et le départ pour Bordeaux, il est préférable de recourir à l'édition synoptique de Jacques Thomas, *L'épisode ardennais de "Renaut de Montauban"*, édition synoptique des versions rimées, Rijksuniversiteit te Gent, Werken uitgegeven door de Faculteit van de Letteren en Wijsbegeerte, 129-31, 3 vol. (Bruges, 1962).

[4]Les remanieurs des 14e et 15e s., se souvenant peut-être de *Lancelot*, imaginent de fait une fresque représentant, dans le palais pontifical qu'occupe plus tard Maugis, l'histoire de Renaud et de ses frères, voir Philippe Verelst, "Texte et iconographie: une curieuse mise en abyme dans un *Renaut de Montauban* inédit", *Romanica Gandensia* 17 (1980), 147-62.

[5]MS D, 154-58, in Thomas, *L'épisode ardennais*, 1:228.

[6]Sur le héros pluriel dans *RM*, voir Jacques Thomas, "Les *quatre fils Aymon*. Structure et origine du thème", *Romanica Gandensia* 18 (1981), 47-72.

[7]MS D, 754-63 in Thomas, *L'épisode ardennais*, 1:246.

[8]Voir Philippe Verelst, "Le personnage de Maugis dans *Renaut de Montauban* (versions rimées traditionnelles)", *Romanica Gandensia* 18 (1981), 135.

[9]Nous ne tenons pas compte ici des deux manuscrits qui nous transmettent le remaniement de la fin du Moyen Age.

[10]Un fragment manuscrit pour *Gormont et Isembard*, un manuscrit unique pour *Raoul de Cambrai*, trois manuscrits pour *Huon de Bordeaux*, cinq pour *Ogier le Danois*.

[11]Thomas, *L'épisode ardennais*, 1:227.

[12]Ibid., 2:233, vv. 371-73.

[13]Ibid., 3:34-35, vv. 804-06.

[14]Éditée, après Castets (*Revue des Langues Romanes* 36 [1892]), par Philippe Vernay (Berne, 1980).

[15]Voir Friedrich Wolfzettel, "Zur Stellung und Bedeutung der *Enfances*", *Zeitschrift für französische Sprache und Literatur* 83 (1973), 317-48; 84 (1974), 1-32.

[16] Ce texte a été édité par Ferdinand Castets in *Revue des Langues Romanes* 30 (1886), 128-63; il a été étudié par Wolfgang Van Emden (qui en prépare une nouvelle édition), "Le personnage du roi dans *Vivien de Monbranc* et ailleurs", in *Charlemagne et l'épopée romane. Actes du VIIe Congrès International de la Société Rencesvals (Liège, 28 août - 4 septembre 1976)* (Liège, 1978), 1, pp. 241-50.

[17]Opinion contraire de Van Emden, "Le personnage", p. 242, qui croit à un poème indépendant.

[18]Cité par Castets in "Maugis d'Aigremont", *Revue des Langues Romanes* 36 (1892), 281 n. 1. La continuation est analysée par Philippe Verelst in *Romanica Gandensia* 18 (1981), 148-52.

[19]Cf. vv. 1232-35 et *RM*, vv. 16583-95.

[20]Voir Verelst, "Le personnage de Maugis", p. 151. Le merveilleux est de type hagiographique: plongé dans une cuve remplie successivement d'huile bouillante, de poix bouillante et de plomb fondu, Maugis reste aussi indemne que peut l'être un saint.

[21]Voir l'étude de Jacques Thomas, *L'épisode ardennais*, 1:31-41 et 116-26. Il s'agit du MS R (Paris, fr. 764) et du MS B (Londres, Brit. Lib., Roy. 16 G II). Ce dernier est un manuscrit mixte, puisqu'il contient tout d'abord les 618 premiers vers du remaniement, puis la vulgate en prose (sans prologue), enfin 1800 vers environ qui racontent les derniers exploits héroï-comiques de Maugis, la mort des frères de Renaud et celle de leur cousin, mais non celle des fils de Renaud.

[22]Voir Léon de Laborde, *Les ducs de Bourgogne*, 3 vol. (Paris, 1849-52), 3:117 (no 5705). L'indication, qui figure dans les Archives de la chambre des comptes de Blois, est tirée des Additional Charters, no 2734, conservées à la British Library. Citée correctement par Jules Guiffrey, *Histoire de la tapisserie depuis le moyen âge jusqu'à nos jours* (Tours, 1886), p. 34, elle a été tronquée par Eugène Müntz, "La légende de Charlemagne dans l'art au moyen âge", *Romania* 14 (1885), 339, ce qui lui ôtait toute valeur probante.

[23]Ainsi, Renaud se trouve à Angorie lorsque ses enfants se rendent à la cour de Charles pour y être adoubés, alors que dans la chanson primitive, c'est le héros qui envoie Yvon et Aymon au roi.

[24]Bibl. Nat., fr. 764, fol. 136a-138d.

[25]Voir Castets, *RM*, pp. 239-42.

[26]Bibl. Nat., fr. 764, fol. 215a-b.

[27]Bibl. Nat., fr. 19176, fol. 169r: "D'icellui Mabrien dira l'istoire ce qu'il en peult avoir veu en cronicque rimee d'ancienneté".

[28]Mabrien est le petit-fils d'Aimon, mais il aura lui-même un fils et un petit-fils.

[29]Voir Émile Besch, "Les adaptations en prose des chansons de geste", *Revue du XVIe siècle* 3 (1915), 155-81; Jean-Marcel Léard, *Étude sur les versions en prose de "Renaud de Montauban" et éd. du MS Ars. 3151* (Thèse de doctorat 3e cycle, Paris, 1974); Jacques Thomas, "Les mises en prose de *Renaud de Montauban*: Classement sommaire et sources", in *Fin du Moyen Age et Renaissance. Mélanges Robert Guiette* (Anvers, 1961), pp. 127-37.

[30]Édité par Marie-Henriette Noterdaeme (Mémoire de licence [Gand, 1973]).

[31]Voir Brian Woledge, *Bibliographie des romans et nouvelles en prose française antérieures à 1500* (Genève, 1954), n° 141, et celle de Léon Gautier, pp. 158-61; pour la Bibliothèque Bleue, voir Alfred Morin, *Catalogue descriptif de la Bibliothèque Bleue de Troyes* (Paris, 1974).

[32]Voir Pierre Brochon, *Le livre de colportage en France depuis le XVIe siècle* (Paris, 1954), et Alexandre Assier, *La Bibliothèque Bleue depuis Jean Oudot Ier jusqu'à M. Baudot, 1600-1863* (Paris, 1874).

[33]Sur *Huon de Bordeaux* imprimé, voir Marguerite Rossi, *Huon de Bordeaux et l'évolution du genre épique au XIIIe siècle* (Paris, 1975), pp. 627-29.

[34]Sur *Valentin et Orson*, voir Arthur Dickson, *Valentine and Orson: A Study in Late Medieval Romance* (New York, 1929).

[35]Ces deux exemplaires sont respectivement les MSS Arsenal 5072-75, complétés par Munich, Gall. 7 - qui ont fait partie de la librairie de Philippe le Bon -, et Pommersfelden, Gräflich Schönbornsche Bibliothek, 311-12 (manuscrits incomplets; manque la seconde partie de l'expédition outre-mer, avec les aventures d'Yvon et d'Aimon, ainsi que *Mabrien*). Le troisième exemplaire est représenté par Bibl. Nat., fr. 19173-77.

[36]La référence est d'ailleurs très précise: lorsque Mabrien arrive à l'île aimantée, l'aimant "traÿ a soy le vaissel et le mena droit au rochier ou Hue de Bordeaux avoit esté mené" (Bibl. Nat., fr. 19177, fol. 119^r).

[37]Celui-ci s'efforce, au cours de la guerre entre Charles et les fils Aimon, de faire périr l'empereur (voir Castets, *Renaud de Montauban*, pp. 197-98); c'est lui qui construit le piège qui se refermera sur Maugis et les frères de Renaud.

[38]Voir Bibl. Nat., fr. 19176, fol. 164^v: "Maiz tant dollent estoit Marcille du deshonneur et du dommage qu'il avoit eu que souvent malgreoit ses dieux, et plus sans comparaison de son poing que Roland luy avoit couppé. Et tant y pensa qu'il jura par tous ses dieux qu'il seroit une foiz vengié de Roland, ou il mourroit en la paine. Hellaz! Ainsi fut il, au plus grief dommage qui oncques advenist en France!"; voir aussi, pour le texte en vers, Bibl. Nat., fr. 764, fol. 214b.

[39]Voir Bibl. Nat., fr. 19177, fol. 43^r-52^v.

[40]Voir Léon Gautier, *Bibliographie des chansons de geste* (Paris, 1897) p. 109: "Icy est contenu les deux tres plaisantes histoires de Guerin de Monglave et de Maugist d'Aigremont, qui furent en leur temps tres nobles et vaillans chevalliers en armes. Et si parle des merveilleux faictz que firent Robastre et Perdigon pour secourir le dit Guerin et ses enfans. Et aussi pareillement de ceulx du dict Maugis". On voit que l'éditeur a retenu ici la présence d'un enchanteur pour réunir les deux récits, imprimés ensuite séparément.

[41]Bibl. Nat. Rés. Y2 337, fol. 108b.

[42]Voir Woledge, *Biblographie*, n° 142; on peut y ajouter une édition de Jean Bogart, à Louvain, avec privilège de 1588 (Lille, Bibl. Munic. 4510).

[43]Voir Gautier, *Bibliographie*, pp. 162-63.

[44]Bibl. Nat., fr. 19177, fol. 37d.

[45]Bibl. Nat. Rés. Y2 75, fol. 38c.

[46]Ibid., prologue A ii. Il serait intéressant d'identifier ces deux personnages; René d'Anjou, en revanche, est connu. Ce n'est pas le roi des Deux-Siciles, comme semble le penser Woledge (voir *Supplément*, p. 92), mais le fils de Louis d'Anjou et d'Anne de La Trémouille, né en 1483 et mort en 1526. Sénéchal du Maine en 1510, il prit part aux expéditons d'Italie; seigneur de Mézières en Brenne, il avait épousé Antoinette de Chabannes, dame de Saint-Fargeau et de Puisaye, d'où les titres qui lui sont donnés dans le prologue de *Mabrian*.

[47]"Apres laquelle premiere victorieuse conqueste, le prince Regnault et ses freres eulx retirerent a Montauban; et ce fait ce ralierent plusieurs vaillans roys et princes leurs parens, et s'en allerent par meure deliberation dela la mer. Mais au chemin eurent grans destourbiers de leurs ennemys, lesquelz ilz subjuguerent tous, comme verrez par l'acteur de l'histoire de la conqueste de Trebizonde..." (éd. Lotrian et Janot, Bibl. Nat. Rés. Y2 585, fol. 1d).

[48]"Et ce fait vint au pays et royaulme d'Angorie, lequel il conquist et tua le roy qui avoit une moult belle fille nommee Synamonde, laquelle il fist espouser au gentil prince Aymon... Et ce fait passa outre et conquist le royaulme de Syrie et la saincte cité de Hierusalem, duquel royaulme il tua le roy qui eut une moult belle fille nommee Ayglentine..." (ibid.).

[49]Voir Gautier, Bibliographie, pp. 161-62; Woledge, *Bibliographie*, n° 143.

[50]Voir Woledge, *Bibliographie*, n° 144, et *Supplément* (Genève, 1975), p. 92; Gautier, *Bibliographie*, p. 162.

[51]Bibl. Nat. Rés. Y2 565, C 1r (éd. Lotrian).

[52]"Fermer et joindre immaculee purité avecques innocente blancheur d'ung indissoluble lax a concatenee ladicte meree hermine avecques elle" (ibid., prologue).

[53]Sur les guerres d'Italie, voir Henri Hauser et Augustin Renaudet, *Les débuts de l'âge moderne* (Paris, 1956), pp. 74-94. Charles VIII porte à son entrée dans Naples, en 1495, les couronnes de France, de Naples, Jérusalem et Constantinople.

[54]Bibl. Nat. Rés. Y2 565, N 4v.

[55]Voir Léon Gautier, *Épopées françaises. Étude sur les origines et l'histoire de la littérature nationale* (Paris, 1892), 2, pp. 629-30.

[56]Le succès de la geste de Renaud en Italie a pu frapper les écrivains familiers des expéditons françaises; mais l'influence des oeuvres italiennes, très différentes des versions françaises, ne peut être qu'indirecte.

Ganelon's Defense

Emanuel J. Mickel, Jr.

As everyone knows, Charlemagne charges Ganelon with treason after the Spanish campaign because of the French baron's alleged role in causing the rear guard's annihilation at Roncevaux. Since no one was present during Ganelon's betrayal, the arrest is made on the basis of strong presumption,[1] especially in the light of Ganelon's attitude when Roland's horn is heard as Charlemagne's army, having cleared the pass, made its way toward France. It was undoubtedly thought that Ganelon would confess to the crime or, perhaps, that he would deny it, given the fact that no one present could possibly prove his complicity. Interestingly enough, Ganelon does not deny his part in Roland's death, but, to everyone's surprise, he does deny the charge of treason, a capital crime, and claims that he merely took vengeance on Roland according to time-honored procedure:

> Dist Guenelon: "Fel seie se jol ceil!
> Rollant me forfist en or e en aveir,
> Pur que je quis sa mort e sun destreit;
> Mais traïsun nule n'en i otrei."[2]

In his speech Ganelon emphasizes that he loves France and would never betray Charlemagne. Roland had wronged him, he argues, and he had defied his stepson, Roland, in open court. As everyone knew, once formal ties of fealty had been broken openly, a man could no longer be accused of oath breaking, and hence treason, if he were to kill his adversary in a subsequent confrontation. Accordingly, Ganelon merely took vengeance

163

on Roland, as one might expect after an open defiance, and should not be charged with more than the crime for homicide.[3]

Because of the outcome of the single combat between Thierry and Pinabel, Ganelon is deemed guilty of the charge in the epic and is punished severely. However, Ganelon's defense has not been lacking in finding modern critics who support the legitimacy of his claim. Some fifty years ago Ruggero M. Ruggieri argued that the dispute between Roland and Ganelon actually comprises the core of the earliest form of the epic and that the complete hostility toward Ganelon is the work of revisionist poets who no longer understood the Germanic foundation of the text. These twelfth-century redactors rewrote it under the religious influence of the later period, which associated Ganelon with Judas, the archetypal traitor.[4] For Ruggieri and many twentieth-century scholars, the Roland reflected in other contemporary versions, such as the *Carmen de Prodicione Guenonis* or Konrad's Middle High German text, are of little significance in analyzing the "real" Roland, because that text is assumed to have had a given form in a much earlier version than that extant today. Ruggieri suggested, and others have since agreed, that the original author was not so hostile to Ganelon. Rather, he intended the conflict to be understood within a framework of Germanic custom. Thus he argued that Ganelon's actions are justifiable when considered against a background of Germanic law. In Ruggieri's view this is the oldest segment of the epic and preserves a text in which Ganelon was the hero of the older Germanic federalism against the centralizing tendencies of Carolingian authority.[5] Thus Ganelon becomes the hero of the barons and aristocracy in their continuing conflict with the king. Smouldering beneath Ganelon's defense is the feeling that German tradition and custom law are being neglected in favor of a dynasty which has a tendency to model itself on Roman ideas. In fact, the idea of permanent monarchy contradicts the basic Germanic familial unit and runs against an innate Germanic hatred of central authority.For Ruggieri the time for such a Germanic unit of government had long since passed in Charlemagne's time, but the deep-seated feeling for it survived in the ninth century and is reflected in the text, which he believed more a product of the eighth and ninth than the eleventh and twelfth centuries. Thus if the barons support Ganelon at the trial, he would argue (and note that only Thierry rejects the defense), it is because they believe deep down that Ganelon is really right and not because they are intimidated by Pinabel or Ganelon's powerful clan (the author's direct statement that fear played a role would be a later addition).

A number of modern critics who feel that Roland is not without blame, tend to agree that Ganelon, if not entirely blameless, certainly had justification for his anger against the bold stepson. Christian Gellinek writes that Ganelon is not really guilty of high treason:

> La raison en est que son crime, malgré sa monstruosité, reste dans le cadre des règles officielles des querelles. D'après les jurés, l'accusé était en droit de se venger publiquement. Selon eux, il était libre d'ébranler publiquement le systéme de pouvoir dans ses fondements.[6]

Certainly the judgement that Ganelon is partially justified in his conduct drastically affects our assessment of the poem and its meaning. It is vital to our evaluation of Roland and may even have an influence on our consideration of the Roland/Olivier question. Before proceeding, however, several factors concerning treason and homicide should be considered.

There is a long-standing, accepted difference between the notion of high treason or lese majesty in a Roman sense and what was deemed treason in the Germanic codes. Because of the quasi-divine nature of authority in imperial Rome, high treason in Roman law need not have involved open rebellion against the state; even blasphemy against the emperor's name or title might have been acceptable grounds for high treason. In any case, the centralized nature of the Roman state made treason a crime against the entire body politic. In Germanic law, treason was related to the feudal nature of the society and reflected its decentralized nature. At the heart of Germanic society, always a federated rather than a centrally oriented entity, was the family bond of blood loyalty and the mutual trust between allies or the oath which bound lord and vassal. To betray in the Germanic sense was less discussed as an act against the crown than as a basic failure to fulfill the oath or fealty owed to friend or kin. Thus treason and oath breaking were virtually synonymous, unless, of course, one were to renounce one's oath openly so that all would know that there was no longer any bond between the individuals in question. This was the formal and legal means of renouncing honorably an agreement which one could no longer maintain in good conscience.

The openness of the deed is crucial to another issue of importance to the text. In the earliest Germanic codes an effort is made to avoid the feuds which caused such havoc among families by their unending cycle of vengeance. The system of fines found in these early *compendia* was an effort to mediate and to conciliate those who have been wronged. A price was placed on each part of the body, and a value was assigned to each man according to his station in life and the value he had as a servant or freeman. Nothing was said of motive or intent. The fine was not less if one caused the man's death accidentally. What was important was the loss sustained by the family, and the fine was charged to the person who caused the physical mishap. This applied as long as the offense was openly acknowledged. Any attempt to hide the crime or to avoid acknowledgement changed the nature of and punishment for the offense. To kill a man openly for recognized dispute was homicide and subject to fine or some amendment. To kill a man by stealth or under cover of darkness was called murder and this was not an amendable offense. The murderer became a pursued man by all of society, and even his kin were forbidden to give him aid. The seriousness of intent can be seen in the frequent warnings against harboring such criminals. To support one's kin when he was charged with assault or homicide was expected, but all society was expected to shun and outlaw the man who sought to take life without justifying his crime openly.

One cannot overemphasize the heinousness of murder to the Germanic mind. It represents the antithesis of the basic Germanic concept of what society was, a mutual trust resting in the oath system. It was not the man's life which was so sacred, but the social order itself. To murder a man, not to make open defiance, not to warn him of his jeopardy, constituted a threat to the fabric of society. It was a rejection of law and the social bond. If tolerated, it would introduce chaos and condone slaughter. It is this that made murder such an intolerable crime and, as one can see, every murder was considered to involve treason. As Philippe de Beaumanoir writes:

> Traïsons si est quant l'en ne moustre pas semblant de haine et l'en het mortelment si que, par la haine, l'en tue ou fet tuer, ou bat ou fet batre . . . celui qu'il het par traïson.
> Nus murtres n'est sans traïson, mes traïsons puet bien estre sans murtre en mout de cas; car murtres n'est pas sans mort d'homme, mes traïsons est pour batre ou pour afoler en trives ou en asseurement ou en aguet apensé ou pour porter faus tesmoing pour celi metre a mort, ou pour li deseriter, ou pour li fere banir, ou pour li fere haïr de son seigneur lige, ou pour mout d'autres cas semblables.[7]

Murder was to homicide what treason was to the open severance of one's ties. It is very clear in the Germanic and later provincial codes that treason involved stealth. In fact, it is stealth which really was the crucial element in treason. In the earliest codes and in those of the thirteenth and fourteenth century, the terms that were used to define treason involved acting at night, stalking from ambush, or striking without warning, even if in the open.

With this concept in mind, another important scene is clarified and helps put the Ganelon trial in perspective. Prior to the attack of the Saracens in the pass, Roland and Olivier have a serious disagreement concerning the best course of action. Olivier has seen the size of the enemy army and urges Roland to blow his horn to summon Charlemagne and the French host before it is too late. Roland's understanding of the situation is different, and he refuses to heed Olivier's advice. The dispute between the two close friends becomes so serious that Olivier later vows that, should they return, Roland would never marry his sister as had been planned:

> Dist Oliver: "Par cest meie barbe,
> Se puis veeir ma gente sorur Alde,
> Ne jerreiez jamais entre sa brace!"
> (vv. 1719-21)

In effect, Olivier has broken the future tie of kinship that would bind them even more closely. Roland is unable to understand why Olivier is so angry. Olivier responds that his error would cost Charlemagne dearly and that Roland's prowess was a curse. If Roland had listened to him, this disaster could have been avoided.

What is important to us at the moment is not whether Olivier's assessment is accurate, but to note the depth of dissension between the two friends. For, later in the battle, when Olivier has been mortally wounded, a most important moment occurs. Marganice has just struck Olivier a fatal blow. Olivier realizes it and avenges the blow on the enemy, then calls out to Roland for help: "Aprés escriet Rollant qu'il li auit" (v. 1964). A laisse later, he again calls to his companion to come to his side:

> Rollant apelet, sun ami e sun per:
> Sire cumpaign, a mei car vus justez!
> A grant dulor ermes hoi desevrez.
> (vv. 1975-77)

Roland sees by his pallor that Olivier is dying. For a moment he loses consciousness because of his grief, and his horse approaches the wounded knight. Olivier strikes the unsuspecting Roland a nearly fatal blow.[8] The author is clear in exculpating Olivier from intent:

> As vus Rollant sur sun cheval pasmet
> E Oliver ki est a mort naffret.
> Tant ad seinet li oil li sunt trublet,
> Ne loinz ne pres ne poet vedeir si cler
> Que reconoistre poisset nuls hom mortel.
> Sun cumpaignun, cum il l'at encuntret,
> Sil fiert amunt sur l'elme a or gemet,

Tut li detrenchet d'ici qu'al nasel,
Mais en la teste ne l'ad mie adeset.
(vv. 1989-97)

Not only is Olivier wounded mortally, but he has bled so much that his eyes are no longer clear. When a figure on horseback draws near, he instinctively protects himself from what might be the approaching enemy. What is important to us, however, is Roland's perception of the incident. He does not have the advantage of the author's comments and is not sure whether Olivier has struck him willingly or not:

A icel colp l'ad Rollant reguardet,
Si li demandet dulcement e suëf:
"Sire cumpain, faites le vos de gred?
Ja est ço Rollant, ki tant vos soelt amer!
Par nule guise ne m'aviez desfiet!''
(vv. 1998-2002)[9]

Despite the blow, Roland asks Olivier the apprehensive question "dulcement e suëf." It is one of the most touching scenes in the Old French *chanson de geste*. What is interesting is that Roland never considers for a moment that Olivier could be justified in striking because of his anger. Roland wonders whether their earlier argument could actually have led Olivier to such a contemptible deed. He asks almost plaintively if he had struck him willing and points out in a sorrowful tone that, if so, Olivier had not even given him warning, he had not even defied him first. This is the crucial point. To the Germanic mind, Olivier's conduct—if willful—is treason in its most contemptible form. He has struck a man with whom he is closely allied without warning or without giving him the opportunity to defend himself. As the author of the *Jostice et de plet* writes around 1260:

Traïson si est quant l'en asaut home dedanz trive, et li cos pert; quant l'en fiert home, et l'en ne voit mie le cop venir. Traïson si est nuit entrée. Traïson si est quant l'en sorprant home, et l'en le fiert, si qu'il ne se puet deffendre.[10]

Roland's gentleness represents the shock he feels that such might be the truth. When Olivier makes it clear that he did not know who he was and asks his pardon, Roland's response is significant. It is not he who begs forgiveness for wrongs he has committed. Rather he pardons Olivier formally for the unintentional misdeed:

Rollant respunt: "Jo n'ai nïent de mel,
Jol vos parduins ici e devant Deu.''

A icel mot l'un a l'altre ad clinet,
Par tel amur as les vus desevred!
(vv. 2006-09)

The clear reconciliation of the two inseparable friends, here separated only by death, is set against their violent dispute and the formal severing of ties when Olivier announced that he no longer wished to be related to Roland. The point that is made, however, is that such disputes do not cause treason among honorable men. Roland and Olivier were still brothers. No argument, no matter how severe, could so warp their relationship. Roland's shocked reaction to Olivier reminds one of his response to Olivier's earlier accusation that Ganelon had betrayed them:

Guenes le sout, li fel, li traïtur,
Ki nus jugat devant l'empereür.
"Tais, Oliver," li quens Rollant respunt,
"Mis parrastre est, ne voeill que mot en suns!"
(vv. 1024-27)

Roland and Ganelon had also argued violently, and Ganelon had severed his ties with his stepson openly. But Roland was unwilling to hear his own kin accused of treason. No matter what the nature of the dispute, treason was contemptible and out of the question. It is one thing to have an argument, even a defiance, but it is another to disgrace oneself and all one's progeny.[11] Only later must Roland ruefully acknowledge that Olivier's accusation must be true.

Ganelon was a clever man, a skilled speaker. The French soldiers recognized this when they approved his selection for the embassy to the Saracens, and he demonstrated it admirably when he argued in the early council scene against Roland's bluntly stated advice. Does he not omit reference to the previous treachery of the Saracens toward Basan and Basilie and does he not argue that only a warmonger would continue to attack someone who wishes to surrender? Ganelon is a sophist, and his trial defense is no exception. Since Ganelon is guilty by presumption, his only defense is to deny the charge by cleverly arguing that he did not really commit treason. When Thierry rejects Ganelon's argument, he points out that Roland was in the service of Charlemagne, and this alone served as protection from attack during the length of his service. To attack someone in the king's service was one of the most serious crimes and may have been high treason.[12] But Ganelon's argument nicely attempts to sidestep the legal question of high treason. Ganelon argues that he meant no harm to Charlemagne whom he loves and that France came away victorious.[13] His

169

is a private quarrel with Roland, one which had been acknowledged before the entire court. He had defied Roland legally and later took vengeance as the old law permitted.

However, Ganelon's argument does not have a semblance of truth even or especially in a Germanic context. True, Ganelon defied Roland, but then he conspired with the enemy to set ambush for his adversary so that he might strike him unannounced and without warning. Ganelon was not only guilty of high treason but of murder and treason together. Ganelon defied Roland openly in court. Because of the circumstances and his impending mission, his defiance could be made with impunity. He had accomplished the easy half of his "honorable" vengeance. To complete the second half without reproach, he had to confront Roland openly in combat for all to see. This he was incapable of doing. Rather, he willingly caused the death of thousands to assuage his murderous rage. Thierry's victory convicted Ganelon of high treason and of treason in the Germanic sense. As we have argued in an earlier paper on the thirty *pleges*,[14] the extraordinary punishment handed out to Ganelon's supporters indicates that the author understood the spuriousness of Ganelon's defense. Here is yet further evidence against the claims that the trial and conflict represent an earlier version with different ethical values. Far from being a noble defense based on the early Germanic codes, it is a base attempt to mask the true nature of the crime behind pretended honorable conduct. The texts cited here which define treason in the Germanic sense are even later than the *Roland*.

Ganelon's use of stealth and attack without warning were treason at the basic level, whether early or late in the Middle Ages. That the *pleges* were also hanged seems to indicate that the author condemned Ganelon's supporters for their conspiracy to commit treason. A *plege*, or perhaps compurgator in this case, did not vouch for the defendant's innocence, since he was not claiming to be witness; rather he stated that he believed the defendant's version of the story. In this case, however, it was not a question of supporting Ganelon's innocence in the role he played at Roncevaux; rather, they concurred in Ganelon's defense and his attempt to sidestep the charge. In executing them, something never done in reality, the author is passing poetic justice on the conspirators and, in so doing, makes a statement concerning Ganelon's defense. It is not a later moralizing Christian writer who condemns Ganelon as the archetypal traitor. It is Ganelon himself who fashions his own mantle as arch-traitor in a Germanic sense. Not only does he commit murder and treason because of his use of stealth, but he would escape the open charge of treason by yet another bit of trickery.

When the author describes the glorious Ganelon just before leaving on his mission of betrayal, he reminds us of Ganelon's previous service and illustrious career. In so doing he accentuates the loss brought about by treason. Just as the Saracens, who invariably are described as having great prowess and magnificent strength, come to nothing because they are not Christian, so are Ganelon's former service and illustrious name totally erased by the murderous, treacherous hate of a single moment.

Notes

[1]Note that a charge based on general belief in a man's guilt was not uncommon and was considered one of the stronger justifications for indictment. See Henry de Bracton, *De legibus et consuetudinibus Angliae*, ed. George E. Woodbine, trans. Samuel E. Thorne, 2 (Cambridge, 1968), p. 403:

> Nunc autem dicendum est de indictatis per famam patriae quae praesumptionem inducit, et cui standum est donec indictatus se a tali suspicione purgaverit. Ex fama quidem oritur suspicio, et ex fama et suspicione oritur gravis praesumptio, tamen probationem admittit in contrarium sive purgationem. Suspicio quidem multiplex esse poterit. Imprimis si fama oriatur apud bonos et graves.

("We must now speak of those indicted by popular rumour [from rumour suspicion arises, and from rumour and suspicion a strong presumption, which must stand until the man indicted has purged himself of such suspicion, since it admits of proof to the contrary, that is, purgation.] Suspicion may be of many kinds. It arises when rumour originates among good and responsible men.")

[2]*The Song of Roland: An Analytical Edition*, ed. Gerard J. Brault, 2 (University Park and London, 1978), vv. 3757-60. Later, Ganelon is even more precise: "Venget m'en sui, mais n'i ad traïsun" (v. 3778). Future citations are drawn from this edition and will be noted in the body of the article.

[3]Ganelon does not actually state as much, but this would be the charge if one were to accept his defense.

[4]Ruggero M. Ruggieri, *Il Processo di Gano nella Chanson de Roland* (Florence, 1936).

[5]Although modern authors such as Erich Köhler and Karl-Heinz Bender (*König und Vasall. Untersuchungen zur Chanson de Geste des XII. Jahrhunderts*, Studia Romanica 13 [Heidelberg, 1967]) do not support Ruggieri's thesis concerning Ganelon as the central figure, their analyses of the social circumstances of the text would provide an appropriate background for such an interpretation.

[6]Christian Gellinek, "A propos du système de pouvoir dans la *Chanson de Roland*," *Cahiers de Civilisation Médiévale* 19 (1976), 41. Other articles that justify Ganelon include John Halverson, "Ganelon's Trial," *Speculum* 42 (1967), 661-69, and John Stranges, "The Character and the Trial of Ganelon," *Romania* 96 (1975), 333-67.

[7]Philippe de Beaumanoir, *Coutumes de Beauvaisis*, ed. Amédée Salmon (Paris, 1899), p. 430, par. 826-27.

[8]Those who would see the clash between Roland and Olivier as a dispute between overweening pride and prudence are tempted to see in this scene a subconscious acting out of their conflict. It has been argued that the scene represents the focal point of the text and that the blow against Roland occurs nearly at the center of the 4000 line epic.

[9]If one is looking for a numerical center of the text as we have it, one might point out that Roland's question occurs exactly at line 2000. The question of Olivier's intent is at the heart of the story, but Roland's question, if understood, places it in a different perspective.

[10]*Li Livres de Jostice et de Plet*, ed. Lewis Nicolas Rapetti (Paris, 1850), p. 297.

[11]Note that the typical punishment for treason involved the disinheritance of the traitor's entire family.

[12]In Germanic law, compensation for crimes was based on a man's *wergeld*, the money value set on a man's life. The sum varied with rank and was significant enough when freemen were involved to be a burden on the family (clan) which had to pay. The twelve-man oath was equated with the *wergeld* of a nobleman. Thus, serious crimes required a twelve-man oath, i.e., eleven compurgators were needed, for clearance. In the most serious crimes, multiples of the twelve-man oath were often required, just as the triple ordeal replaced the single ordeal for crimes of magnitude. It is most interesting that a provision of the *Lex Salica*, perhaps revised in its current form in the ninth century, established that anyone who is killed while in the king's service must be assessed at triple the ordinary nobleman's *wergeld*. In such a case triple compurgation or thirty-six compurgators would be required precisely because Roland had been in the king's service, a point made specifically by Thierry in his affirmation that Ganelon's crime was treason and no other.

[13]His supporters even point out that continuing the quarrel with Ganelon can only be destructive and cannot restore Roland.

[14]Emanuel J. Mickel, Jr., "The Thirty *Pleges* for Ganelon," *Olifant* 6 (1979), 293-304.

Three Old French Magicians:
Maugis, Basin, and Auberon

William W. Kibler

If, for the sake of discussion, one were to attempt to distinguish the subject matter of the *chansons de geste* from that of romance, one might posit that the *chansons de geste* portray heroes representing great families (which is one of the definitions of *geste*) who are fighting to preserve their homeland and their religion, while romances present individual heroes whose exploits are primarily undertaken to enhance their own personal reputations. The epic hero is a social archetype as well as an individual one. He embodies social and moral virtues necessary for the proper functioning of the community. His victories are also those of his society and, in the case of the *chansons de geste*, of his Christian religion. An epic hero is static; his character does not grow or change; his ideals are fixed from the beginning. What change he does undergo is not of character but condition.[1] In William Calin's felicitous phrase, "he does not *become* great but is slowly and surely recognized to *be* so."[2] A romance hero, on the other hand, through a series of adventures reaches a new self-identity. He *becomes* what he was previously only in potentiality. Where the epic hero is sure of his right and status from the beginning, the romance hero's quest is one of self-discovery and self-realization. Although the romance heroes are French and Christian, to be sure, with the exception of a Perceval or a Galahad this is only incidental to their self-identity, and not their very essence.

It is widely recognized that by the second generation of epic production, that period extending from about 1190 to 1230, many of the elements that characterize romance—giants and dwarfs, magic rings and horns, the love interest—have made their appearance in the *chansons de geste*.[3] In the present study, I propose to consider only one of these elements, the appearance of the magician, but would like to extrapolate from the role assigned him some general comments regarding the reworking of epic material to incorporate romance elements. In the first part of this paper I shall study two epic magicians, Maugis d'Aigremont and Basin de Gennes. In the final part, I shall contrast them with Auberon, a romance sorcerer whose presence in *Huon de Bordeaux* suggests that we may no longer be dealing with a true *chanson de geste*.

Miracles, the marvelous, and magic are all supernatural phenomena which are to be found in the *chansons de geste*,[4] but an initial distinction must be made among them. The miraculous, sometimes referred to as the "Christian *merveilleux*," is a manifestation of the special relationship which the epic hero enjoys with the God for whom he fights. It is constant throughout the *chansons de geste*. In the earliest extant epic, the *Song of Roland*, God sends his angel Gabriel to receive Roland's proferred glove (laisses 175-76); in the same epic, God stops the sun in its path to allow Charlemagne to complete his victory over Marsile's army (laisses 179-80). In the second generation epic *La Chanson des Saisnes*,[5] the walls of the city of Saint-Herbert-du-Rhin collapse miraculously before Charlemagne (laisse 79); later, a stag pursued by hounds appears as a miraculous sign to Charlemagne to instruct him where to build a bridge across the Rhine (laisses 158-60). In the fourteenth-century epic *Lion de Bourges*,[6] one of the last verse epics we have, Lion's mother Alis, disguised as a man, is miraculously aided by God in slaying a fearful giant:

> Per la vertu de Dieu qui miraicle y moustroit,
> Hauber ne armure, nulle rien n'y valloit;
> Playne palme et demie ains ou cor li antroit.
> (vv. 1742-44)

And, shortly thereafter, when the daughter of the pagan emir wishes to marry her—thinking her to be a man—Alis is saved when she heeds the advice of a voice from heaven. Thus we can say that miraculous events are those in which God intervenes directly on behalf of the hero, as an answer to an expressed or unexpressed prayer, and without the use of a mortal go-between.

The marvelous is an element of literary description used in part to whet the public's appetite and to create a certain atmosphere which is most usually associated with romance: carbuncles that light up the night, invincible weapons, stones with healing or protective properties; giants, dwarfs

174

and fairies; fantastic castles with splendid trappings, and the like, are all manifestations of the romance marvelous.

Magic is a third manifestation of the broad category of the supernatural; it does not occur in the earliest *chansons de geste*,[7] and when it does make its appearance it is important to distinguish the magical from the miraculous on the one hand and from the romance marvelous on the other. Magicians, as we define them here, are men with publicly acknowledged special gifts which allow them to perform deeds which go beyond normally recognized behavior. In the *chansons de geste*, magicians function on the side of good as well as on the side of evil; in the former case, their actions are generally qualified as being performed "par la Dieu volenté"; in the latter, their powers are recognized as demonic, although they are never to be thought of as "possessed" by the devil.[8] Magic is typically an accessory and non-essential motif in the Old French epic. It does not *replace* the Christian miraculous, but functions along with it as an added element in the design of many later *chansons de geste*.

In a recent study of the character of the magician Maugis d'Aigremont, Philippe Verelst has analysed and classified the principal magicians who appear in published Old French epics.[9] He sees *Huon de Bordeaux* as marking an important turning point in the use of the magician figure in the Old French epic. Before *Huon*, the magician had a minor role and was always a normal man. After *Huon*, the role of the magician was greatly enhanced and many had unusual physical properties (great age, dwarf-like stature, incredible speed, etc.). Moreover, the powers of the pre-Huon magicians were quite different from those after *Huon*.[10] For pre-Huon enchanters Verelst isolates six powers:

1. the ability to cast victims into a deep sleep;
2. the art of unbolting doors;
3. the art of escape;
4. the ability to become invisible;
5. knowledge of herbs;
6. use of disguise.

Many post-Huon enchanters had the following powers:

1. the ability to cause frightening visions in the victim's mind;
2. the capability of causing objects such as castles or food to appear;
3. the capability of moving from place to place at incredible speed;
4. the gift of metamorphosis;
5. the gift of holding anyone who speaks to him in his power;
6. the gift of omniscience;
7. the ability to command devils.

175

Although both Maugis d'Aigremont in *Renaut de Montauban* and *Maugis d'Aigremont* and Basin de Gennes in *Jehan de Lanson*, the two most powerful magicians in the Old French epic, are technically post-Huon creations, it is remarkable that their powers are strictly those of pre-Huon magicians.

As a complement to Verelst's study, I would like to approach the roles of these magicians from another angle. I, too, consider *Huon de Bordeaux* to be a key text, but for a different reason. *Huon* indeed gave new prominence to the role of the magician: after its appearance, magicians could function as a principal character (Maugis) or even as *the* principal character (Basin in *Jehan de Lanson*); yet it did not alter the basic depiction of the *chanson de geste* magician. In enhancing the importance of the magician it did not fundamentally affect his functions. Only minor epic magicians (Galopin in *Elie de Saint-Gille*; Espiet and Noiron in *Maugis d'Aigremont*, etc.) possess any of the seven new powers—and they generally possess at least one of the old powers as well.[11] To endow a *chanson de geste* magician with the powers of Auberon is to put him beyond the confines of the genre. This, I contend, is precisely what has occurred in *Huon de Bordeaux*; and this, I would argue, is why in other Old French epics only minor magicians can possess such powers.

Let us turn, then, to a consideration of Maugis and Basin, two truly epic magicians whose functions, we shall see, contrast markedly with those of Auberon.

Maugis d'Aigremont, the most famous magician in the Old French epic, appears first in *Beuves d'Aigremont*, a prologue to *Renaut de Montauban*, where he is mentioned as Beuve's son.[12] In the Ardennes section he appears in one important passage.[13] After a quarrel in which Renaud de Montauban, one of Aymon de Dordonne's four sons, kills Charlemagne's nephew Bertolais, the "quatre fils Aymon" flee from Charles' court into the Ardennes forest, where they construct the castle Montessor. After it is laid waste by Charlemagne, the brothers return to Dordonne to seek a reconciliation with their father, who has remained loyal to Charlemagne. Following a bitter quarrel, Aymon leaves his sons to their mother's care, and they re-provision themselves and are about to set off again when their cousin Maugis makes his appearance:

> Atant es vos Maugis qui fu preuz et senez,
> Et repa(r)ire de France ou il or conversez;
> En la cité d'Orliens ot .j. tresor emblez
> Que Karles l'emperer i avoit assemblez.
> Trois somers i avoit d'or et d'argent trossez.[14]

176

The adjectives used here to characterize Maugis, *preuz* and *senez*, are those that would describe any other warrior of noble lineage, and there is no indication as yet that he is a magician. The treasure he has stolen was collected by Charlemagne, and this theft cements his commitment to his cousins, who welcome him warmly. He is qualified throughout as *li bons lerres* and uses his cunning to re-provision the brothers (vv. 4788-89) as well as to steal Charlemagne's crown, eagle tent ornament, sword, and treasure. Although he makes use of disguise to facilitate his thieving, there is nothing in all of this that would distinguish Maugis from any number of clever knights in the *chanson de geste*.

In the Vaucouleurs episode, Maugis for the first time assumes a major role in the epic. Aymon's four sons come to Vaucouleurs with Yon de Gascogne, who has betrayed them to Charles. They fall into the trap but, after a brief struggle, are able to escape to Roche Mabon. There they lament the absence of Maugis who, alone, has the power to save them. When Maugis learns of their fate, he uses a charm to escape from Yon's men:

> Donc commença .j. charme a basete raison,
> Que toz sunt endormiz la gent au rois Yon
> (D, f⁰ 80r⁰; cited by Verelst, p. 96)

Maugis rallies the faithful Gascons and rescues the brothers. As Verelst has pointed out, Maugis appears here principally in his role as a doughty warrior: "Il apparaît ici davantage comme un chevalier brave et courageux...." He rescues the four brothers "par la force des armes et non pas à coup de charmes! C'est d'ailleurs la première fois que nous voyons Maugis se battre avec autant d'ardeur; il reproche même à Allard et Guichard de ne pas être assez courageux."[15]

Although upon the field of battle Maugis relied solely on his strength, it is significant that he did use a magic charm to effectuate his escape from Yon's men. It is, indeed, his use of charms and magic herbs that makes Maugis so different from other heroes. On two subsequent occasions Maugis uses his enchantments to put Charlemagne himself to sleep.

On the first, Maugis has been captured by Olivier and heavily enchained by the emperor, who has vowed to put him to death. At midnight, with great concentration, Maugis works a charm that not only puts Charlemagne and all his men to sleep, but also allows Maugis to slip effortlessly out of the chains:

> Donc commence son charme Maugis sanz demorrer,
> Tot issi com il puet son visage torner
> Sont Franceis endormiz, ne s'en porrent garder;

177

Meïsmes Ka*rll*em*aine* fist en .j. lit verser,
Tant fort le so[ut Ma]ug*is* souduire *et* enchant*er*.
Amaug*is* [commença si fort] a conjurer,
Charchanz, buies [et cl]és co*m*mence*n*t a voler. . . .
      (D, f⁰ 110v°; cited by Verelst, p. 109)

On the second occasion, Maugis captures Charlemagne by putting him to sleep, then carrying him off over his shoulders to Montauban:

Et Maugis s'en torna, si vint au maistre tré.
Il comence son carme; ses a si encantez
Qu'il ne disisent mot por les membres coper.
Maugis vint à Charlon, droit au lit où il ert;
A son col l'encarja, o lui l'en a porté.[16]

In the so-called "horserace" episode, Maugis first shows his knowledge of magic herbs. Charlemagne wishes at all costs to find a horse large enough to carry his nephew Roland. Naimes proposes a race in Paris, with the winner to receive the imperial crown, four hundred silver marks, and a hundred precious cloths. In order for Renaud to participate in the race with his fine horse Bayard and not be recognized, Maugis employs a special herb that not only transforms Bayard's color to pure white, but also makes Renaud appear as if he were no older than fifteen (vv. 4800-07). After several near recognitions, Renaud wins the race on Bayard, seizes the crown, reveals his identity to the emperor and, disdaining Charlemagne's anger, returns safely to Montauban.

Maugis employs magic herbs again after having escaped from Charlemagne's chains in the episode recounted above. Once free, Maugis steals Charles's royal crown as well as the swords belonging to the emperor and his peers. He then uses a herb to awaken Charles to ask his leave!

Puis si a p*ris* d'une herbe, Ka*rll*es p*ris*t a forter,
Et Ka*rll*es si commence tantost a deschanter.
Sire, a v*ost*re congié, dist Amaug*is* li ber,
Ersoir vos di je bien, q*ua*nt vint a l'avesprer
Que ge ne m'en iroie sanz co*n*gié demander!''
      (D, f⁰ 110v°; cited by Verelst, p. 109)

Although Maugis appears relatively late in *Renaut de Montauban*, he quickly assumes a major role, effectively forcing Renaud's brothers into the background. He alone accompanies Renaud on his pilgrimage to the Holy Land; both he and Renaud end their lives in the odor of sanctity, and their deaths mark the final stages of the poem. His knowledge of charms and herbs marks him as different from and superior to the four brothers; yet throughout, as Verelst clearly demonstrates, the emphasis is on Maugis' human, knightly qualities.[17]

From a minor character at the beginning of *Renaut de Montauban*, Maugis developed into a hero to equal Renaud himself. The character was so successful, in fact, that a mini-cycle of poems grew up around it. A short epic devoted to his death, *La Mort de Maugis*, appears in a single manuscript.[18] He appears once again as an ideal knight, a councilor, and a magician, but it is his piety that is particularly stressed.

Two later poems, composed to serve as prologues to *Renaud de Montauban*, are devoted to Maugis's early years: *Maugis d'Aigremont*[19] and *Vivien de Monbranc.*[20]

Maugis d'Aigremont, in telling about Maugis's youthful adventures, follows an *enfance* plot found also in poems such as *Doon de Maience*, *Parise la Duchesse, Tristan de Nanteuil, Boeve de Hamtone,* and (inevitably) *Lion de Bourges*. Shortly after his birth Maugis is separated from his twin brother Vivien and his parents because of a war being waged by the Saracens against his father, Bueves d'Aigremont. Maugis is carried off by a slave girl, who is soon devoured by a lion and leopard, which next kill one another when they cannot agree which will have the child for dessert. Maugis is then rescued by the fairy Oriande, who has him raised under the tutelage of her brother Baudris, who had studied the seven arts in Toledo. When he learns he is adopted, Maugis sets off to discover his true parents, passing through a series of adventures during which he frequently extricates himself from difficult situations thanks to his knowledge of herbs and charms. A single example will suffice: while in the service of the pagan ruler Marsile, Maugis begins making love to Marsile's queen. When they are discovered in a compromising situation, Maugis casts a spell that causes Marsile and his men to believe he is not a man, but a doe with fifteen-point antlers, each of which shines with precious stones like a candelabrum. While Marsile is bedazzled by this apparition, Maugis makes good his escape. From this example alone we can see that the charms in *Maugis d'Aigremont* are more imaginative than those in *Renaut de Montauban*; however, there is relatively little use of magic until the culminating battle against Vivien and his magician Noiron. This battle of magicians was to become a set piece in subsequent epics and bears some attention here.

Maugis' brother Vivien, who has still not discovered his identity, has been raised as a Saracen and is attacking their father, Bueves d'Aigremont. Help finally arrives for Bueves from every direction at once, notably that of his son Maugis, who first intervenes in the battle by casting a spell over Vivien's troops that makes them believe they are beset by more than a thousand dragons and lions. Vivien responds by engaging the services of the dreadful magician Noiron, who causes his devils to sow confusion throughout Aigremont. Maugis, too, engages demons to work for him, but it is carefully pointed out that he does this only through the will of God:

> Car Maugis le larron n'est pas de lui [=Noiron] pior
> De l'art de l'ingromance, et est bon ferreor;
> Si n'est pas au deable home ne servitor,
> Ainz les destrainst par Deu le pere creator,
> Quant il en a mestier et il en a loissor.
> (vv. 7990-94)

There follows an amusing war of spells: after Noiron makes the Christians believe they are drowning, Maugis causes him to think he is burning in a fire. Noiron calls forth the demons of hell in the form of ravens (*corbel noir*), while Maugis invokes God's angels to prevent the devils from rescuing Noiron. In their frustration, the devils tear down a tower, then rush upon Charlemagne like Alfred Hitchcock's birds and rip apart his clothing; they lift Naimes and Ogier into the air, then drop them back upon the hard earth. Although Noiron convinces Maugis that he is being attacked by a dragon, Maugis eventually gets the better of him, slays him, and catapults his corpse over the city's walls and into Vivien's camp.

At this point the battle once again takes on more human proportions as Maugis and Vivien meet one another in single combat. Maugis finally overcomes his brother, and when he brings him back within the city, their mother recognizes them both by magic rings that she had placed in their ears just after their births. The poem ends with the requisite reconciliations and conversions, before the principals disperse to their own lands.

Whereas Maugis in *Renaut de Montauban* works his magic largely at the expense of Charlemagne, in *Jehan de Lanson*[21] Charlemagne is greatly helped by the magician/thief Basin de Gennes.[22] This Basin is included in the list of peers at the beginning of the poem alongside such luminaries as Roland, Ogier, and Olivier (vv. 21-30). Like Maugis, Basin has studied in Toledo (v. 2675) and is skilled in *encanterie* and the *ars d'ingremance* (vv. 171-72). Like the Maugis of the *Renaut de Montauban*, he is also able to use charms to escape from chains (vv. 1969-75) and is a master of disguise. The epic *Jehan de Lanson* tells of Charlemagne's prolonged siege of Lanson, occasioned by Jehan's refusal to acknowledge Charlemagne as his overlord. Charles first sends his twelve peers to compel Jehan to submit, but they are cornered and hard pressed by Jehan. This first stage of the siege is highlighted by Basin's battle of enchantments against Jehan's master magician, Malaquin: Malaquin first uses a spell to open the gates of Lanson, which has been occupied by Charlemagne's peers. He then slips into the city, makes off with the twelve peers' swords, and cuts off the sleeping Basin's beard in provocation. In the course of their combat, Basin casts a spell which causes Malaquin to believe that he is tied to a holly tree (*jarris*) within a burning castle; this hallucination induces Malaquin to throw himself into a nearby stream, to the immense delight of Basin and the peers. Malaquin's reply is a spell that causes Basin to believe he is shipwrecked and drowning. The enchantment ends, and Basin beheads Malaquin (vv. 2349-715). Although similar spells are used, the combat in *Jehan de Lanson* is not well-developed and is poorly integrated into the rest of the battle. When the peers are unsuccessful in subduing Jehan, they send Basin disguised as a pilgrim to seek aid from Charles himself. But when Charlemagne arrives before Lanson, he is captured by Jehan with the connivance of the traitorous Ganelon. In keeping with the central role he occupies throughout the *chanson de geste*, it is appropriate that Basin be the one to rescue Charlemagne. He does this with a final enchantment, which puts Jehan and his men to sleep and allows Charlemagne to capture Jehan and carry him upon his shoulders out of Lanson.

In the poems we have been examining thus far, the magician is wholly adapted to his epic context. His appearance at all may indicate some romance influence, but this "epic" magician is probably of Germanic origin (although there is even an Egyptian representative of the type in Herodotus).[23] Unlike the wizzened and elderly Merlin of the romance, Maugis and Basin are in the prime of life and have every attribute of the feudal knight. Maugis, we recall, is first qualified as *preuz et senez*, and is noted throughout for his skills in battle. Descriptions of him underscore his martial qualities:

> N'ot plus bel chevalier jusqu'en Carfanaon;
> Tel josteor de lance ne trovast l'on el mont;
> N'ot plus maistre larron desi à Besençon,
> Mais ainc n'embla vilain vaillant .i. esperon.
> par fu preus Maugis, molt ot bele raison
> Por alever tos ceux qui de sa geste sont. . . .
> (L, 9873-78; cited by Verelst, p. 105)

Basin, a *noble duc sené* and peer of Charlemagne, is a first-rate warrior, and the blows he strikes with his steel-edged sword echo those of every epic warrior before him. For these men, magic is only an added dimension, a skill learned in Toledo that sets them apart *in degree*[24] from other men, but which does not alter their essential humanity. They employ magic only as a last resort or when confronted themselves by supernatural powers; they are members of noted aristocratic families and serve as peers or vassals of the emperor.

Auberon, the magician of *Huon de Bordeaux*,[25] is of another species altogether: he differs *in kind* from ordinary mortals. He is a dwarf-like fairy king of unsurpassed beauty, standing only three feet high, an off-spring of the union of Julius Caesar with Morgan the Fay.[26] He was born before Christ (v. 3447) and is not subject to aging (v. 3581); he will even be able to choose the time of his death (vv. 3582-83, 10509-14). As presented in *Huon de Bordeaux*, Auberon is much closer to the Merlin archetype and to the mysterious dwarfs that populate the Arthurian world.[27] He is no longer a creature of the high mimetic epic world, but is a denizen of the romance. In addition to being skilled in the loosening of bonds and in creating illusions through the casting of spells, gifts that he shares with Maugis and Basin, Auberon is a shape-changer who operates in a sort of time warp.[28] He has the power to transform those who have the misfortune to cross him into *luitons* and other odd spirits; when Auberon wishes to travel, he need only formulate the wish to be in a certain locale in order to appear there instantly. Where Basin and Maugis were skilled fighters, Auberon is never seen with a weapon, preferring to use magic as his first and only resort. Auberon is never incorporated into the epic context; his role is always tangential and, to use Marguerite Rossi's word, "ornamental." Professor Rossi, in her lengthy and important study of *Huon de Bordeaux*, has pointed out a further distinction between Maugis and Auberon:

> Par ailleurs, une différence d'allures et de ton très grande sépare Auberon de Maugis. Ce dernier est d'une verve jaillissante, d'un caractère inventif, d'une richesse affective qui manquent quelque peu à Auberon; Maugis a toute la hardiesse et le caractère de sympathique bravade du faible luttant avec ses moyens propres contre le fort brutal, ce qui donne un intérêt humain à son rôle: Auberon, plus fort que tous ses adversaires, apportant partout une aide uniforme et agissant dans un cadre juridique strict, apparaît en face de lui comme dénué de poésie.[29]

While *Huon de Bordeaux* retains the exterior form of a *chanson de geste*,[30] its hero is engaged upon a mission that will serve him alone. Having killed Charlemagne's nephew Charlot in legitimate self-defense and his champion Amauri in judicial combat (an opening which closely resembles that of *Renaut de Montauban*), Huon can only be reconciled

182

with Charlemagne after fulfilling the following conditions: he must travel
to Babylon to the court of the pagan emir Gaudisse, where he must behead
the first knight he encounters at the emir's table, kiss the emir's daughter
three times, and return with a thousand falcons, a thousand bears, a
thousand hunting dogs, a thousand youths, a thousand maidens,
Gaudisse's moustache and four of his molars.[31] On his adventure Huon is
befriended by Auberon, who subsequently uses his magical powers to help
him accomplish the impossible. His entire adventure, however, is undertaken for his own purposes, and the great twin *chanson de geste* themes of
country and religion are only secondary. A few pagans are slain, but the
East remains a Saracen stronghold; Huon regains his patrimony of Bordeaux, but he will soon abandon it to succeed Auberon as King of the
Fairies. His adventure, as both Alfred Adler and William Calin have
skillfully shown,[32] is a search for self-identity, and the entire poem is a
series of personal adventures that, except for their exotic setting, are very
much akin to those of an Erec, a Gawain, or a Lancelot. The romance
elements are taken over with very little alteration, to such an extent that
Huon de Bordeaux hardly qualifies as a true *chanson de geste*.[33]

The roles of the magicians Maugis d'Aigremont, Basin de Gennes,
and Auberon have thus led us to distinguish two distinct types of magicians
in Old French epic literature. *Renaut de Montauban, Maugis d'Aigremont*, and *Jehan de Lanson* are conservative in their use of the figure,
preferring to fit their magicians into the standard epic configuration.
Maugis and Basin are truly human, but with an added, magical dimension.
They embody the moral and social values of the community, and their
talents are given to help the good triumph over the wicked. The most
notable innovation in these poems is the "combat of magicians," which
not only moulds the magician to the epic context, but also renews the
traditional one-on-one combat motif by infusing it with colorful, fantastic,
and occasionally humorous traits.

In *Huon de Bordeaux*, on the other hand, we have a degree of
innovation that sets this poem apart from other *chansons de geste* of the
period. *Huon de Bordeaux* incorporates into its epic framework a number
of romance elements without significant adaptation. This is particularly
evident in the characterization of Auberon, a fairy spirit whose size,
background, and skills set him entirely apart from ordinary mortals. By
refusing to adapt the elements to the genre, the unknown poet of *Huon de
Bordeaux* has in effect adapted the genre to the times: he has created a
new, composite text that is neither romance nor epic, but which in its
numerous avatars was destined for a long and successful life. Works of
this type we might call, for want of a better term, *chansons d'aventure* or
"adventure epics."[34]

Notes

[1]See William Calin, *The Epic Quest* (Baltimore, 1966), esp. pp. 27-28. Professor Calin is discussing *Aymeri de Narbonne*, but his comments are valid for other *chansons de geste* heroes as well.

[2]Ibid.

[3]Many works deal with this problem. Among the more useful is *Chanson de geste und höfischer Roman, Heidelberger Kolloquium, 30 Januar 1961*, Studia Romanica, 4 (Heidelberg, 1963). Particularly valuable are the contributions by Erich Köhler, "Quelques observations d'ordre historico-sociologique sur les rapports entre la chanson de geste et le roman courtois" (pp. 21-36) and Hans-Robert Jauß, "Chanson de geste et roman courtois" (pp. 61-77 and discussion, pp. 78-83). See also Ellen Rose Woods, *Aye d'Avignon: A Study of Genre and Society*, Histoire des idées et critique littéraire, 172 (Geneva, 1978), and Marie-Louise Ollier, "Demande sociale et constitution d'un 'genre': La situation dans la France au XIIe siècle," *Mosaic* 8/4 (1975), 207-16. Still useful is Erich Auerbach, *Mimesis*, trans. Willard R. Trask (Princeton, 1953), chaps. 5-6.

[4]On supernatural phenomena in the *chansons de geste*, consult Adolphe J. Dickmann, *Le rôle du surnaturel dans les chansons de geste* (Iowa City, 1925). Ralph C. Williams, *The Merveilleux in the Epic* (Paris, 1925), gives only fleeting mention of the Middle Ages.

[5]*Jean Bodels Saxenlied*, ed. Friedrich Menzel and Edmund Stengel, Ausgaben und Abhandlungen aus dem Gebiete der Romanischen Philologie, 99-100 (Marburg, 1906-09).

[6]*Lion de Bourges*, ed. William W. Kibler, Jean-Louis G. Picherit, Thelma S. Fenster, Textes Littéraires Français, 285 (Geneva, 1980).

[7]A Saracen magician, Siglorel, is mentioned in the *Chanson de Roland* (ed. Gerard J. Brault [University Park and London, 1978], vv. 1390-92), but plays no role.

[8]See Norman R. C. Cohn, *Europe's Inner Demons: An Enquiry Inspired by the Great Witch-Hunt* (New York, n.d. [1975]) and especially Edward Peters, *The Magician, the Witch, and the Law* ([Philadelphia], 1978). Magicians, wizards, and necromancers—unlike witches, around whom a considerable body of literature has arisen—have received relatively little attention. One reason is that historical source material abounds for witches, whereas there is very little solid evidence outside of literature for the practices of the magicians and their ilk. The best-known medieval magicians—Merlin, Simon Magus, and Auberon—are essentially literary creations. On the one hand, medieval magicians have been confused with the practitioners of learned, priestly magic, and on the other they have frequently been treated indiscriminately as a part of the large category of "witches." But magicians are not to be confused with witches, who did not appear as a significant cultural phenomenon until the very end of the Middle Ages and who had their heyday in the late fifteenth through the seventeenth centuries. A very different figure from the witch, the magician was "more often male than female, a com-

mander of demons rather than their servant, [and] a specialist skilled in a most elaborate technique" (Cohn, *Europe's Inner Demons*, p. 164).

[9]Two of the promised three parts of Verelst's study have appeared: "L'enchanteur d'épopée: Prolégomènes à une étude sur Maugis," in *Romanica Gandensia* 16 (1976), 19-162; and "Le personnage de Maugis dans *Renaut de Montauban* (versions rimées traditionnelles)," in *Romanica Gandensia* 18 (1981), 73-152. A third section, on Maugis in the later texts, was announced in the initial article, p. 121. All are based on his *mémoire de licence*, "Le personnage de Maugis dans l'épopée médiévale" (Ghent, 1972).

[10]For the classification and powers of the magicians, see Verelst, "L'enchanteur," pp. 155-61.

[11]See chart in Verelst, "L'Enchanteur," p. 159.

[12]See Verelst, "Le personnage," p. 75 n. 3.

[13]Jacques Thomas has divided *Renaut de Montauban* into five major sections: prologue, Ardennes section, Gascony section, Rhine section, and epilogue. He has published an excellent synoptic text of the Ardennes section, which I have used where possible in preference to the older Castets edition: Jacques Thomas, *L'épisode ardennais de "Renaut de Montauban," édition synoptique des versions rimées*, Rijksuniversiteit te Gent, Werken uitgegeven door de Faculteit van de Letteren en Wijsbegeerte, 129-31 (Bruges, 1962). I have also used Ferdinand Castets, *La Chanson des Quatre Fils Aymon*, Publications de la Société pour l'étude des langues romanes, 23 (Montpellier, 1909).

[14]Citations from manuscript D (Oxford, Bodl. Douce 121) are based on the transcriptions in Verelst, "Le personnage."

[15]Verelst, "Le personnage," p. 98.

[16]Ed. Castets, vv. 12546-50.

[17]Verelst, "Le personnage," especially pp. 134-45.

[18]Edited by Ferdinand Castets, in "Maugis d'Aigremont," *Revue des Langues Romanes* 36 (1892), 281-314 (text) and 401-15 (notes).

[19]Ed. Ferdinand Castets (Montpellier, 1893).

[20]Ed. Ferdinand Castets, in *Revue des Langues Romanes* 30 (1886), 128-63.

[21]*Jehan de Lanson*, ed. John V. Myers, North Carolina Studies in the Romance Languages and Literatures, 53 (Chapel Hill, N.C., 1965).

[22]The story of Basin is itself rather complicated. He was widely known in the Old French epic, and seems initially to have been one of the peers and duke of Geneva (Genoa?). In a lost Old French poem listed among the volumes of the library of the Dukes of Burgundy as *le Rommant Basin*, and known today only through allusions in several Old French epics and translations into German, Dutch, and Icelandic, this Basin was unjustly banished by Charlemagne. He was forced to live as a sort of early Robin Hood, stealing from the rich nobles and churchmen, until Charlemagne was told in a vision to become a robber himself. He joins forces with Basin and soon discovers the latter's loyalty. From this the author of *Jehan de Lanson* and, after him, the poet of *Maugis d'Aigremont* took the name Basin and

made of him a robber/magician. Basin "li bons lerres" is alluded to in *Elie de Saint-Gille*, *Wistasse li Moines*, *Bertran du Guesclin*, *Auberi le Bourguignon*, *Restor du Paon*, and *Le Chevalier au Cygne*, as well as in *Renaut de Montauban* and *Maugis d'Aigremont*. Although the poems are lost and proof is thus impossible, it seems that the peer Basin was first transformed into a robber, then into a robber/magician, which is how he appears in most of the known poems, including those studied here. The classic studies on the development of the character Basin are those by Gaston Paris, in *Romania* 21 (1891), 296-98, and in *Romania* 24 (1895), 317-18, and Charles Bonnier, in *Romania* 29 (1900), 425-26. This material is summarized by Gaston Paris, *Histoire poétique de Charlemagne*, 2d ed. (Paris, 1905), pp. 315-22. Evidence for the existence of the lost *Chanson de Basin* is reviewed in the present volume, pp. 103-14, by Constance B. Hieatt, "Reconstructing the Lost *Chanson de Basin*: was it a *Couronnement de Charlemagne*?" However, in none of these studies are his magical powers considered *per se*.

[23]On the history of the *larron enchanteur*, see Marie Ramondt, *Karel ende Elegast, oorspronkelijk? Proeve van toegepaste sprookjeskunde* (Utrecht, 1917). I have not consulted this work, which is cited by Verelst, "L'enchanteur," p. 126.

[24]I have adapted Northrup Frye's useful distinctions *in kind* vs. *in degree* from his *Anatomy of Criticism: Four Essays* (Princeton, 1957).

[25]*Huon de Bordeaux*, ed. Pierre Ruelle, Université Libre de Bruxelles, Travaux de la Faculté de Philosophie et Lettres, 20 (Brussels, 1960). Auberon is also featured in the *Roman d'Auberon*, *Esclarmonde*, and *Lion de Bourges*.

[26]*Huon de Bordeaux*, vv. 6-18, 26-28.

[27]On Merlin, see Paul Zumthor, *Merlin le prophète* (Lausanne, 1943). On the relationship of Merlin to Auberon, consult Marguerite Rossi, *Huon de Bordeaux et l'évolution du genre épique au XIIIᵉ siècle* (Paris, 1975), pp. 377-79.

[28]For good examples of Auberon's shape-changing, see our edition of *Lion de Bourges* (ed. cit.), vv. 20834-929. For a complete listing of Auberon's physical and moral qualities, consult Marguerite Rossi, *Huon de Bordeaux*, pp. 324-32.

[29]Rossi, *Huon de Bordeaux*, p. 380.

[30]Rossi, *Huon de Bordeaux*, esp. chap. 4.

[31]Vv. 2332-70.

[32]Alfred Adler, chap. 7 of *Rückzug in epischer Parade*, Analecta Romanica, 11 (Frankfurt a.M., 1963), and Calin, chap. 4 of *The Epic Quest*. Rossi, however, opposes their conclusions, notably in part C (pp. 382-423) of her chap. 6.

[33]See vv. 10488-506. In comparing *Huon de Bordeaux* with the *Geste des Lorrains*, which served as one of its immediate sources, Rossi points out the essential distinctions between the "adventure romance" of *Huon de Bordeaux* and its *chanson de geste* source:

> Alors que toutes les épopées lorraines sont entièrement consacrées au
> récit de querelles féodales, il ne reste de celle-ci qu'un souvenir
> insignifiant et d'une importance secondaire dans ce dernier poème
> [i.e., in *Huon*] où les lignages et les parentés ne jouent d'ailleurs
aucun rôle; or, dans la *Geste des Lorrains*, c'est la solidarité entre

hommes d'un même lignage qui détermine toutes les attitudes, y compris le comportement des féodaux à l'égard du roi de France que chacun espère intéresser dans sa propre querelle: par contre, les relations entre Huon de Bordeaux et le roi sont essentielles, et non accidentelles.... Ainsi, tout en puisant largement son inspiration dans l'épopée lorraine, *Huon de Bordeaux* ne la continue pas, puisqu'aucun des thèmes essentiels du cycle ne se retrouve dans le poème: un roman individuel se substitue à d'interminables récits de vendettas familiales, la guerre, de réalité douloureuse et passionnante devient thème de roman d'aventures.... (pp. 64-65)

Even in its techniques, *Huon de Bordeaux* is less *chanson de geste* than it may initially appear: although written in laisses, these tend to be very long and the majority assonate in -é. Laisse 74 has 1139 lines, and 7287 of *Huon de Bordeaux*'s 10553 lines assonate in -é. The laisse has thus lost its thematic unity and lyric function and has become entirely narrative. The traditional epic themes are totally absent (there is not even a war in *Huon de Bordeaux*!), and epic motifs are consistently abbreviated, dislocated or otherwise altered (see Rossi, *Huon de Bordeaux*, chap. 4, "La technique épique et son utilisation").

[34]Romance influence in *Huon de Bordeaux* has been noted by most critics who have studied the poem. But where Rossi on the one hand sees the poem as basically epic, Calin and Adler on the other believe "that the poem belongs first and foremost in the domain of romance." (Calin, *The Epic Quest*, p. 174). I would argue that it is neither, but rather the most illustrious representative of an as yet unidentified genre, the *chansons d'aventures* or "adventure epics."

Several other poems that fall into this classification are *Aye d'Avignon*, *Boeve de Hamtone*, *Floovant*, and *Lion de Bourges*. They are set in epic form and have an epic opening and framework but soon devolve into adventure stories (see Rossi, *Huon de Bordeaux*, p. 205). On the question of the distinction of genres in the Middle Ages, see Jean Frappier, "Remarques sur la structure du lai," in *La littérature narrative d'imagination. Colloque de Strasbourg, 23-25 avril 1959* (Paris, 1961), pp. 23-29. The term *chanson d'aventures* appears to have been coined by Larry S. Crist in his review of S. J. Borg's edition of *Aye d'Avignon* (Geneva, 1967) in *Le Moyen Age* 75 (1969), 575. See also my article, "La chanson d'aventures," in *Essor et fortune de la chanson de geste dans l'Europe et l'Orient latin*, Actes du IXe Congrès International de la Société Rencesvals pour l'Étude des Épopées Romanes (Padoue-Venise, 29 août - 4 septembre 1982), 2 vols. (Modena, 1984) 2:508-15.

Saracen Heroes in Adenet le Roi

Peter S. Noble

In his two epic poems, *Buevon de Conmarchis* and *Les Enfances Ogier*, Adenet drew heavily on the work of two much earlier poets, whose work survives in the *Siège de Barbastre* and *La Chevalerie Ogier.*[1] *Buevon* is very closely related to the *Siège*, but the later *Enfances* shows considerably more independence of the *Chevalerie*, in that the second part of the *Enfances* is almost entirely of Adenet's devising, as the last 4,000 or so lines of his poem correspond to about 100 lines of the earlier poet.

One of the few areas in which Adenet does show some originality is in his treatment of the Saracens, both male and female, whose role in his poems is expanded when compared with the earlier poems and given a different interpretation. There was already a long tradition of respect for certain Saracens in epic poetry. In the *Roland* itself, Margariz is described particularly favourably,[2] while the tradition of the beautiful Saracen in love with a Christian goes back to Guibourc, the wife of Guillaume, formerly the Saracen Orable, not that she is wholly typical. "Orable est mariée, elle n'est ni coquette ni impudique, et ne se mêle pas de sorcellerie."[3] This tradition was recognized many years ago by W. W. Comfort: "The Saracen maid does not differ essentially from her Christian sister. The *trouvères* were no more able to imagine a Saracen type of female beauty and charm distinct from that of the Christian than they were able to create a Saracen hero who should not be identical with a Christian chevalier.... They are all paragons of beauty, they are usually more forward in their amorous declarations than we would have them, and they end regularly by being baptized and marrying the hero.... But the *trou-*

189

vère expended all his talent upon these foreign beauties...."[4] More recently Bernard Guidot has described one particular Saracen, Augaiete in *Guibert d'Andrenas*, written probably some sixty years before Adenet towards the beginning of the thirteenth century. His description of Augaiete will serve for the type. "Augaiete, pour sa part, singularise *Guibert d'Andrenas*. Sarrasine, elle n'est pas dévergondée mais sage; obligée de trahir sa famille par amour, elle franchit le pas sans devenir odieuse. Spontanée, vive, autoritaire mais aussi perfide et dissimulatrice, elle entre immédiatement dans le jeu du Destin, attend son heure en ne perdant jamais de vue sa seule préoccupation: épouser Guibert."[5] With both female and male characters Adenet had plenty of material to draw on.

In *Buevon* the Saracen hero is Limbanor, the son of the amirant d'Espagne, described as "preus et vassaus esprouvés" (v. 708), and he is summoned by his father to marry Malatrie, the daughter of the "amustant" de Cordres, who is leading the attack on the Narbonnais. Despite the epic background and theme of the poem, Limbanor behaves like a knight of romance. He treats Malatrie with great courtesy, going to meet her when she arrives at the camp of the Saracen army (vv. 2182-84), coming at her bidding when she summons him to her tent (vv. 2389-97), and, as they walk together in the meadow beyond the stream, which they have crossed to challenge the besieged Christians, they make a wreath of flowers (v. 2427). The love which Limbanor feels for Malatrie is constantly mentioned. Already at their first meeting he rejoices that he is to marry her (vv. 2251-52). Later when she challenges him to prove himself to her, he is very pleased (vv. 2289-307), and he is decidedly dry about her enthusiastic praise for the Christian knight who has accepted their challenge (vv. 2522-25). His pride has been touched, and he is perhaps jealous. Despite this love for Malatrie, Limbanor, in the initial exchange with his opponent, Gerart, offers to surrender Malatrie if Gerart will convert (v. 2564), and Adenet betrays his ignorance of Arab life by making Limbanor describe her as her father's heiress. As Gerart is unwilling to convert and Limbanor is more than ready for battle, they fight, but Limbanor cuts a poor figure, quickly knocked into the stream and saved only by the generosity of his opponent, who fishes him out. He plays no further role in the poem as we have it.

This elegant, courteous but overall unimpressive figure is very close to the original Limbanor in the *Siège*. The touches which are Adenet's own have the effect of weakening the character. In the *Siège*, for example, he is able to clamber out of the stream himself and he had actually arrived in the Saracen camp after Malatrie, so that there is no scene in which he goes to meet her. Thus, in the earlier poem, the action is quickened, as Limbanor arrives, is challenged by Malatrie and rides out to joust the morning after his arrival. The shorter, sharper speeches give the impression of greater firmness and authority than the longer, courtly phrases of Adenet, whose Saracen fails to convince as a serious rival to the aggressive Gerart.

Malatrie is a much more interesting character, clearly in the tradition of Augaiete. She is forceful, cunning, and afraid of nobody. The lengthy description of her (vv. 2096-103) is courtly in tone, emphasising her intellectual as well as her physical qualities. When her father tells her that she is to be queen of France, she politely but with unmistakeable irony asks how he proposes to conquer France when a mere two hundred men are holding him up (vv. 2219-21). Although well aware of Limbanor's quality, she wants him to prove it before her eyes before she promises to marry him (vv. 2268-69). Observing the proprieties but still controlling the action, she sends one of her maidens to induce him to escort her across the stream and challenge the Christians, and when they do cross, it is she who sees the approaching Gerart—she has her eyes fixed on Barbastre— and praises him at length (vv. 2512-21). Gerart's victory causes her to fall in love (vv. 2656-58). There is no false modesty about her. "Par fine amour" (v. 2680) she asks him to take her away, promising to be converted and advising haste as the Saracens are about to try to rescue her. When she is recaptured and hauled before her furious father, she answers him with a cool impudence which enrages him, as she puts the blame firmly on him for choosing such a poor defender (vv. 2966-67). Her love for Gerart is discovered by Flandrine, one of her ladies, who devises the plan to bring Gerart to Malatrie's tent, a plan which Malatrie immediately puts into action. When Gerart comes, he, like Limbanor before him, is hers to command (vv. 3700-01). This deepens her love for him, and, when they realise that the Saracens have discovered the Christian guards, posted nearby, her only worry is that Gerart may suspect her of treason. Well aware that her fate is sealed amongst her own people, she is determined to follow Gerart (vv. 3762-63).

Much of this was in Adenet's source, but he has introduced several differences. Malatrie is no longer in love with Gerart on his reputation alone. She falls in love with the victorious Christian challenger and is then pleased to discover that it is Gerart. The character of Flandrine is invented by Adenet to soften perhaps the ruthless manipulation of others by Malatrie found in the Siège, where she plans the second meeting herself. Her language in the Siège is even more outspoken: "Pute soit la pucele qui ert a son costé" (v. 2361) whereas Adenet preferred the less robust "Honnie" (v. 2967). Adenet makes her send a messenger to Limbanor to summon him to ride out against the Christians. In the Siège she went herself. These alterations all have the effect of making Malatrie behave

191

with rather more of the decorum to be expected of a great princess, although there is, of course, no pretence at realism. Nevertheless the vigorous, unscrupulous, self-reliant girl of the *Siège* is turned into someone equally determined to get her own way, but rather more aware of the conventions to be observed. Working within the conventions of polite behaviour in no way hampers her, and her elegant language, her shrewd observations and the slightly greater psychological realism of having her fall in love with Gerart after she has met him and not before make her in many ways the dominant figure in the poem, which is not the case in the corresponding part of the *Siège*.

In the *Enfances Ogier* there are three attractive Saracens, the kings Carahués and Sadoine and Carahués's fiancée Gloriande. Sadoine does appear in the earlier poem as a friend of Carahués eagerly summoning Carahués to encounter Ogier, joining him in the battle against Ogier and Charlot, where he does not perform very well, and speaking fiercely in defence of Carahués at Corsuble's court. His role in Adenet is different although the opening description is very similar (vv. 1482-83). His force as a warrior is made clear from the moment that he and Charlot unhorse each other, while his prudence is revealed when he advises Carahués to withdraw before they are surrounded (v. 1795). He is thrilled that he will fight Charlot in the duel and here shows himself to be far superior as a warrior, as Charlot is saved only by the intervention of Ogier. Sadoine is so badly wounded that thereafter he plays little part in the poem except to lament his absence from the great battle and to be with Gloriande at the end so that he, too, is able to leave Rome with Carahués, Gloriande, and the remnants of the Saracen army. An attractive figure, shrewd, practical, and extremely courageous, he recalls to some extent Oliver in the *Roland*, although his role is much less important.

Carahués is a much more striking figure than Limbanor. For a start he is a very successful warrior, and there can be no question that the Christians have no champion to match him except Ogier, with whom he is extremely anxious to match himself. Not only is he a great warrior but he is also courtly (vv. 1510-12). His passionate attachment to honour leads him to surrender himself to Charles after Gloriande's brother has treacherously interrupted his duel against Ogier and captured Ogier. His motives for undertaking this combat are mixed. His main motive seems to be love (v. 2188), which is not in Adenet's source. He claims this when challenging the Christians, adding that the winner will take the girl. This seems a remarkably casual way to treat his fiancée of over a year, but it is clearly not meant as a point for criticism. The offer was, of course, in the source. When Ogier accepts the challenge, Carahués is delighted, but his sense of propriety is offended by the ill-mannered intervention of Charlot claiming the honour for himself. Carahués rebukes him sharply (vv. 2243-45), but suggests that Charlot should fight Sadoine instead. The second motive emerges later when, speaking to Corsuble, Carahués says "Bataille empris pour plus vous honorer" (v. 3128). Carahués is protesting at the treason which has resulted in the capture of Ogier, but Corsuble is not interested in his protest. Only when Ogier has killed Brunamon, Carahués's rival for Gloriande, does Corsuble agree to release Ogier. Throughout the second part of the poem great stress is put on the mutual esteem and affection of Ogier and Carahués who carefully avoid each other in battle, until, with the defeat of the Saracens, Ogier arrives just in time to save Carahués, who is resisting to the last against overwhelming numbers. Carahués always treats Gloriande with the utmost respect and is, in part, inspired by love for her. The ending for them at least is reasonably happy as they return to their own countries where they marry.

Carahués seems to combine the best qualities of the epic hero and the knight of romance. Fearless and second only to Ogier in battle, he is courteous and a loving suitor, which is Adenet's main contribution. His offer of Gloriande as the prize of the combat is partly because of its presence in the source, but Adenet has changed the circumstances by making it clearly a mark of Carahués' confidence and an attempt to flush out a Christian challenger with such an attractive prize. His sense of honour, his courage and his magnanimity are all outstanding, and his success is summed up in the line "Forment le prise de France li barnés" (v. 3558), which shows that his enemies all respected him. His role in the poem is to bring out the greatness of Ogier, the only man able to master him in battle. Where Adenet had failed to create an interesting figure with Limbanor, he has definitely succeeded with Carahués, who is more his own creation, although he uses all the material that was already in the source. He adapts it confidently, however, and as Albert Henry remarks "Nous sommes loin du remanieur timide de *Buevon de Conmarchis*...."[6] Carahués stands out in marked contrast to the other Saracens, the treacherous Danemon, the ferocious Brunamon, and Christians such as Charlot. His loyalty to his cause, unwavering even in defeat, and his desperate defence when all seems lost must guarantee the sympathy of the audience. He may not be able to defeat Ogier in battle, but he seems to interest the poet and perhaps the audience more than Ogier.

Gloriande differs from Malatrie in that she is less masterful and intriguing, and indeed less true to the type already described, but not in any way insipid. Beautiful with a skin like roses and lilies, learned and courtly (vv. 1468-75), she shows none of Malatrie's fondness for a handsome Christian knight. Although she does not incite her father to the attack by saying that she will come to watch the battle as in the *Chevalerie*

193

(vv. 1054-58), she has considerable influence with her father and persuades him to excuse the first attack by Sadoine and Carahués on the Christians (vv. 1906-18). Her love for Carahués seems very real. She weeps when he leaves (vv. 2036-37), and her gaze follows him. She willingly accepts his decision that she is to watch his combat with Ogier from a tent nearby so that the winner can carry her off, and her beauty makes Ogier desire her (v. 2705). His remark inflames Carahués so that the combat begins almost immediately. It is her beauty, too, which has made Brunamon fall in love with her and makes him so jealous of Carahués. The sight of Carahués flat on the ground with Ogier ready to administer the coup de grace terrifies her into calling on Mahomet for aid (vv. 2872-75). There is no sign in the *Enfances* of any love for Ogier, which there was in the *Chevalerie*. She does not give Ogier flowers before the battle; she does not speak to him at all. She seems to bear him affection because he is a friend of Carahués, but the thought of being carried off by him to live among the Christians does not attract her at all. Her courage and resourcefulness emerge after the combat when she secures the guardianship of the prisoner Ogier for herself and then proceeds to treat him extremely well (v. 3109). This is to protect him from the other Saracens. She is willing to be championed by Ogier against Brunamon, which after all is common sense in the absence of Carahués, and she arranges to send a messenger to alert Carahués to what is happening at the Saracen court. This alliance of noble spirits knows no barriers of race or creed, and they unite against the less noble of whichever side. Inevitably once the main battle begins, she fades into the background, comforting Sadoine on his inability to join in the battle (vv. 4899-900). Thereafter she says little, seeking refuge with Sadoine in a fortified gate when the Christians seize Rome, bravely concealing her unhappiness when she and Carahués leave Rome, and dutifully mourning her father and her brother when the news of their deaths is broken to her. As with Malatrie, Adenet shows his ignorance of Saracen customs by making Gloriande inherit all her father's possessions, and her story ends with her marriage to Carahués.

Beautiful, wise, and dignified Gloriande is a person who matters in the Saracen court and, with Sadoine and Carahués, is a force for good. Her adherence to the highest standards of personal behaviour never wavers, and she excites the admiration of all who meet her. Her role is less active than that of Malatrie, but physically and morally she would grace any romance as its heroine and is not out of place in a poem that is supposedly epic. She stands out from other Saracen princesses, as Comfort saw: " . . . Adenet surprises us by keeping Gloriande faithful to her first lover, whom she finally marries. . . ."[7]

The role of the admirable Saracen characters in these two poems tells us several things about Adenet. Although he followed his sources carefully, he was writing at a period when the ideas and norms of romance were well established and had long been influencing epic. He was writing at a period when the taste for the exotic was well established, too, and for patrons who had been involved in or interested in the Crusades and therefore were aware of the East and of its peoples. Nevertheless, there is little sign in Adenet of any knowledge of the Arabs. The descriptions given of them are standard romance descriptions. Their way of life, their laws of inheritance are exactly the same as those of their Christian opponents. Their women have a freedom and an initiative certainly not allowed to Arab girls and probably to few Christian upper-class girls of the period. This is all part of the escapism which is such an essential part of Adenet's work and which will reach its fullest expression in *Cléomadès*. The battles and the Christian-Saracen conflict are epic; but the tone in which the individual duels are conducted, the fact that the Saracen champions are accompanied by their women for whom they are fighting (this was, of course, in the sources) and more explicitly for whose love they are fighting, all show how far the influence of romance has spread. The language of all the main characters is the language of romance, however empty phrases such as *fine amour* have become.

Adenet's progress as an adaptor can be seen clearly by comparing the two poems. Limbanor is not a successful creation, although Malatrie is, even if the changes introduced by Adenet do little to strengthen Malatrie and effectively weaken Limbanor. Carahués, Sadoine, and Gloriande come to life vividly and attractively, threatening to take over the poem as the main source of interest. The desperate struggle of Carahués for a doomed cause is more interesting than the almost inevitable victories of Ogier, and the loyalty of Sadoine and the love of Gloriande effectively complement this picture. The lack of interest in the religious nature of the conflict, the concentration on the "exotic" Saracen heroes and heroines, the attention devoted to the female characters all demonstrate just how far Adenet has moved from epic poetry, whatever he himself may have thought of his role as an epic poet.

Appendix

SIEGE DE BARBASTRE

A Libanor mon fil, le neveu Moadas   (v. 465)

Comment cuidiez François de la terre giter
Qui encor sont en France por lor terre garder
Qant je por cent François vos voi ci arester?   (vv. 1714-16)

La pucelle [Malatrie] descent o le viaire cler   (v. 1706)

- Sire, dist la pucele, ne veil plus demender,
Mes que devant la vile en alez ja jouster.   (vv. 1756-57)

Et la pucele i monte, qui n'a song de targier...
Juque au tref Libanor ne fina de coitier.   (vv. 1825-29)

....

Mahom! con il est biaus, cortois et acesmez!
Con li siet li haubers et li hiaumes dorez,
Li escuz a son col con s'il i fust plantez!
Vez quele enforcheüre, quel piz et quieus costez!
Con liee ert la pucele de cui il est privez!   (vv. 1948-52)

- Bele, dist Libanor, ce ert sanz demorer...
Je vos ferai la joste que vos oi desirrer.   (vv. 1758-63)

....

- Bele, dit li baron, trop l'avroiz hui loé.
Encui le vos rendrai, s'il ne muert a joster
Par itel covenant c'un besier me donez.   (vv. 1956-58)

Por la teue amistié...   (v. 2070)

M'amie te donrai a la clere façon   (v. 1991)

Hahi! quel mariage m'aviez ordoné:
Pute soit la pucele qui ert a son costé!   (vv. 2360-61)

La grant biauté de lui vos veil bien acointier;
Les cheveus ot luisanz plus c'argent en gravier,
Les euz vairs et rianz si conme ostoir müer,
La color de sa face pase flor de rosier
Et la bouche espesete et por estroit besier,
Les mameletes dures con pome de pomier.   (vv. 1812-17)

- Bele, ce dit Girart, si con vos commendez...
Ja mes del duc Buevon n'en serai rencuné,
Que ge n'en face auques de vostre volenté.   (vv. 2560-63)

....

196

BUEVON DE CONMARCHIS

Car Limbanors est preus et vassaus esprouvés;
Quant France arons conquise, rois en iert coronnés. (vv. 708-09)

Contre celi qu'il cuide bien avoir a amie
S'en va moult liement, parmi la praierie.
Malatrie encontrerent pres a liue et demie. (vv. 2182-84)

Droit au tre Malatrie s'en vint par la bruiere....
Limbanors la salue et dist: "Amie chiere,
Vostre conmant vueil faire, n'i couvient par priiere". (vv. 2389-97)

Un chapel de floretes vont entre aus deus faisant. (v. 2427)

Vint Limbanors el tre, moult lié et esbaudis,
Car d'avoir Malatrie cuide estre trestous fis. (vv. 2251-52)

Grant joie ot Limbanors quant il ot la devise
Que la pucele ot dit, forment l'en aime et prise.
"Bele, fait il, ja fust faite vo conmandise,
Se ça fors fust as chans cele gens Conmarchise; ... (vv. 2289-92)
[This speech continues to v. 2307]

"Bele, dist Limbanors, forment le me loés;
Cis vous sera ja tost, se je puis, delivrés,
Se il n'est au jouster de mon espiel tués,
Par un tel couvenant c'un baisier me donrés". (vv. 2522-25)

M'amie vous donrai qui a les cheveus blons (v. 2564)

Plus bele ne plus gente de li ne fut trouvee;
Sage fu et courtoise, a raison enparlee,
Et fu blanche et vermeille, a point encoloree,
D'ieus vairs, gais et rians fu tres bien acesmee;
Le chief avoit si blont de blondeur esmeree
Que ce sambloit fins ors quant ert desgalonnee;
Droite fu et bien faite de bon grant compassee,
Et fu selonc sa loi tres bien endoctrinee; (vv. 2096-103)

Mais volentiers saroie, s'il vous plaisoit, comment
Cuidiés France conquerre, quant un pou de lor gent
Tienent ci un chastel enmi vo tenement; (vv. 2219-21)

Ainçois de mon cors soiiés dou tout saisis,
Verrai comment vous estes d'armes duis et apris (vv. 2268-69)

Et il meïsmes samble hom de tres grans fiertés,
Bien est seans en armes et bien est acesmés,
Bien li siet en son chief ses vers hiaumes gemés
Et li escus au col si qu'il i fust plantés,
Sa lance porte droite com hom asseüres,
Moult samble qu'il soit bien et tailliés et mollés;
Com lie est la pucele a cui il est donnés!
Moul doit bien de li estre conjois et amés,
De paradis samble estre angles tous empenés,
S'il n'est hardis et preus, ja mais ne me creés. (vv. 2512-21)

Quant voit Gerart venir, tous le cuers li sautele,
S'amour li a donnee mais il n'en set nouvele;
L'amours de lui li touche au cuer souz la mamele. (vv. 2656-58)

. . . Par fine amour . . . (v. 2680)

Ahi! quel mariage m'avez or trouvé!
Honnie soie je s'il gist a mon costé. (vv. 2966-67)

Dist Gerars: "Douce amie, or soit a vo talant,
Tout entierement vueil faire vostre connant". (vv. 3700-01)

Aprés vous m'en irai, li consaus en est pris,
Car se me tient mes peres, mes cors est mal baillis. (vv. 3762-63)

CHEVALERIE OGIER	
Des Sarrasins i vint un Nubïant, Nom ot Sadones, fix le roi Quiquevant; Fors fu et fiers, orgillous e poissans; (vv. 762-64)	Es Gloriände qui le cors ot a droit... Les elx ot vairs, ben colorés a droit, Bouce petite come enfant aroit. (vv. 1033-44)
Prist Karaeus par son resne a or mier; [This is to attract his attention, not to restrain him] (v. 1315)	....
Karaeus fu mult prodon et cortois; (v. 1464)	....
....	...[No exact equivalent, but he does accept a flower from her] (v. 1796)
"Vassal, dist il, trop es desmesurés. Tant has hui dit qu'il t'iert guerredoné: (vv. 1554-55)	....
Je combatoie por la vestre amistié E por la loi Mahomet esaucier. (vv. 2028-29)	...[No exact equivalent, although she does get Ogier as her prisoner by tricking his guards]
Dient François: "Cis Paiens est gentis''. (v. 2148)	

199

ENFANCES OGIER

Uns Sarrazins qui moult fist a cremit
Non ot Sadoines, fieus le roi de Monmir.   (vv. 1482-83)

Ez vous Sadoine, qui par le frain l'a [Carahués] pris
K'entour lui voit trop de ses anemis.   (vv. 1795-96)

Car moult ert biaus et gens et parcreüs,
Courtois et sages et de bonnes vertus
Selonc sa loi, dont il estoit tenus;   (vv. 1510-12)

Por soie amour me vorrai esprouver . . .   (v. 2188)

Vassal, plains estes d'outrageus escïent
Qui a Ogier parlez si folement,
Mal fait li rois quant il le vous consent   (vv. 2243-45)

Bataille enpris pour vous plus honnorer   (v. 3238)

Forment le prise de France li barnés   (v. 3558)

Car tant ert bele, de biauté adercie,
Que dou veoir estoit grant melodie.
Com flours de lis estoit blanche et polie
Et plus vermeille que n'est rose espanie,
Si mist au faire Nature sa maistrie
Que puis ne fu plus bele riens choisie;
Sage et courtoise fu et bien ensaignie,
Selonc sa loi estoit bien entechie.   (vv. 1468-75)

Dist Gloriande: "Sire, mal en parlés,
Joene gent sont, vraiement le savés;
C'est a grant tort se vous les en blasmés,
K'onnour doit querre li noviaus adoubés,
Si que feïstes, sire, quant fustes tes;
Vous conquesistes honnor, pour ce l'avés,
Que n'eüssiez pas, se fussiez remés;
Se en tans n'est non d'onnour conquestés,
A paines mais puet estre recouvrés.
Pour ce vous pri, sire, se tant m'amés,
S'il ont meffait que vous leur pardonnés
Et quant il vienent, bon samblant lor moustrés,
Ne ne soiez pas envers us irés.   (vv. 1906-18)

Au partir pleure Gloriande un tres poi;
Tant qu'ele pot, li fist des ieus convoi   (vv. 2036-37)

Dieus me doinst grace que la puisse baisier!   (v. 2705)

Dist Gloriande: "Mahommet, que fais tu?
Lasse, dolente, que m'est il avenu,
Quant Carahuel le courtois ai perdu
Dont fait avoie mon ami et mon dru!   (vv. 2872-75)

Moult doucement l'ala reconfortant
Coume pucele courtoise et bien sachant.   (vv. 4899-900)

Moult forment l'a la pucele honnoré   (v. 3109)

Notes

[1]*La Chevalerie d'Ogier de Danemarche*, ed. Mario Eusebi, Testi e Documenti di Letteratura Moderna 6 (Milan, 1963); *Le Siège de Barbastre*, ed. J. L. Perrier, CFMA 54 (Paris, 1926); *Les Oeuvres d'Adenet le Roi*, ed. Albert Henry, 2, *Buevon de Conmarchis* (Bruges, 1953), and 3, *Les Enfances Ogier* (Bruges, 1965). All references are to these editions. The lines cited in this article are quoted in the Appendix, where I have also given the corresponding passages, when they exist, from the *Siège* and the *Chevalerie*.

[2]*La Chanson de Roland*, ed. Frederick Whitehead (Oxford, 1965): "Margariz est mult vaillant chevalers E bels e forz e isnels e legers" (vv. 1311-12).

[3] Charles A. Knudson, "Le thème de la princesse sarrasine dans *La Prise d'Orange*," *Romance Philology* 22 (1968-69), 461.

[4]W. W. Comfort, "Types in the Chanson de Geste," *Publications of the Modern Language Association of America* 21 (1906), 420-22.

[5]Bernard Guidot, "Figures féminines et chanson de geste," in *Mélanges de Philologie et de Littérature Romanes offerts à Jeanne Wathelet-Willem* (Liège, 1978), pp. 204-05.

[6]Henry, *Enfances Ogier*, p. 47.

[7]Comfort, "Types," 427.

On the Saracens in Early Italian Chivalric Literature

Antonio Franceschetti

This essay partially covers some aspects of more extensive research that the writer hopes to be able to complete in the future; that is, the relations between real life and Italian chivalric tradition from the Middle Ages to the Renaissance.[1] Naturally, the Saracens occupy a very relevant place in this research: they were the enemies of Christian Europe for almost a thousand years, from the time of the Arab invasions of Spain and Sicily, through the period of the Crusades, to the Turks' conquest of the empire of Constantinople and their subsequent efforts to extend their domination of Eastern Europe. The importance of the Saracens' historical role is reflected in the numerous works of the Carolingian cycle which deal with the continuous wars fought by the knights of Charlemagne either to defend Italy and France or to conquer part of the pagan world, the so-called *Pagania*, that is, Spain, Africa, and Asia.

Considering the vastness of the subject matter, I must restrict myself to only a few points and a limited number of particularly significant examples. We may begin with *L'Entrée d'Espagne*, written between the years 1300 and 1340, the best known and artistically most important poem of the *franco-veneta* literature.[2] It cannot be said that it started a pattern, since we have no idea of the Italian oral texts which precede it; but at least it represents one of the earliest documents we have. The poem deals with the last war fought by Roland for the conquest of Spain, which led to the tragic epilogue of Roncesvals.[3] During this war the young hero comes into conflict with his uncle, Charlemagne, and, leaving the Christian army, heads for the Orient alone. This is the most interesting part of the poem because it shows for the first time in the Italian tradition a Carolingian character transformed into an Arthurian wandering knight: a prelude of the total fusion of the two cycles which will be completed in the following century.

During the subsequent adventures of the hero among the Saracens, there is little doubt about the author's feelings towards the infidels. In brief, they can be divided into three categories: 1) they are good natured, honest, and decent persons, and sooner or later they will accept baptism and become Christians; 2) they are such bad, arrogant, and untrustworthy rascals that the only solution is to kill them; 3) particularly among the lower classes, they are poor and simple people who are destined to follow the destinies of their rulers, that is, to become Christians if they are good or to be killed if they are bad. Only occasionally can they avoid such a fate—when the author forgets about them! The first two choices naturally show an instinctive rejection of a foreign and religious enemy, oversimplifying the situation of good and evil. The third is, I feel, a reflection of the lower class audiences to which this kind of legend was originally directed in their oral versions. That public, used and often abused by its rulers, was not unwilling to accept the idea that poor and simple people can be found everywhere and always follow the destinies of rulers. Besides, it was obviously very exciting to see those poor souls saved from the devil and ready to go to Paradise, as well as to see those nasty enemies of the Christian name slaughtered like animals by a very valiant knight.[4]

In the *Entrée*, the errant Roland first meets and slays two Saracen merchants who despise him because he says he is poor;[5] he defends the young daughter of the king of Persia against an aged pursuer and kills in a duel the latter's proud and arrogant nephew, who becomes a frightened coward the moment he knows the real name of his opponent;[6] he converts all Persians to Christianity[7] and goes back to Spain to continue the war, although an old hermit warns him of his imminent death within seven years.[8] In this last episode there is a particularly interesting and meaningful moment: after a short hesitation upon hearing of his impending death, the hero proudly expresses his intention to kill all of "la pute gent ahie" in Spain, Africa, and Asia, a thought that the author considers "valoreus e plain de vigorie." Here we confront an irrational, instinctive feeling of hatred that has its roots only in the difference of religion.

The unfinished *Entrée d'Espagne* was continued by another writer in the so-called *Prise de Pampelune*, written around 1340, which we have in only one incomplete manuscript.[9] From the point of view of our topic, this poem contains a very instructive situation. Maoçeris, king of Pamplona, and his son Isoriés, after the conquest of the city, are taken prisoners and accept baptism in order to save their lives. During the night preceding the ceremony, however, the king cannot sleep. Disappointed because he was not accepted to be one of the twelve French Peers, he regrets having abandoned his gods and his lord, King Marsille, and decides to flee and join him to keep on fighting.[10] Undoubtedly, this presents a very human and touching situation: Maoçeris can accept the idea of becoming a Christian under the threat of death, but alone in his bed, during the silence of the night, he cannot avoid feeling guilty for his behaviour. In an opposite situation, in the case of a French knight taken prisoner by the Saracens, we can bet that his repentance would have been considered a sign from Heaven by a Christian author; as for Maoçeris, the poet sees in his attitude only an indication of his villany, "sa felonie." Conversely, his son Isoriés, who becomes a faithful Christian, is considered "loyal and brave" and should be sorry and ashamed of his father's behaviour.

On the same line, in Li fatti de Spagna[11] (a romance in prose of uncertain date on the same subject matter) Galeant, grandson of the king of Portugal, is sent by him to help Marsille at Roncesvals with three hundred knights. But upon learning that he is the son of Oliver, not only does he decide to deny his god and not to fight against his father (something that the "loyal and brave" Isoriés continues to do without any moral problem), but he also offers his followers the choice of joining forces with Roland and attacking the army of the very king they have come to help, or remaining pagan; but, of course, they all follow their leader. Obviously, there is no doubt in the mind of the Christian author that Galeant is a noble hero.

In the category of conversions, there is the example of the Saracen who faces a Christian knight in a duel and eventually asks for baptism. This situation became one of the most common in the Italian chivalric tradition. Only a few alternatives were possible: the request for conversion could precede the duel, in which case the Saracen's life was spared (as it happens to Morgante with Orlando in the anonymous poem used by Pulci as his main source[12]); otherwise, the same request could follow a fatal blow, in which case it depended upon tradition or the author's will to decide if, after becoming a Christian, the infidel would die (the most common solution) or survive (as does Fierabraccia in the Cantare di Fierabraccia e Ulivieri).[13] Probably the most famous example of this kind of conversion is the duel of Roland and Ferragu during the war of Spain: in the version of the Entrée it lasts approximately 2600 lines (from 1630 to 4213), making it one of the longest duels in the history of Italian literature. But even if for approximately 400 lines the two knights engage in theological arguments about which religion is superior to the other, we never reach the request for baptism before the death of Ferragu. This innovation was introduced in *Li Fatti de Spagna* and, later, in a Tuscan poem in octaves on the same subject entitled *La Spagna*, which we have in two partially different texts, both of the first half of the fifteenth century. In this work Ferragu is represented as a noble and brave knight who is not afraid to duel with the strongest warriors of Charlemagne and is very humane to those who become his prisoners. His only limits are his violent, primitive soul and his pride, by which he feels sure he can conquer all Christendom by himself and make his horse eat on the altar of St. Peter in Rome. Quite different from Ferragu, his mother is a real monster: after he has been mortally wounded and baptized by Roland, his last concern is for saving his prisoners from her fury. Thus, before dying, he instructs Roland on how to kill her and save his friends.[14] Once again, it seems that the converted Saracen loses any feelings of filial attachment and respect he might have had for his parents.

In the sequence to this episode, we find another interesting detail. Following Ferragu's advice, Roland exchanges armour with the corpse and enters his city and palace impersonating the dead knight. The rejoicing of the mother is as great as the despair of the Christian prisoners. Only one of them, Astolfo, the French Estaut, shows a quite different reaction, justified on the basis of his personality, since in the Italian tradition he tends increasingly to become a comic character.[15] Convinced he is facing Ferragu and the corpse of Roland, he first congratulates the winner for having eliminated "the bastard who wanted to dominate everybody";[16] then he offers to guide and accompany him in the conquest of all of Charlemagne's empire. The author excuses this apparent betrayal by Astolfo through his great fear of being killed and his light and superficial personality; yet even in this situation, Astolfo feels that he has to make one limiting condition: he refuses to convert to Islam and asserts his intention to remain faithful to Christ. Obviously, the case of a Christian knight who declares his intention to abandon his faith was considered so terrible and shocking (even if it happened quite often in reality) that it was no matter to be introduced as a joke. In order to reach such a stage, the easy-going Astolfo will have to wait for a later poem, the *Orlando Innamorato*, written by a much more liberated author for a much more sophisticated audience.[17] This culminated in the absurd situation presented in the undated *Cantari di Rinaldo da Monte Albano*, the Tuscan version of the French *Renaut de Montauban*.[18] Here, even the holy Roman emperor, the senile and hysterical Charlemagne, promises a Saracen king that he will deny the Christian faith in exchange for his help against his always turbulent vassal.

A highly dramatic conversion to Islam by a Christian knight is that of Gherardo da Fratta, lord of Vienne: change of editor, It. Vienn*a* being the

French city of Vienn*e* on the Rhône river. After fighting for a very long time against Charlemagne, whom he refuses to recognize as legitimate emperor, he falls into despair when he sees his strongest grandchild killed by Roland in a duel, breaks a cross to pieces, and decides to escape on Muslim soil in order to find help to continue fighting against his hated enemy. We can read this episode, written with a sad and almost tragic tone, in a Tuscan romance after a French *chanson*, *Aspremont*.[19] Its author, Andrea da Barberino, who lived approximately between 1370 and 1432, was the most prolific writer in prose of Italian chivalric literature; his works, in abridged and modified versions, remained popular for centuries. He, too, somehow put himself in line with the tradition, evidencing a definite preference for the Christians over the Saracens; but his effort to assume the aspect and the tone of a historian rather than a storyteller determined a number of changes worthy of being stressed, since I believe they made a substantial contribution to the different attitude towards the Saracens that was accepted by following generations.

As for duels, fights, or wars on battlefields, there is little doubt that—generally speaking—for Andrea da Barberino, Christians are morally better than Saracens.[20] During peace, however, in their elegant palaces or simple and humble dwellings, with their courteous and generous sense of hospitality, it is quite often clear that the Saracens have nothing to envy in their Christian counterparts. One feels at times that there is such a 'social' assimilation as to leave very little to 'religious' alternatives; it makes no difference if one believes in Christ or in Mohammed, the difference is determined only by the nature and the character of the individual, who can be good or bad, no matter in what or in whom he believes.

Andrea's sense of ethics appears somehow independent from any religious interference: dishonesty is wrong in itself and must always be condemned, no matter what the motivation, purposes, and the consequences of a specific act. When the ten Saracen guards in charge of the prison of Bueve d'Antone plan to escape with him and become Christian, the young hero, unaware of their decision, kills all of them; Andrea has no word of sympathy for their fate and no reproach for Bueve's behaviour.[21] They were betraying the trust of their master, they were doing something wrong, they deserved a punishment; the fact that they were saving a Christian knight and thinking of becoming Christians themselves is no excuse.

The development of these circumstances during the course of the fifteenth century shows a definite improvement in the attitude of Italian writers towards the Saracens. Omitting the presentation in the poems of Pulci and Boiardo, with whom we enter the world of the Renaissance, the writer will give only two examples from two works of uncertain date, but which certainly belong to the medieval tradition in format, style and structure. In the *Falconetto*, the protagonist, a young Asian prince, is killed by Roland after he bravely enters a fight wearing only part of his armour.[22] This same situation is found in the *Aspramonte* by Andrea da Barberino, with the substantial difference that there the killer was an African king and the victim a Christian hero.[23] An episode of another poem, *L'Inamoramento di Carlo Magno*, offers an apotheosis of the bravery and just self-esteem of a Saracen hero, the Asian emperor Gargatai. Abandoned by his friends and soldiers, surrounded by the Christian winners who invite him to accept baptism, he first reminds them of the many crimes committed in that poem by Charlemagne; then, after stating that he does not want to have anything in common with them, he kills his horse and throws himself on his own sword, saying these words: "Nulo di voi vo' che si vanti / d'aver conquisa la mia gaiardia" ('I do not want anyone of you / To claim to have won my vigor').[24]

This situation is even more surprising when we consider that Italian witnesses and historians became generally more embittered and aggressive towards the Turks and their habits at the time of the fall of Constantinople in 1453.[25] The successes of their traditional religious enemies were sensed as a real threat to the safety of the peninsula; there was an almost unanimous agreement about the necessity of a new crusade to free the capital of the ancient Roman Eastern Empire and re-establish that bulwark of Western political and religious freedom. Among the numerous available references, I will only quote a passage from a letter of Enea Silvio Piccolomini, the future Pope Pius II, regarding the Byzantine empire: "[Greek culture] will be in a quite different situation under the rule of the Turks, the most cruel men, enemies of civilized living and of letters . . . an infamous and unknown people, addicted to prostitution and rape, supporters of brothels, they eat all kinds of abominable food and use neither wine, nor wheat, nor salt . . . Wallowed in lust, they give little consideration to the study of letters and proudly despise them. . . ."[26] In the humanistic world to which Piccolomini belonged, this accusation was probably the worst of all. But for some reason, these and other similar comments do not seem to have left any trace in the contemporary works of Italian chivalric literature. Obviously, tradition had established a pattern by that time which neither concrete historical fears, nor slandering propaganda were able to shake.

In conclusion, I would like to suggest that there is apparently not much relation between historical Saracens and those depicted in Italian chivalric literature. Obviously, there must have been a great many differences between the Arabs of Spain, the African Muslims, and the Turks who established their empire in Constantinople. But these differences totally disappear in the literary tradition, where Saracens act and behave like Christians. They all seem to belong to an identical, idealized world; they wear the same kind of armour, use the same rituals, share the same ideals, enjoy hunting, dancing, parties in the same way and always live in similar, beautiful castles, palaces, and gardens. Even for a city like Venice, which was for centuries in direct commercial and political contact with Saracen countries, historical reality never affected the many works of this genre prepared or printed in the region. As just mentioned, several documents show that Italians were terrified by the Turks who conquered Constantinople, but chivalric texts provide very little evidence on the subject. As a consequence, a closer look at the relations between the Saracens in history and those in the chivalric tradition could throw some very important and interesting light on the overall attitude towards them by the Italian public and contemporary writers.

Notes

[1]A work of similar but not identical purposes has recently been published, dealing mostly with English tradition: *Chivalric Literature: Essays on relations between literature and life in the later middle ages*, ed. Larry D. Benson and John Leyerle (Kalamazoo, Mich., 1980). Not used in this study is Paul Bancourt's "Le thème du Sarrasin dans l'épopée," *Perspectives Médiévales* 8 (1982), 107-16.

[2]Published in two volumes by Antoine Thomas (Paris, 1913; rpt. New York, 1968). On this work see Alberto Limentani, "L'epica in *Lengue de France*: *l'Entrée d'Espagne* e Niccolò da Verona," in *Storia della cultura veneta*, II, *Il Trecento* (Vicenza, 1976), pp. 338-68: other bibliography can be found in this essay. Particularly relevant for this poem and the subsequent developments of the same legend in the Italian chivalric tradition is Carlo Dionisotti, "*Entrée d'Espagne, Spagna, Rotta di Roncisvalle*," in *Studi in onore di Angelo Monteverdi*, 1 (Modena, 1959), pp. 207-41.

[3]The conquest itself is justified by religious rather than political reasons: the main purpose is to free for pilgrims the way to reach the sanctuary of St. James in Compostella (see the beginning of the poem, vv. 1-95).

[4]Any feeling of compassion for these scenes of massacre is virtually unknown in early Italian chivalric tradition: it will be found only later, during the Renaissance, particularly in Ariosto and after.

[5]Vv. 11497-563. Merchants, whether Christian or Saracen, did not enjoy a particularly high esteem in Italian chivalric tradition: it is a very common topos that, when a knight errs during a duel, his adversary immediately accuses him of being the son of a merchant, rather than the offspring of noble blood.

[6]Vv. 11946-13171.

[7]We cannot tell precisely how this episode (which is, however, clear from

what follows) took place, since there is a lacuna in the only extant manuscript of the poem.

[8]Vv. 15126-64.

[9]Published by Adolf Mussafia in *Altfranzösische Gedichte aus venezianischen Handschriften*, I, *La Prise de Pampelune*; II, *Macaire* (Vienna, 1864).

[10]Vv. 597-668.

[11]Li *Fatti de Spagna*, ed. Ruggero M. Ruggieri (Modena, 1951), pp. li-lii.

[12]See *"Orlando". Die Vorlage zu Pulci's "Morgante,"* ed. Johannes Hübscher, 2 (Marburg, 1886), pp. 3-7.

[13]See *Die Gestaltung der Chanson de Geste "Fierabras" im Italienischen*, ed. Carl Buhlmann (Marburg, 1880), canto III, octave 37 - canto IV, octave 24.

[14]See *La Spagna*, ed. Michele Catalano, 3 (Bologna, 1940), canto II, octave 31 - canto V, octave 40. In *Li Fatti de Spagna*, the dangerous woman against whom the dying Ferragu warns Roland is his sister, not his mother (see canto XXV). For the Italian tradition of the various legends concerning the conquest of Spain and the death of Roland and the relations among the various surviving texts, Catalano's study, which occupies the whole first volume of his edition, is still fundamental.

[15]See Giuseppe Guido Ferrero, "Astolfo (Storia di un personaggio)," *Convivium* 29 (1961), 513-30.

[16]"lo sterpone / che volia sogiogar tutte persone" (canto VI, octave 26). For the whole episode see canto VI, octaves 16-40.

[17]See Matteo Maria Boiardo, *Orlando Innamorato. Sonetti e Canzoni*, ed. Aldo Scaglione (Turin, 1951), I, vii, 63. Boiardo's attitude on this point is discussed in my *L'Orlando Innamorato e le sue componenti tematiche e strutturali* (Florence, 1975), pp. 102-09.

[18]*I cantari di Rinaldo da Monte Albano*, ed. Elio Melli (Bologna, 1973), canto XLII, octaves 28-30. For the relations between the Tuscan poem and French epic see Melli's introduction, pp. vii-xxiii, and the bibliography quoted there.

[19]See Andrea da Barberino, *L'Aspramonte*, ed. Marco Boni (Bologna, 1951), book III, chaps. cxliv-cxlvi.

[20]This, of course, does not happen in the case of a Christian character who turns traitor (for thirst for power, ambition, envy, love, etc.) to his fellowmen: particularly obvious is the situation of the members of the family of Magance who, according to a pattern which became customary in Italian chivalric tradition, are always untrustworthy and ready to commit any kind of treason. This pattern clearly originated from the case of Ganelon, the betrayor in the *Chanson de Roland*.

[21]See Andrea da Barberino, *I Reali di Francia*, ed. Guiseppe Vandelli and Giovanni Gambarin (Bari, 1947), book IV, chapter xxi.

[22]There are no modern editions of this poem. One can read this episode in the incunabulum printed in Milan in 1483, p. 103, or in the different version in octaves printed in Venice in 1500, canto IV, octave 28.

[23]Riccieri di Risa is killed in this manner by Almonte during the conquest of

his city (*L'Aspramonte*, book I, chapter xlii).

[24]For this poem, too, there are no modern editions. The episode can be seen in the incunabulum printed in Venice in 1491, canto XXXVII; the lines quoted are in octave 17.

[25]See the numerous documents collected in two volumes by Agostino Pertusi, *La Caduta di Costantinopoli*, 1, *Le testimonianze dei contemporanei* (Milan, 1076), and 2, *L'eco nel mondo*.

[26]"Nunc sub Turchorum imperio secus eveniet, saevissimorum hominum, bonorum morum atque litterarum hostium . . . Gens ignominiosa et incognita, fornicaria in cunctis struprorum generibus, lupanarium cultrix, quae abhominabilia quaequae comedit, ignara vini, frumenti atque salis . . . In libidinem provoluti sunt, litterarum studia parvi faciunt, incredibili fastu superbiunt. . . ." From a letter to Cardinal Nicholas of Cues of 21 July 1453, in Agostino Pertusi, *La Caduta di Costantinopoli*, 2:52-54.

La imagen del rey en el *Cantar de Mio Cid*

†Aristóbulo Pardo

Por alguna razón que se me escapa, los reyes no son figuras épicas en las obras o leyendas que de este género se nos han conservado de la edad media española[1]. Es extraño que los hechos heroicos de reyes como Alfonso VI, Fernando III, Alfonso XI, para dar apenas unos ejemplos, no hayan instigado el numen épico de los españoles. La extrañeza es mayor al notar que los reyes, cuando aparecen en los textos épicos - sean prístinos o refundidos -, presentan trazos antiheroicos de traición y engaño en el cumplimiento de sus pactos y promesas. Alfonso el Casto incumple repetidamente la promesa que ha hecho a Bernardo, su héroe, de darle libertad a su padre. Una carta traidora de la reina de León a su hermano el rey de Navarra induce una jugada también engañosa de éste, en la cual apresa al conde Fernán González. En la leyenda y menciones del cerco de Zamora, pese a la voz honrada de Arias Gonzalo, muy poca duda queda de la complicidad primaria de Urraca y secundaria de Alfonso en la muerte de su hermano el rey Sancho II de Castilla. En el *Poema de Alfonso Onceno*[2], el rey deja de cumplir con su promesa de matrimonio con Constanza Manuel, y no es ésa la única infidencia del rey en su poema.

Cuando no es la condición astuta y escurridiza, es la llaneza imprevisora, como acontece con el rey Sancho II en el *Cerco de Zamora*. Incautamente, el soberano se confía a Vellido Dolfos, un recién llegado que le promete enseñarle un punto débil en la muralla zamorana. El rey marcha solo con él en una caminata exploratoria y, en la más indefensa y chabacana de las situaciones posibles, se pone a merced del extraño

213

sujeto[3]. El resultado es, en efecto, la muerte del rey a manos de aquel desconocido. Semejante rasgo campechano del rey Sancho II parece obedecer más a velada intención política que a designio genuino de arte literario. La historia no ha podido ser así. La situación es demasiado absurda para ser histórica. Los reyes tenían una noción clara del decoro correspondiente a su alta investidura. El hecho de llevar en su mano el venablo de plata indica que en ningún momento el rey se olvida de su calidad de soberano[4]. No es concebible que un rey se confiara en forma tan incauta a un desconocido y que el cortejo real desertara tan completamente. La historia es, en este caso, juglaresca - sin duda. Una flecha traidora habrá dado muerte al rey, sí, pero no a la vista de todos como supone Carola Reig[5], ni mucho menos como se narra en la chabacana escena acríticamente plasmada por las historias y los restos del *Cantar de Zamora*. De ese modo han dado al traste con la ingeniatura de las posibilidades épicas para el rey Sancho, justamente cuando se acercaba a quedar encuadrado dentro de eventos heroicos propios de su persona y su linaje.

Más sensible es lo que sucede en el *Poema de Alfonso XI*, donde la incompetencia del juglar no es suficiente para explicar la esfumadura que desdibuja la gesta heroica del rey, sobre todo si se considera que aún la muerte del monarca es consecuencia de su agitada militancia contra los musulmanes.

Esta especie de *capitis deminutio* que se aplica a los reyes en la esfera de la épica española no significa, sin embargo, que la imagen del rey ni la noción de la majestad regia se hallasen en condición de deterioro. Juan de Salesburi dice que el rey es "in terris, quaedam divinae maiestatis imago"[6]. Nada diferente puede decirse de la imagen del rey en España durante los siglos de activa creación épica[7]. La idea de que el rey lo es "por la gracia de Dios"[8] sigue vigente a pesar de que a la épica se le haya pasado la mano en el adumbramiento de los reyes.

La única gesta en que se halla una figura de rey conscientemente trazada para producir efectos de semántica ideológica es el *Cantar de Mio Cid*. Sin embargo, por circunstancias especiales, que no es del caso discernir aquí, la imagen que del rey Alfonso VI se ha generalizado concuerda con los datos históricos y no con la que se desprende de los datos del *Cantar*. El curso de las cosas ha podido ser éste o quizás uno muy cercano: (1) *En la España del Cid* (prim. ed. 1929) don Ramón Menéndez Pidal pone al Cap. XVI un epílogo titulado "La invidencia del Emperador"[9], donde se muestra la tozuda actitud negativa del rey en sus últimos quince años de reinado para con los éxitos militares del Campeador; (2) años después, en "Mio Cid el de Valencia" (1943)[10], don Ramón recalca la invidencia del rey Alfonso VI; y (3) al año siguiente, en su artículo sobre "La crítica cidiana y la historia medieval"[11], el insigne abanderado de Mio Cid subraya la actitud invidente del rey frente a las afortunadas campañas del Cid. La confianza que han merecido los datos aportados por el venerado maestro del romanismo hispánico ha despejado toda duda sobre la invidencia histórica de Alfonso VI para con el Cid de Vivar. Pero conste que Menéndez Pidal no trasladó la invidencia alfonsina a sus estudios de crítica literaria sobre el *Cantar*. Otros lo han hecho respaldándose en Menéndez Pidal y su crítica histórica. Y justamente por ello es importante aclarar el equívoco. Hay que leer la figura del rey con los rasgos deducibles del poema mismo.

Parte de tales rasgos ha sido entrevista ya por Gustavo Correa[12], por Edmund de Chasca[13] y otros. Pero ha sido Roger M. Walker[14] quien ha mostrado cómo el rey, injusto al comienzo, se vuelve justo y comprensivo para con el Cid, con lo cual se crea la circunstancia poética propicia para responder como se debe al desideratum del famoso verso 20: "Dios, que buen vassallo, si oviesse buen señor"[15]. En el tratamiento que Walker da al problema, el señorío del rey mejora en el grado y medida en que se funda más y más en la justicia. Y, aunque no es su propósito el abocetar una figura del rey, Walker contribuye provechosamente al entendimiento de la imagen del rey en el *Cantar*[16].

Es el caso que el rey del poema, además de buen señor, y justo, acusa una objetividad política muy perspicaz y se muestra magnánimo. Estas dos cualidades son armónicas con las dos primeras. Hay que destacarlas porque sin ellas es menos visible el trasfondo de proyecciones patrióticas y religiosas que acompaña la imagen del rey Alfonso VI en el *Cantar*. Ahora bien, se trata de proyecciones presentadas en tal forma que no comprometen la credibilidad humana ni las proporciones terrenas de los acontecimientos. No es difícil advertir la manera como estas características del rey se entrelazan y matizan en el curso de los hechos.

Al llegar Minaya ante el rey con el primer presente del Cid (vv. 781-78), el rey sonríe complacido: "fermoso sonrisava" (v. 873). Aquella sonrisa abre la puerta al diálogo con Minaya, quien explica el obsequio y pide al rey "quel [sc. al Cid] ayades merced". El rey esquiva la petición alegando que es muy pronto para ello, pero acepta el presente porque ha sido tomado a los moros (v. 884), lo cual es una prudente expresión del carácter que el rey atribuye a la actividad del Cid en esas tierras de morisma; y para subrayarlo, agrega: "aun me plaze de mio Cid que fizo tal ganancia" (v. 885). La frase es calculada. Con ella da acogida benévola a la manifestación de vasallaje del Cid y connota que éste ha abierto un capítulo que puede llegar a ser historia, por lo cual conviene dejar las cosas en suspensión, en espera de desarrollos ulteriores. Si la acción prospera, habrá nuevas gestiones, nuevas embajadas del Cid y situaciones nuevas. El rey se muestra como político objetivo y prudente. Se muestra asimismo generoso al corresponder de su parte al presente del Cid: (1) "a vos quito, Minaya", o sea que lo declara limpio aun de la sospecha de deslealtad o de infracción; (2) le condona tierras y honores; (3) le extiende un salvoconducto incondicional para que pueda entrar en el reino de Castilla cuando y cuantas veces lo tenga a bien; (4) franquea cuerpos y heredades a cuantos súbditos del reino quieran marcharse a luchar junto con el Cid (vv. 886-94). En su actitud no es posible leer ni brizna de envidia o de resentimiento para con el Cid.

Cuando Minaya regresa con presente del Cid, el rey respeta la promesa hecha - cosa que es de notarse - y recibe con agrado la embajada. Escucha atentamente el relato de las batallas campales que el Cid ha vencido, se admira de "tan fieras ganancias como ha fechas el Campeador" (v. 1341) y se alegra de "las nuevas que faze", sin que pueda advertirse ni el más leve detalle de reserva o de incomodidad por los éxitos cidianos que Minaya le cuenta. El poeta resalta en ese punto la dispar actitud del rey y de García Ordóñez: "Maguer plogo al rey, mucho peso a Garci Ordoñez" (v. 1345). En retribución al Cid el rey concede: (1) que la familia de Ruy Díaz vaya a reunirse con él en Valencia; (2) que mientras Ximena y sus hijas transiten los caminos del reino, la Corona les brindará honores y protección; (3) que el Campeador no debe perder nada de lo que tiene, y mucho menos hombres, por lo cual restituye las heredades a quienes militan bajo órdenes del Cid (vv. 1362-64); (4) que tanto como sus bienes, les asegura los cuerpos contra cualquier asechanza u ocasión; y, 5) para rematar, confirma el permiso general para que quienes quieran ir a Valencia a luchar junto al Cid lo hagan sin temor alguno y con franquicias plenas (vv. 1369-70). Al terminar sus concesiones, el rey sonríe como asegurándose de que había estado en lo cierto cuando la primera embajada y que lo está también ahora. Con esa seguridad íntima hace callar a García Ordóñez que ha hecho una observación impertinente y envidiosa: "dexad essa razon, / que en todas guisas mijor me sirve que vos" (v. 1349). La facultad justiciera del rey se ha zafado de las redes en que antes estuvo embrollada. El rey justo se ve ahora con perfil nítido. Y de igual modo aparece el rey político, a quien no se le oculta que "Mas ganaremos en esto que en otra desamor" (v. 1371). El rey actúa con circunspección, con tino, pero con mano abierta y generosa. En las concesiones excede con creces al regalo en caballos. Hay en todo ello mucho más que mera valía pecuniaria. Hay cierta lumbre magnánima y un seguro tacto político. Su sonrisa significa mucho más que mera complacencia por el valor material del obsequio recibido.

Al llegar la tercera embajada del Cid con doscientas cabalgaduras de presente, el rey está de antemano dispuesto a otorgar el perdón. Su reacción es inmediata. Le encarga a Minaya que diga a "Roy Diaz, el que en buen ora nascio, / quel ire a vistas do aguisado fore" (vv. 1910-11). Con esas palabras empieza el acceso a la cumbre del empeño del Cid, que ha sido el recobro del amor de su rey. La otra parte del mensaje es el arreglo de los esponsales de las hijas del héroe con los infantes de Carrión. Un acto de justicia y un acto político. Con el acto justiciero crece la virtud señorial del rey. Con el acto político se reconoce una realidad imponente: el Cid es ahora cabeza de un reino conquistado por sus manos, y sólo una devotísima lealtad a la corona de Castilla le ha impedido erigirse en soberano[17]. De todos modos, el Cid es un poderoso del reino castellano y es de suponerse que su poderío crecerá. De otro lado, el rey se da buena cuenta de que los Vanigómez no van a cejar en su empecinamiento anticidiano. Lo más indicado es constituir un vínculo de familia entre los dos bandos - el de los Vanigómez y el del Cid -, a objeto de precautelar tensiones y desavenencias.

Todo este proceso culmina en la escena del perdón, junto al Tajo: "aqui vos perdono e dovos mi amor, / e en todo mio reyno, parte desde oy" (vv. 2034-35). La ceremonia se encuadra dentro de pasos rituales que el poeta del *Cantar* despliega sin economía de pormenores. Comparando el comportamiento del Cid en esta ceremonia con el de los Vanigómez en el desarrollo de las Cortes de Toledo, el espectador del *Cantar* percibe sin esfuerzo una intención de fondo. Es el obvio desequilibrio entre la humildad - casi ostentosa - del Cid ante su señor y el descoco de todos los Vanigómez ante su señor y ante la Corte. Leyendo la situación en su balance general, no es difícil advertir que el rey ha establecido un equilibrio entre el Cid, que ahora tiene parte en el reino, y los Vanigómez, que son "mucho urgullosos e an part en la cort" (v. 1938), como ha dicho el propio Cid.

No obstante, el equilibrio buscado resulta precario. La afrenta de Corpes lo pone en peligro decisivo, ya que no es solamente una infamia contra las dos hijas del Cid sino, sobre todo, un atentado contra la honra del héroe victorioso. El equilibrio de honores se resquebraja, pero no el de poderes, y el rey ve claramente el significado de semejante situación. Por eso convoca a cortes y no a vistas. Las Cortes de Toledo son el tribunal de reparación para la falta de los infantes. Siendo las Cortes una extensión funcional de la Corte, el bando carrionense es poderoso en ellas. El rey tiene que agenciárselas para que haya equilibrio de poder en ellas y, por lo tanto, derecho para el Cid. Sólo así podrá prevalecer la justicia, que es prioritaria para el éxito del rey. ¿Como obtener ese equilibrio sin posibilidad alguna de fracaso? El rey nombra como alcaldes de primera instancia a sus dos yernos, los condes don Anrric y don Remond (v. 3135), y se designa a sí mismo juez, en instancia de casación. Además, para que sus cortesanos tengan las cosas claras, el rey exhibe ciertos detalles para con el Cid: lo invita a sentarse a su lado compartiendo el escaño regio y manifiesta que el escaño le ha sido regalado por el Cid; hace saber expresamente que aquellas Cortes no tienen más objeto sino que el Cid "reciba derecho de infantes de Carrion" (v. 3133). De esta manera, el soberano está seguro que el fiel de la balanza estará en vilo. Un error de justicia puede desencadenar estados de beligerancia, con riesgo para el reino. No puede haber yerros decisorios. El Cid ha de recibir derecho de los ofensores. Todo el decoro escénico está dispuesto para que el Cid despliegue sus talentos de jurisperito. Con ello se crea un aire estremecido de lances y visajes de emoción humana y el juego político queda recatado detrás de aquella esfera de intereses. En la última fase de las Cortes, cuando se concreta el duelo entre "vasallos" del Cid y los hermanos carrionenses para limpiar mancillas de la sangre, el rey se constituye en garante y protector de la seguridad de los justadores del Cid. Es un gesto con el cual el soberano aparece, entonces, justo, buen señor y magnánimo. Nada invidente.

Al comienzo del *Cantar*, un dictum poético presenta al Cid llorando, reducido a la impotencia, frente a sus heredamientos estragados también. Aquello es un reflejo del dictum del rey, que ha extrañado al Cid y lo ha destituido de sus privilegios y derechos; únicamente la vida le ha sido conservada, y eso como gracia, no como derecho; no puede, pues, ni siquiera vivirla con los suyos. El rey se siente allí como poder remoto, inhumano, injusto, pues el varón que mira sus heredades en escombro y que marcha hacia el destierro no puede volver los ojos a su rey ni elevar a él su queja. Dios le está más cerca, y a El dirige sus palabras. Por virtuosismo poético, es en esa escena donde el Cid ofrenda su primer acto de lealtad al rey: no pone la culpa de lo que le sucede en la cuenta del rey sino en la de "mios enemigos malos". El Cid sabe que, por fuero, no ha podido ser el rey quien le ha estragado sus bienes: ". . . quando ovier el Rico ome a salir de la tierra, . . . el Rey non le deve facer mal ninguno en sus compañas nin en sus algos que han por la tierra"[18]. Pero si el ricohombre comenzara a guerrear contra el rey, éste podrá destruirles, a él y a quienes con él van, toda clase de bienes, y aun talarles los montes; "mas los solares e las eredades non los deve el rey entrar para si, mas deven fincar para ellos e para sus erederos"[19]. De manera que no pudiendo ser el rey, razona el Cid, solamente sus enemigos malos pueden haberlo hecho. Pero a pesar de la generosa hipótesis del Cid, el espectador del *Cantar* sospecha que el rey consiente el abuso de fuerza ejercido contra los bienes del vasallo. La desconfianza se refuerza con el duro tenor de la carta del rey a los de Burgos, puesto que, en esa materia, el Fuero dispone que "quando ovier el Rico ome a salir de la tierra . . . el rey devel' dar vianda por sus dineros, e non gela deben encarecer mas de quanto andava ante que fuese echado de la tierra''[20]. Pero la carte del rey manda que para el Cid ni sal ni agua ni techo. Es patente que la facultad regia para el ejercicio de la justicia está desgobernada. Los burgaleses, buenos conocedores de sus fueros, hacían la inferencia correcta; la prohibición era excesiva. Es por eso por lo que quisieran vociferar su desacuerdo con el empecinamiento del rey; pero las amenazas de la carta los fuerzan a mantener físicamente cerradas las puertas y las ventanas, lo mismo que las gargantas, mientras el Cid y los suyos van de paso por Burgos ''la ciudad''. Lo cual no quita autenticidad poética a la protesta del famoso verso 20. Lo injusto de la prohibición motiva eficazmente el engaño de las arcas de arena, que viene enseguida del vacío total con que Burgos ha tenido que humillar al Cid. La crítica ha visto que el Cid, allí en la glera de Burgos, planeando y ejerciendo el engaño, desciende a su mínima expresión moral; pues es, precisamente, cuando el rey es menos rey porque se ha hecho inaccesible a los suyos y se ha convertido, como repercusión, en instrumento de la iniquidad.

Los pasos del *Cantar* van ordenados de allí adelante en tal forma que el Cid se va haciendo más y más acepto al rey, quien, simultáneamente, se va haciendo más y más merecedor del vasallo que es ahora objeto de su injusticia y dureza. Los trabajos de Correa[21], de De Chasca[22] y de Walker[23] muestran bien el proceso de merecimientos por parte del rey y de su vasallo. El resultado será, como Walker lo pone presente[24], que el Cid es buen vasallo, cosa sabida, y que el rey es también buen señor - *quod erat demonstrandum* - según el desideratum del verso 20. Señor y vasallo pasan las pruebas a satisfacción recíproca y también a satisfacción del espectador del poema. En esa forma se desarrolla el paradigma central de la gesta, consistente en la relación entre señor y vasallo, que es feudal por excelencia[25].

La caracterización de la presencia regia en el curso de dicha relación necesita examen. En el comienzo del *Cantar*, la presencia del rey es por ausencia, si se permite el oxímoro, en tanto que los personajes son presencia total; son humanidad, en tanto que el rey es únicamente poder; los personajes hablan, van y vienen, sufren, se agitan y se refrenan, movidos por intereses materiales y espirituales, en tanto que el rey es distancia, es un decreto o una carta. Así aparece el rey en la gesta.

En persona, el rey aparece cuando llega el primer regalo del Cid y, de nuevo, quienes se hallan a su alrededor son animados, activos, al paso que el rey es una voz, una sonrisa, una cautela. Un cierto hieratismo que emana del rey domina lo visual de la escena. Lo político del acto va subtendido, inmerso en los trazos que abocetan el prestigio del rey: la sonrisa, la condescendencia, el poder de dar y conceder sin que lo parezca, todo ello correspondido por la docilidad y la aceptación de quienes le rodean y le sirven y le escuchan. Al recibir el segundo regalo del Cid, Alfonso se muestra, aunque todavía en ademán de majestad hierática, algo más humano que en la primera entrevista con Minaya. Ahora se santigua de admiración por las ganancias que ha hecho el Cid, le place de corazón el éxito de quien se profesa su vasallo y recibe con gusto las cien cabalgaduras "quem enbia en don" (v. 1344). Ante la tercera embajada del Cid, con doscientos caballos en agradecimiento por el permiso para trasladar la familia a Valencia, - "por amor de mi mugier e de mis fijas amas, / porque assi las enbio dond ellas son pagadas" (vv. 1811-12) -, el rey deja el hieratismo en un segundo plano mientras el manipulador político se adueña de la escena. Se trata del perdón y del casamiento de las hijas del Cid, en lo cual aparece el rey en un acto consciente de acerca-miento al plano de su vasallo. El manejo del perdón es genial. Podría muy bien el rey invitar al Cid a la Corte y pronunciar su perdón; pero en esa forma sólo se mostraría su decisión de rectificar un decreto equivocado; en cambio, cuando el rey ofrece ir a vistas con el Cid donde a éste le parezca bien, lo que resalta es la magnanimidad regia.

Se ha mencionado a veces el ritualismo que domina la escena del perdón[26], y se ha notado igualmente que el hieratismo emana allí sobre todo del Cid, quien actúa frente al rey como un oficiante ante el altar impetrando perdón de la divinidad. Para el Cid del *Cantar* ésta es la ocasión cumbre de su gesta. El la ha dispuesto y llevado a cabo con tesonería ejemplar, con la vida constantemente en vilo, justamente para este momento del perdón. Para el vasallo, la figura del rey se alza muchos codos en este instante, como proyectado sobre tradiciones que proceden por igual de las fuentes romanas y de las raíces hondas de la realeza germánica[27], en la cual el rey se consagraba con un ceremonial casi idéntico al de los obispos. Hay, pues, un poco más que mera relación de señor a vasallo. Hay un trasunto de la relación entre el señor y Dios, que es en alguna forma similar a la existente entre señor y vasallo[28]. No sor-prende, entonces, que el Cid se hinque de hinojos y manos y hasta muerda las yerbas (vv. 2021-22), ni que llore del "gozo mayor" al rendir sus homenajes de humildad a Alfonso su señor. Llega a tal grado que aunque el rey le ordena levantarse, el Cid insiste en que el rey lo perdone "assi estando", de suerte que lo escuchen todos cuantos se encuentran allí (vv. 2025-32b).

Cumple destacar que el rey aparece sin insignias, o por lo menos no se hace mención de ellas: ni corona, ni cetro ni nada. Su prestancia no deriva de los símbolos de la realeza, sino de su propia persona[29]. El ritualismo del Cid habla un idioma y la majestad real responde sin recurrir a los símbolos visuales convencionalizados. Hay una sintaxis - porque no es una proporción, ni una proyección figurativa - que el Cid ordena con su ritualismo, y es esa sutil analogía entre Rey y Dios, pero sin salirse de los límites humanos y sin llegar a la insinuación de que el rey sea un "elegido de Dios", como sí occurre en torno a Carlomagno, según lo han expuesto los estudiosos del *Karlsmythus*[30].

Por contraste, el rey se muestra más humano que antes, casi tierno. Pero sentimos que aquella benevolencia llega como de lo alto. Tenemos la impresión de que hay cierta grandiosidad calculada tanto en la veneración del vasallo a su señor como en la magnanimidad humana del perdón. Parece haber un mensaje que trasciende del perdón y de la justicia; tal vez un mensaje de transparencias para los grandes del reino como también para las entendederas regias de tiempos por venir. La seguridad confiada con que el rey actúa puede entenderse como parte del mensaje. El rey justiciero tiene asegurada su prestancia y la aceptación de los suyos. Entre buen señor y buen vasallo no hay lugar para el recelo. El reino está bien cuando esta relación se ordena bien. Estas connotaciones ocupan el primer plano de la atención del lector o del oyente, lo que permite velar, asordinar, la motricidad política del acto del perdón en el *Cantar*.

En la última aparición personal del rey, en las Cortes de Toledo, el ritualismo es algo difuso pero existe. Allí, por el contrario, el ajetreo político y judicial se sobreponen al plano de fondo en que se mueven las figuras de los actores. Hay una actitud de ritualismo hierático procedente de todos y que converge en la persona del rey. Los únicos que se manifiestan con irreverencia para con el rey y con la solemnidad de las Cortes son los Vanigómez. Para los demás, el respeto, la obediencia, el asentimiento a la voz del soberano mediatizan convenientemente la figura de éste pero iluminándola con un halo de prestigio. Como logro visual, el cuadro es portentoso. La figura del rey se alza ante todos, mientras las miradas confluyen por un tiempo en la persona del Cid. Y es en la dinámica del acto judicial donde el rey termina adueñándose del lote de atención que le corresponde en el poema. Como juez de última alzada, sus decisiones son inapelables[31]. Más aún, no son cuestionables y, por lo tanto, el rey no tiene que explicarlas. Su ejercicio judicial evoca la calidad de las sentencias de Dios. Esta situación de finales del *Cantar* se corresponde con lo acontecido a comienzos, donde el rey ha decidido el extrañamiento del Cid, y como ello era un acto de su majestad no tenía que explicarlo. Tampoco tiene que razonar Dios - al menos en la teología cristiana - por qué expele a alguien del paraíso ni cuando condena las almas al infierno. Análogamente, el rey no siente que debe justificar cuando priva a algien de los derechos y privilegios que ha tenido. Y del mismo modo que cuando Dios condena un alma hay que suponer que esa alma carece de virtud, así también cuando el rey despoja a un súbdito suyo de derechos y prerrogativas hay que entender que esa persona carece de honra. ¿No se transparenta en esto una cierta homología paradigmática Dios-hombre y rey-vasallo?

Un punto más puede acentuar el parecido - no por distante menos real - entre la conducta del vasallo y la del cristiano en el plano religioso. El Cid, a pesar de que sabe que no ha cometido desafuero contra su señor, hilvana en su gesta los requisitos del perdón en el plano religioso, a saber: (1) confesión de boca - o sea reiteración de sincera lealtad al rey Alfonso -; (2) contrición de corazón - o sea la barba intonsa por el dolor que le causa el desamor de su rey -; y (3) satisfacción de obra - o sea los presentes al señor y el acatamiento incondicional. El Cid ha aprendido en las más duras circunstancias que no basta con tener razón.

La imagen del rey en el *Cantar* es el resultado de un consciente proyecto poético. La figura del rey en esta gesta es muy diferente de la de los otros reyes que aparecen en la épica española. Sin embargo, no tiene atributos de personaje épico. Pero en la construcción del *Cantar*, el crecimiento del Cid carecería de la grandeza que le prodiga la evolución de la imagen del rey. Piénsese por un momento en lo que serían las hazañas del héroe sin ese telón de fondo, sin la imagen regia, desde el comienzo hasta el fin.

Al principio, una especie de leviatán ha postrado al Cid y lo pisotea sin que nada ni nadie lo pueda evitar. El brazo del leviatán es el poder del rey. En el curso de los sucesos de la gesta, el leviatán se desvanece y el rey se restablece en su función justiciera, con rasgos cada vez mas humanos, pero sin pérdida de su prestancia ni prestigio. Lo curioso es que a medida que el rey se humaniza gana en intensidad su dimensión trascendente hacia planos concordes con el régimen de los príncipes cristianos deseables para la salud de España. Desde un ángulo peninsular, el rey Alfonso del *Cantar de Mio Cid* responde al ideal medieval europeo de *unus Deus*, *unus rex*.

Notas

[1]Véase Louis Chalon, *L'Histoire et l'épopée castillane du moyen âge. Le Cycle du Cid - Le Cycle des comtes de Castille* (Paris, 1976). Ramón Menéndez Pidal, *La España del Cid*, 2 vol., 4a. ed. totalmente revisada y añadida (Madrid, 1947). Ramón Menéndez Pidal, *Reliquias de la poesía épica española* (Madrid, 1947). María E. Lacarra, *Poema de Mio Cid: Realidad, historia e ideología* (Madrid, 1980).

[2]*Poema de Alfonso Onceno, rey de Castilla y de León*, ed. Florencio Janer (Madrid, 1863). En 1864 incluyó Janer el mismo texto en el tomo de *Poetas castellanos anteriores al siglo XV*, ed. Tomás Antonio Sánchez, cont. por Pedro José Pidal, Biblioteca de Autores Españoles, 57 (reimp. Madrid, 1966), pp.

471-551. Véase también la ed. crít. por Yo Ten Cate, en *Revista de Filología Española*, anejo 65 (Madrid, 1956).

[3]Véase [*Primera*] *Crónica general de España*, ed. Ramón Menéndez Pidal, 2 (1906; Madrid, 1955), cap. 836. Y, con leves variantes, el cap. 28, que transcribe Carola Reig del MS 2-E-4 Mod 429, Biblioteca Nacional, de la misma *Crónica*, en su obra *El cantar de Sancho II y cerco de Zamora*, en *Revista de Filología Española*, anejo 37 (Madrid, 1947), pp. 248-49. En la misma obra, p. 24, dice la Dra. Reig: "Un soldado valiente que sale de la plaza sitiada, exponiendo su vida para librar a la ciudad de su enemigo y que, a vista de todos, le atraviesa con su lanza, consiguiendo después refugiarse en la ciudad". ¿En qué se funda para tales hipotesis? Tal vez en la falta de convicción con que quedamos muchos al leer y releer la leyenda de como dió muerte Dolfos a don Sancho. Pero de ahí a afirmar lo del "soldado valiente" y aquello de "a vista de todos", hay un trayecto que debería fundamentarse de alguna manera.

[4]Pese a la observación de Percy E. Schramm, *Las insignias de la realeza en la Edad Media española*, trad. Luís Vázquez de Parga (Madrid, 1960), p. 63: "Podemos comprobar que en los reinos hispánicos los atributos [insigniales] de la realeza juegan un papel menos importante que en el resto de Occidente...". En la p. 68, afirma Schramm de nuevo: "...en Castilla disminuye aún más la importancia de las insignias reales, ya que apenas se da ocasión de que el rey se muestre ante el pueblo revestido con ellas".

[5]Véase supra nota 3.

[6]*Policraticus*, libro 4, cap. 1, PL 199:513-14, citado por Thomas R. Hart, Jr. en su artículo "Hierarchical patterns in the *Cantar de Mio Cid*", *Romanic Review* 53 (1962), 162. Véase también William A. Chaney, *The Cult of Kingship in Anglo-Saxon England: The Transition from Paganism to Christianity* (Berkeley, 1970), p. 49: "This image of the earthly king ruling under the heavenly one runs throughout the old English period after the coronation".

[7]Véase *Las Siete Partidas*, Partida II, Tit. I, Ley V, cuyo título ya reza: "Qué cosa es rey, et como es puesto en lugar de Dios". (Cito por la ed. de la Academia de la Historia, Madrid, 1807). Véase también Juan Manuel, *Libro infinido*, cap. 4: "Vos debedes saber que los reyes en la tierra son a semejanza de Dios", Biblioteca de Autores Españoles, 51 (Madrid, 1952), p. 208.

[8]Me tomo la libertad de citar varios pasajes documentales tomados de Alfonso García Gallo, "El imperio medieval español", *Arbor* 11 (1945), 199-228: "Ego Adefonsus Dei gratia Toletanus imperator" (documentos de 1097 y 1099). Pero ya en 1079, sus áulicos le decían "divina misericordia imperator totius Hispaniae". En el año 974, el Conde Garci Fernández firma "Ego Garssia Fernandi, gratia Dei comes et imperator Castille" al otorgar el Fuero de Castrojeriz. Y en 987, el mismo Conde: "Ego Garcia Fernandiz comes, et donna Aba cometissa, comitis imperatores in domino Deo et aeterna salute".

[9]Menéndez Pidal, *La España del Cid*, pp. 589-92.

[10]Conferencia pronunciada en el Paraninfo de la Universidad de Valencia, 15 Dic. 1940, en conmemoración del VIII centenario del *Poema de Mio Cid*, ed.

original y separada (Valencia, 1943; reimpr. in *Castilla: La tradición y el idioma*, col. Austral, 501 [Buenos Aires, 1945], pp. 141-69).

[11]"Filología e Historia: De crítica cidiana", *Zeitschrift für romanische Philologie* 64 (1944), 211-32 (reimpr. en *Castilla: La tradición y el idioma*, pp. 95-139).

[12]Gustavo Correa, "Estructura y forma en el *Poema de Mio Cid*", *Hispanic Review* 25 (1957), 280-90.

[13]Edmund de Chasca, "The King-Vassal Relationship in *El Poema de Mio Cid*", *Hispanic Review* 21 (1953), 183-92. Véase también el mismo autor en su obra *El arte juglaresco en el "Cantar de Mio Cid"*, Biblioteca Románica Hispánica: Estudios y Ensayos, 101, 2a. ed. aum. (Madrid, 1972), pp. 67-78, 149-58.

[14]Roger M. Walker, "The Role of the King and the Poet's Intentions in the *Poema de Mio Cid*", en *Medieval Hispanic Studies Presented to Rita Hamilton*, ed. Alan D. Deyermond (London, 1976), pp. 257-66, y espte. p. 265.

[15]*Cantar de Mio Cid*, 3, *Texto del "Cantar"*, ed. Ramón Menéndez Pidal (Madrid, 1946). En este escrito, todas las citas del *Cantar* van por esta edición.

[16]Por otra parte, Walker diseña una perspectiva nueva para examinar la estructura del *Cantar* y arroja luz sobre la tesis del paradigma arquetípico que había sido presentado por Hart, "Hierarchical patterns", pp. 161-73.

[17]Parece haber habido una línea política del papado tendiente a disuadir la creación de nuevos reinos y, en casos *de facto*, postergarlos. Con todo, el Cid procede como rey (o par de rey) en su conquista: hace el repartimiento, se hace de una corte de hecho, crea una sede episcopal; esto último era privilegio real. Véase vv. 1245-47, 1298-99 y 1305-06.

[18]*El fuero Viejo de Castilla*, ed. Ignacio Jordán de Asso y del Río y Miguel de Manuel y Rodríguez (Madrid, 1771), lib. 1, tít.4, aparte 2, p. 14.

[19]Ibid., p. 15.

[20]Ibid., p. 14.

[21]Gustavo Correa, "El tema de la honra en el *Poema de Mio Cid*", *Hispanic Review* 20 (1952), 185-99.

[22]Edmund de Chasca, "The King-Vassal Relationship", según nota 13, supra.

[23]Walker, "The Role", según nota 14, supra.

[24]Ibid., p. 265.

[25]Véase Karl-Heinz Bender, *König und Vasall. Untersuchungen zur Chanson de Geste des XII. Jahrhunderts*, Studia Romanica 13 (Heidelberg, 1967), p. 19.

[26]Américo Castro, "Poesía y realidad en el *Poema del Cid*", en *Semblanzas y estudios españoles* (Princeton, 1956), pp. 3-15, y espte. p. 12. Ramón Menéndez Pidal, *Cantar de Mio Cid*, nota al v. 2022, se refiere a "morder las yerbas" como una costumbre.

[27]Véase Percy E. Schramm, *A History of English Coronation*, trans. Leopold G. W. Legg (Oxford, 1937), pp. 2, 9, 11, 13, 20. Y Ramón Menéndez Pidal, "La

historiografía medieval sobre Alfonso II'', en *Estudios sobre la monarquía asturiana*, ed. Instituto de Estudios Asturianos (Oviedo, 1947), p. 17: Alfonso II el Casto ''es el primer rey nuevo [es decir de la nueva serie gótica] de quien las crónicas dicen que subió al trono consagrado por la unción sacerdotal: *unctus est in regno*''. En la misma página agrega don Ramón: ''La consagración vino a ser el distintivo de superioridad que elevó a los reyes astur-leoneses sobre otros creados más tarde en España. Los reyes de Navarra, establecidos en 905, no se ungían, se levantaban sobre el escudo a modo militar''. Y de nuevo Schramm, *English Coronation*, p. 25: ''The monarch, . . . is, from the eighth century onwards, distinguished by the title *Dei gratia*; he is now *Vicarius Dei* here on earth''. Un poco más adelante, misma página: ''The formula *Dei gratia* is to be found in England even earlier than on the Continent. The anointing was adopted a generation after its introduction among the Franks''.

[28]Véase Bender, *König und Vasall*, p. 19: ''Weil Charlemagne, der keinen irdischen Lehnsherrn anerkennt, für Gott streitet und dieser seinen Kämpfer unterstützt, bezeichnet Aebischer Gott als den Lehnsherrn des Kaisers''. La referencia a Paul Aebischer es al estudio ''Pour la défense et l'illustration de l'épisode de Baligant'', en *Mélanges de philologie romane et de littérature médiévale offerts à Ernest Hoepffner par ses élèves et ses amis* (Paris, 1949), pp. 173-82.

[29] Anota Luís Vasquez de Parga en el Prólogo a su traducción de *Las insignias de la realeza en la Edad Media española* (Madrid, 1960), p. 8, que para el autor, Percy E. Schramm, ''durante la Edad Media no ha habido un vocablo que aparezca como generalmente aceptado para designar lo que nosotros llamamos el 'Estado'. Esto no quiere decir que la cosa en sí no haya existido; lo que sucede es que el Estado se encarnaba para el hombre medieval en la persona del Monarca: 'El Rey es el signo del Estado'''.

[30]Véase Bender, *König und Vasall*, p. 16.

[31]Véase lo que dice William A. Chaney, *The Cult of Kingship*, p. 177: ''As in a Norse kenning the King is called 'justice', so in Anglo-Saxon law he reflects still the ancient Germanic royal rôle of the judge the breaking of whose decrees looses the wrath of God upon the offender''.

The Economy of *Mio Cid*

Miguel Garci-Gómez

It is a basic assumption in this article that pre-existent socio-economic conditions are influential on thought and artistic creation.[1] Also basic is the belief that the *Cantar de Mio Cid*, far from being eminently historical, is a work of artistic creation composed towards the end of the twelfth century. Let me affirm at the outset, then, that the poet of the *Cantar* himself invented or selected from historical records and traditional lore the names, roles, events, episodes, etc. that he freely arranged to fit into his artistic purpose. But there was something he did not, could not invent: the economic structure of the world he created and its linguistic expression, for he inherited the economic values of his community. The author of *Mio Cid,* portrayed by many scholars as a typical epic poet, was, in more appropriate terminology, a poet-economist. References to the Cid in this study are to the protagonist of the *Cantar*, not the historical Rodrigo Diaz de Vivar; *Cantar* refers to its First Part: Exile, Conquest of Valencia, and Weddings.[2]

The *Cantar de Mio Cid* was obviously composed with the public of Burgos in mind. Burgos in the twelfth century was the vigorous capital of the ever expanding Castile, hence the most important commercial city of Spain north of the Guadarrama Mountains. It was also a most important station for the pilgrims on their way to Santiago de Compostela. These pilgrims, one of them tells us in the *Codex Calixtinus*, consisted of religious travellers and merchants—*peregrini cursorii et peregrini nego-tiatores*.[3]

227

The *Cantar de Mio Cid* is replete with commercial language and trading activities: buying, selling, exporting, importing, money-lending, money-changing, pawning, accounting. All transactions are valued in terms of a unique monetary unit: the mark—the only denomination specified in the *Cantar*, where it reigns as the supreme good. The mark becomes the measure of all things material and spiritual, the measure that lends homogeneity to the most heterogeneous world: the sand-filled chests are traded for marks; the Castle of Alcoçer is sold for a sum of marks. The mark secures prayers and masses; marks for the Monastery of Saint Peter serve concomitantly as a guaranty of haven and investment in heaven.

The reader of *Mio Cid* can easily discern the extent to which wealth is an obsession. To increase their wealth, the Infantes of Carrion sought to marry the Cid's daughters; the girls—very young—speak only once in the entire first part of the *Cantar*, in a comment on their marriages that is contained in a single line clearly meant to make their father very proud: "Quando vos nos casáredes bien seremos ricas" (v. 2195). They know very well their father will only give them in marriage if through it they become very rich. Don Jerónimo, upon being installed bishop of Valencia, becomes "very rich" (v. 1304).

Traditional criticism has primarily focused on the bellicose aspects of the *Cantar de Mio Cid*: on the conflicts between the Cid and his king, the Cid against the court, the Cid against the Jews, the Cid against the Moors, the Cid against the Count of Barcelona, etc. Consequently, the action of the *Cantar* has been viewed in the sole perspective of a war, a Crusade, a Reconquest; such criticism has thus overlooked the core of the narrative movement, its life-giving sap: the rise of the Cid from the most abject poverty to an incalculable richness that, respectively, gives cause to the bitter tears of the first line of the *Cantar* and the joy of its last.

Traditional criticism has projected the *Cantar* over the external world of religious wars between Christians and Moors for the possession of the land, an external war that had some validity for eleventh-century Burgos and the historical Cid. In so doing, it has overlooked sociological changes the public of Burgos had undergone by the last part of the twelfth century, when the *Cantar* was written. Burgos had become a commercial city, an emporium—the most important center of trade, for example, between Spain and Flanders. It had attracted and retained great masses of foreigners; many "Francos" (French) had established themselves in the city to become successful merchants. It is curious that the names of the merchants who appear in the old documents of the cathedral and monasteries are foreign.

Twelfth-century Burgos, as its counterparts in other European regions, experienced the rise to prominence of the bourgeoisie, a new social class of influential citizens who earned their living by trading, speaking, writing, and teaching (i.e., by persuading others). The leading exponent of the new class was the merchant, whose behavior was greatly influenced by commercial interest and the love of money. Such were the social-economic conditions prevalent in twelfth-century Burgos that influenced the creation of the *Cantar of Mio Cid*, which, if read in this cultural context, leads to the conclusion that it is indeed a very special type of song with a special type of epic hero: the epic song and the epic hero of the bourgeoisie.

The merchant is defined in the *Partidas* (5, tít.7, 1-2) as the man who travels from one place to another, motivated in his actions by his intent to make a lot of money: "ganar algo." The ever travelling merchant may have found no problem in identifying with the Cid, who early in the narrative solemnly proclaims in a sententious line: "¡Qui en un lugar mora siempre, lo suyo puede menguar!" (v. 948). If the religious pilgrim had problems in accepting the exemplarity of the Cid in cheating his two close friends, Rachel and Vidas, the merchant could have easily identifed with the man needing to make a "quick buck."

From the very beginning in the narrative, the writer attempts to shape the frame of mind of his readers. We are presented with the most moving scene of the whole work: a nine-year-old girl stands in front of the armed and irate Cid to calm him and make him understand why the citizens of Burgos will not come to his aid; if they do, they will be deprived of their homes and possessions. From his recent experience, the Cid knows only too well what that would mean. To the little girl, possessions secure life; the hero is left with trust in God as his only recourse.

Some of today's leading historians of twelfth-century Europe have pointed to several phenomena that serve to illustrate the meaningfulness of the economy of *Mio Cid*. The twelfth-century economy has been characterized in Europe—Castile, of course, included[4]—as a monetary economy that is expressed in the *Cantar*'s "haberes monedados" and "marcos." The most dominant motive of the first part, the more functional motive, is undoubtedly shame and fear of poverty, with the hope and strife to become rich, very rich. The ultimate message of the work—in the twelfth century and thereafter—was to go forth and become rich rather than go forth and fight the Moors. The poet hoped the reader would become vicariously rich—very rich—along with the protagonist. There was no place in the writer's mind for the "Blessed are the poor" of the Gospel; poverty was a curse, and its place had been taken by the *Ecclesiastes, pecuniae obediunt omnia* (Ec. 10:19), i.e., money talks. Money helped to restore honor and respect; money helped to increase love and loyalty; with money, one was a better vassal, a better lord, a better bishop, a better wife, a better father, a better husband, a better Christian.

The reader of the *Cantar* cannot but concur with Georges Duby when he insists that "money had become the most potent instrument of power by the second half of the twelfth century."[5] Prior to this period, the center of power had gravitated around real estate: land, palaces, castles, a type of wealth that confined the owner's influence to a specific region. Conversely, money was mobile, compact, lasting, knowing no boundaries. Alan of Lille, a contemporary of the poet of *Mio Cid*, has told us of the craze for money that had turned the Christian doxology into a fashionable parody: "Christus vincit, Christus regnat, Christus imperat. Nummus vincit, nummus mundum regit, nummus imperat universis."[6] The world had turned chrematistic, creating the illusion that "wealth consisted of a quantity of money," to use Aristotle's explanation.

This economic change that occurred in the twelfth century is beautifully allegorized in the introductory episode of the *Cantar*: the hero's palace has been demolished; with the dirt, he fills two chests and manages to exchange them for 600 marks, 300 in gold and 300 in silver. From that moment the hero will resemble Midas, converting into gold—specifically, marks—everything he touches. Real estate has yielded to metals, to marks.

But, why marks? Why should the Castilian poet omit mentioning any of the local monetary denominations and speak solely of marks? Georges Duby attests that after the middle of the twelfth century the mark "became the standard unit of value" (p. 251). We may conclude that the poet of *Mio Cid* was a well-informed economist. It is safe to assume that the historical Rodrigo Diaz de Vivar never used marks in his transactions, for this monetary unit does not seem to appear in Spanish documents until the twelfth century. A unit of value weighing half a pound, the mark was used only in large transactions by those merchants whose activities, as Duby clarifies, "reached beyond the confines of a small region" (p. 251). The historian's characterization of these merchants is of great interest to the reader of *Mio Cid*:

> Merchants had a common culture and a certain common attitude towards worldly values. They could read and write; above all, they were numerate. For them wealth was expressed by means of figures and precise references to monetary units (p. 253).

The Cid of the *Cantar* fits this pattern; to being literate he adds being numerate or, to use his own expression, "contado." He likes to express quantity with precise figures; he likes to fix labels with the exact price: 30 marks, 50 marks, 100 marks, 200 marks, 300 marks, 600 marks, 3,000 marks, 5,000 marks. The price given may be inflated; it should not be forgotten that the author was both accountant and poet. However, all things considered, the different figures keep a remarkable proportion when compared to each other in the *Cantar*.

Comparisons help us to better understand the originality of a given work; in this respect, the uniqueness of the realism and preciseness of the Castilian poet is better appreciated when contrasted with the astronomic amounts or generic pricing of the French author of the *Chanson de Roland*. For the latter, for example, the sword Durendal was more valuable than fine gold; for the former, the sword Colada was worth over 1,000 marks.

Literary critics and students feel somewhat frustrated when, assuming that the *Cantar de Mio Cid* is an epic poem, they can hardly formulate a definition of epic into which the *Cantar* properly fits. That frustration is best shown in Menéndez Pidal's tripartite division of the *Cantar* in which he entitles the *gesta* per se as *Cantar de las Bodas*. Under what canon of epic does the wedding of the hero's daughters constitute such a great deed? Such weddings, however, add to the spirit of the twelfth-century bourgeoisie, the *nouveaux riches* whose aspirations were to see their children marry into the aristocracy. Duby assures us that such were the aspirations of the wealthy families of France, England, and Germany (p. 260), not realizing how exalted such weddings had been in Castile; the Cid of the *Cantar* manages to have his daughters marry counts the first time, kings, the second. In his *The Medieval World: Europe 1100-1350*, Friedrich Heer explains how in those days "a man 'took' a wife, calculating her value as an object for political and economic ends" (p. 21). With that calculation, we are told by the poet-economist of *Mio Cid*, did the Infantes of Carrion 'take' the Cid's daughters; with that intention were the latter given by their father. The Cid was a hero without illusions, delusions, or unreachable dreams; as a father, he reveals at the very outset the objectives of a businessman: to find husbands for his daughters and time and place to serve his wife (vv. 282-84).

What endemic malady affects us that we judge "making money" as a prosaic, egotistical, un-Christian aspiration, while "waging war" is the courageous, patriotic, Christian call and destiny? So often those who directed the war were waging it to make money, a tacit goal hidden from the common soldier, a meagre *solidus* who was expected to risk his life at very little cost to the king.

The Cid of the *Cantar*, direct and pragmatic, fights for the booty. At the very beginning, when he enlists the first men, he tells them in a mundane paraphrase of the Gospel that those who leave their homes and possessions will some day be repaid twofold:

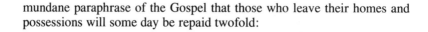

> vos, que por mí dexades casas y heredades enantes que yo
> muera, algún bien vos pueda far, lo que perdedes doblado
> vos lo cobrar.
>
> (vv. 301-03)

Admirers of the bellicose Christian hero have found 450 expressions of piety in the 3,730 lines of the *Cantar of Mio Cid* but have failed to demonstrate that those expressions were much more than food for contemplation. There are no miracles in the *Cantar*, only mundane economy. At the beginning of the action the Cid, in the direst of need, finds in a moment of meditation the inspiration to cheat his close friends in a matter of life or death and makes 600 marks. His need of bread justifies the first encounters with the Moors:

> De Castilla la gentil exidos somos acá,
> si con moros no lidiáremos, no nos darán del pan.
>
> (vv. 672-73)

After some land has been acquired, war is justified as *defensive*; the Cid tells his men how they should protect themselves in a narrow land:

> por lanças y por espadas habemos de guarir,
> si no, en esta tierra angosta no podríemos vivir.
>
> (vv. 834-35)

By verse 1086, the Cid and his men already consider themselves ''ricos,'' but decide they should continue to fight to increase their wealth, for the goods belong to the stronger: the outcome of battle will determine who deserves the goods. The war that begins as a means to survive continues as a defensive means to protect what has been gained, then is turned into an outright offensive campaign under the rationale that the Moors are people from foreign lands:

> aparejados me sed a caballos y armas,
> iremos ver aquella su almofalla,
> como homnes exidos de tierra estraña;
> allí pareçrá el que mereçe la soldada.
>
> (vv. 1123-26)

The Cid's thirst for wealth is clearly insatiable; the men are not about to stop and enjoy what they have accumulated; they will continue to fight to enlarge it: "agora habemos riqueza, más habremos adelante" (v. 1269). Why are they so certain of success? Since God and Saint James are on their side, there are no psychological or moral limits to how profound a wound they should inflict on the Moors. It should be deep enough as to prevent that they ever regain the bread:

> . . . .
> ir los hemos ferir en el nombre del Criador y del
>   apóstol Santi Yaguo,
> más vale que nos los vezcamos, que ellos cojan
>   el pan.
>
>   (vv. 1689-90)

What an admirable language is the original language of the *Cantar*! The Cid was conceived by a poet-economist with clarity of vision and of expression. Such a hero could not fail; a hero with such a realistic, such a chrematistic mind could not fail. Conversely, in search of an illusion, Roland meets a tragic end. Now we understand better why, in his galloping ascension to great wealth, the Cid does not stop and return to Burgos to reclaim two chests full of sand. It would have been ridiculous. But Rachel and Vidas have not been entirely forgotten, as we shall see.

More than enough has been said about the Cid's antagonism towards his king, the nobles, the Moors, the Jews, the "Francos," etc. Little or nothing has been said about the Cid's most precious qualities: his ability to persuade, his interest and success in negotiation—in short, the qualities of a good businessman.

The poet of the *Cantar de Mio Cid* betrays himself as a bourgeois in his portrayal of the persuasive hero. It is by persuasion that the Cid wins his first and most difficult encounter with Rachel and Vidas, luring them into taking and keeping the sand-filled chests as a pledge for 600 marks—300 in gold, 300 in silver. Immediately after, the hero enters into delicate negotiations with the abbot of the Monastery of Saint Peter. He has little more than promises to offer the abbot for the keeping and protection of his wife and two very young daughters for an indefinite period of time, yet he succeeds. He will soon negotiate with the Moors: when he conquers Castejón, he sells them his share of the spoils for 3,000 silver marks (v. 521). Shortly after he conquers Alcoçer, he sells its fort for 3,000 silver marks. Then follows an admirable gesture of clemency on the Cid's part:

233

he will not follow the custom of decapitating the conquered Moors, for there is no *gain* in it; instead, he decides to occupy their homes and make them his servants:

> Los moros y las moras vender no los podremos,
> que los descabeçemos nada no ganaremos,
> cojámoslos de dentro, ca el señorío tenemos,
> posaremos en sus casas y d'ellos nos serviremos.
>   (vv. 619-22)

Evidently the Moors are grateful, for they line along the road and bless the passing Cid.[7] Later, it is only through persuasion and persistent negotiation that the Cid finally wins the heart of the defeated and imprisoned Count of Barcelona. Obviously, the hero's negotiations with his irate king, carried out gradually and astutely, were more important: first, he will regain the king's friendship; later, he will regain his confiscated patrimony; finally, he will gain two aristocratic husbands for his daughters.

Having established the socio-economic ambience of twelfth-century Burgos and the chrematistic mentality of the poet of *Mio Cid*, I would like to offer a new interpretation of the second appearance of Rachel and Vidas, i.e., their encounter with Minaya Alvar Fáñez. Rachel and Vidas, we surmise from the text, were two successful merchants, two of the leading financiers of Burgos. The Cid gives them two sand-filled chests as a pledge for 600 marks, but fails to redeem them within the one-year term specified in their agreement. Sometime later, Minaya, the man in charge of the Cid's shuttle diplomacy with the king, travels to the monastery of Saint Peter in order to bring back to Valencia the Cid's wife and daughters with their servants. Rachel and Vidas, the two *caros amigos*, appear in the monastery not only to bid farewell to the Cid's family, but also to remind Minaya of their unfinished business with the conqueror of Valencia since he had failed to pick up the chests and repay the debt. Aware of this, Minaya responds with an implied enticement:

> Yo lo veré con el Çid, si Dios me lieva allá,
> por lo que habedes fecho buen cosimente hy habrá.
>   (vv. 1435-36)

('I will see to it, God willing; I am sure the Cid will fulfill his promise for what you have done').

Then Rachel and Vidas state:

> ....El Criador lo mande.
> Si no, dexaremos Burgos, ir lo hemos buscar.
> (vv. 1437-38)

('Blessed be the Creator; in that case, we are ready to leave Burgos and go to Valencia in search of the Cid').

Immediately, the voice of the narrator informs us that many, many people leave Burgos for Valencia. The phrase *si no* of v. 1438 is still correctly and widely used today to express correction through which one rectifies or clarifies what was said or implied in a previous sentence.[8] With this interpretation, the once unintelligible passage acquires full meaning and the narrative movement gains a triumphal dimension: the Cid, who had extended from Burgos to Valencia Castile's military structure with his "mesnadas," Castile's religious structure with the bishop Don Jerónimo, Castile's aristocratic structure with his daughters' husbands, extends with the financiers Rachel and Vidas Castile's economic structure.

Roland the idealistic epic hero and his *Chanson* are sublime; the Cid and his *Cantar* are chrematistic. Longinus, in his *Treatise on the Sublime*, argues that "sublimity is the polar opposite of economy, and that the effect of sublime language is transport, while the effect of economy is persuasion."[9] Those who teach the *Cantar de Mio Cid* should not catapult their students into a transport of honor and religious duty; rather, accepting the earthliness of the *Cantar*'s language and values, they should dwell on the verification and realization of Euripides' old saying: "Gold weighs more with men than countless words" (*Medea*, v. 965). The Cid leaves Burgos without a protest against his king, confident that Alfonso will some day be persuaded by a bombardment of gifts. True enough: the weight of the many gifts sent by the Cid makes the king solemnly proclaim "aquí vos perdono y dovos mi amor" (v. 2034).

Noel Stock has remarked of Ezra Pound that he admired Homer, Dante, and Shakespeare inasmuch as they were poet-economists,[10] suggesting that only literature about economics is worth reading and basing his evaluation of a writer on whether or not he mentions money. Pound would have been fascinated with the *Cantar de Mio Cid* and its Castilian poet-economist.

Notes

[1]For discussion on this subject see Marc Shell, *The Economy of Literature* (Baltimore, 1978).

[2]I of course accept the division of the *Cantar de Mio Cid* in two distinguishable parts, following the indication of the texts itself, where it says: "Las coplas d'este cantar aquí se van acabando" (v. 2276). That division was accepted by the editors Sanchez, Hinard, Janer, Wollmöller, and Restori. For further discussion on this matter, see my book *Mio Cid. Estudios de endocrítica* (Barcelona, 1975), pp. 155-71. I adopted this division in my own edition of the *Cantar de Mio Cid* (Madrid, 1977), from which all textual quotations are taken.

[3]The impact of the French, both pilgrims and merchants, is a topic widely treated in my book *El Burgos de Mio Cid* (Burgos, 1977), to which I refer the reader interested in more ample information on the matter of the economy in the *Cantar*.

[4]Cf. R. Pastor de Togneri, "Ganadería y precios: consideraciones sobre la economía de León y Castilla (siglos XI-XIII)," *Cuadernos de Historia de España* 35-36 (1962), 55.

[5]Georges Duby, *The Early Growth of the European Economy*, trans. Howard B. Clarke (Ithaca, N.Y., 1974), p. 253. Future references to this work will incorporate the page(s) in the text.

[6]Cf. PL 210:464. For more information and bibliographical references on the polemics over money and poverty, see Lester K. Little, *Religious Poverty and the Profit Economy in Medieval Europe* (Ithaca, 1978), pp. 38, 228 and *passim*.

[7]Friedrich Heer, *The Medieval World: Europe 1100-1350*, trans. Janet Sondheimer (1962; rpt. New York and Washington, 1969), has singled out the conduct of the Cid as a shining example of compassion: "exquisite courtesy," "gentle treatment," "readiness to come to terms" with the defeated Moors (p. 117).

[8]The key word seems to be "cosimente." The editors of the *Glossarium Mediae Latinitatis Cataloniae* (Barcelona, 1965-), M. Bassols di Climent *et al.*, have helped to clarify the meaning of *cosimentum* in the Latin texts of the period as that of "asegurar (garantizar) el señor al vasallo el cumplimiento de lo convenido" (s.v. *cosimentum*).

[9]This is the comment of Marc Shell, who offers an interesting discussion on the matter (*The Economy of Literature*, pp. 102ff.).

[10]Noel Stock, *The Life of Ezra Pound* (New York, 1970), p. 344; reference taken from Marc Shell, *The Economy of Literature*, n. on p. 2.

Contributors

J. L. Roland Bélanger, fms, is Professor of French literature and civilization at Marist College, Poughkeepsie, New York. His *Damedieus: The Religious Context of the Loherain Cycle* was published in 1975; a second volume on the religious context of the William Cycle is in preparation. He has a particular interest in the future of religion and the mythical/mystic elements of religion and poetry.

Nancy Bradley-Cromey is currently Associate Professor of French and Italian at Sweet Briar College, Virginia. She has published articles and reviews on Franco-Italian literature, aspects of the Twelfth Century Renaissance, and Froissart; presently, she is completing a book on *L'Entrée d'Espagne*.

William Calin is Professor of French at the University of Oregon. His interests center on medieval French literature and French poetry since the Renaissance. A recipient of NEH, Guggenheim, ACLS, American Philosophical Society, and Fulbright awards, a Visiting Professor at the University of Poitiers and Visiting Fellow of Clare, Cambridge, he has written or edited eight books (including studies of *chansons de geste*, Guillaume de Machaut, and the baroque poet Pierre Le Moyne), as well as some fifty articles. His most recent volumes are *A Muse for Heroes: Nine Centuries of the Epic in France* (Toronto, 1983), which was awarded the Gilbert Chinard First Literary Prize, and *In Defense of French Poetry: An Essay in Revaluation* (Philadelphia, 1986). From 1973-76 he was president of the American-Canadian branch of the Société Internationale Rencesvals, and in 1987 he was elected president of the International Guillaume de Machaut Society.

237

Alice M. Colby-Hall, Professor of Romance Studies at Cornell University, is best known for her book *The Portrait in Twelfth-Century French Literature: An Example of the Stylistic Originality of Chrétien de Troyes* (Geneva, 1965). While visiting Provence in 1976, she was startled by a telltale resemblance between Arles and the city of Orange as portrayed in the *Prise d'Orange*; this discovery led her to concentrate her research efforts on the literature, history, geography, and archeology of the lower Rhône valley. To date, this research has resulted in eight articles. Professor Colby-Hall currently serves as president of the American-Canadian Branch of the Société Internationale Rencesvals.

Larry S. Crist is Professor of French at Vanderbilt University. He has published an edition of the prose *Saladin* (Geneva, 1972) and, with Robert F. Cook (University of Virginia), has done a study on *Le Deuxième Cycle de la Croisade* (Geneva, 1972). At present his long work on an edition of *Baudouin de Sebourc* is nearing completion. Methodologically, he is working on semiotic approaches to medieval French literature and in that connection has done a number of studies on the epic, lyric, and theatre. From 1976-78 he served as president of the American-Canadian branch of the Société Internationale Rencesvals.

Antonio Franceschetti is Professor of Italian at Scarborough College, University of Toronto. He is the author of *L'"Orlando Innamorato" e le sue componenti tematiche e strutturali* (Florence, 1975) and several articles on various aspects of Italian literature from the Middle Ages to the eighteenth century.

Miguel Garci-Gómez, Professor of Spanish at Duke University, has written numerous articles of philological and literary interest on the marqués de Santillana, *El Cantar de Mio Cid*, *La Celestina*, the *romance*, and traditional lyric. His major works include *Mio Cid: Estudios de endocrítica* (1975) and *El Burgos de Mio Cid: Temas socio-económicos y escolásticos* (1982), both of which were awarded literary prizes. He has published two critical editions: *Cantar de Mio Cid* (1977) and *Proemios y cartas literarias del Marqués de Santillana* (1984).

Edward A. Heinemann has taught since 1966 at the University of Toronto, where he is currently Associate Professor of French. His recent articles include "Aperçus sur quelques rythmes sémantiques dans les versions *A*, *B* et *D* du *Charroi de Nîmes*" (1981), "'Composite Laisse' and Echo as Organizing Principles: The Case of Laisse I of the *Charroi de Nîmes*"

(1983), and "Mémoire, répétition, système esthétique dans la chanson de geste" (1985).

Constance B. Hieatt, Professor of English at the University of Western Ontario, has published a translation of *Beowulf and Other Old English Poems* (revised and enlarged 2d edition, New York, 1983) as well as of the lengthy *Karlamagnús saga* (Toronto, 1975-80) and her edition *Curye on Inglysh: English Culinary Manuscripts of the Fourteenth Century including the "Forme of Cury"* for the E.E.T.S. (London and New York, 1985), written in collaboration with the late Sharon Butler. She is currently working on an edition of Anglo-Norman medical recipes for publication by the A.N.T.S. in collaboration with Robin Jones, with whom she edited the Anglo-Norman recipes that appeared in *Speculum* (October 1986).

Hans-Erich Keller is Professor of French at The Ohio State University. Next to five books on French philology and some eighty articles, he has edited the two-volume *Studia Occitanica in memoriam Paul Remy* (Kalamazoo, 1986) and a festschrift. At present he has finished his edition of *La vie de sainte Marguerite* (to be published in 1988) and is continuing work on his book *"The Song of Roland" in European Literature from Past to Present*. In 1987 he received the Distinguished Scholar Award of The Ohio State University. The organizer 1981-87 of annual symposia on the Romance epic within the framework of the International Congresses on Medieval Studies of the Medieval Institute of Western Michigan University, he served as president of the American-Canadian branch of the Société Internationale Rencesvals 1982-85; since 1981, he has been a vice-president of the Association Internationale d'Études Occitanes.

William W. Kibler, Superior Oil-Linward Shivers Centennial Professor of French at the University of Texas at Austin, has worked extensively in the field of the Old French epic, contributing articles and reviews on the subject to distinguished journals in this country and abroad. His edition/translation of Guillaume de Machaut's *Jugement du roy de Behaigne* and *Remede de Fortune*, with James I. Wimsatt, will be published in 1987. He has currently begun work on *Medieval France: An Encyclopedia* for Garland Press. With Jean-Louis Picherit and Thelma Fenster, he published the late epic *Lion de Bourges* (Geneva, 1980); he has also published an edition and translation of Chrétien de Troyes's *Lancelot* (New York, 1981), and an *Introduction to Old French* (New York, 1984). From 1978-82, he served as president of the American-Canadian branch of the Société Internationale Rencesvals.

André de Mandach teaches Medieval French and Comparative Literature at the University of Neuchâtel, Switzerland. He specializes in medieval civilization, especially in the fields of the *chansons de geste* and the Tristan legend. His main work, constituting five volumes to date, is *Naissance et développement de la chanson de geste en Europe*, concentrating especially on the *geste* of Charlemagne and of Roland, the *Pseudo-Turpin* and the *Chanson d'Aspremont*. The fifth volume contains heretofore unpublished thirteenth-century texts of *Fierabras* and orally transmitted Latin-American adaptations of it.

Emanuel J. Mickel, Jr., Professor of French, Chairman of the Department of French and Italian, and Director of the Medieval Studies Institute at Indiana University, has written more than thirty-five articles on medieval and nineteenth-century French literature. With Jan A. Nelson (University of Alabama), he is co-editing a projected ten-volume series, *The Old French Crusade Cycle*. He has also written three books: *The Artificial Paradises in French Literature* (1969), *Marie de France* (1974), and *Eugène Fromentin* (1982).

Barbara Schurfranz Moorman is currently Associate Professor of French and Latin at the University of Southern Mississippi. She has written articles on the Lorraine and William cycles for *Romance Philology* and *Romance Notes*. Work in progress includes studies of the manuscript tradition of the Lorraine cycle and allusions by other works to *Garin le Lorrain*.

Peter S. Noble is at present Reader in French Studies at the University of Reading, England. He has published articles in a variety of journals on different aspects of medieval romance, the Tristan legend, medieval epic, fifteenth-century language, and French Canadian literature. One of the editors of *Reading Medieval Studies*, he has also edited three festschriften and published three books: *Le Voyatge d'Oultremer a Jherusalem de Nompar Seigneur de Caumont* (1975), *Love and Marriage in Chrétien de Troyes* (1983), and *Beroul and "La Folie Tristan" de Berne* (1982).

Aristóbulo Pardo was Associate Professor of Spanish at The Ohio State University at the time of his sudden demise in 1984. Former director of the Seminario Andrés Bello, Instituto Caro y Cuervo, Bogotá, Vice-Minister of Education in Bogotá, and consultant for the Ministeries of Education in Costa Rica and Venezuela, his publications include articles about the *Cantar de Mio Cid*, Alfonso the Wise, the poetry of the marqués of Santillana, and the medieval Spanish studies of the Venezuelan poet and scholar Andrés Bello. His book *Serranas, pastorelas y serranillas de los poetas peninsulares en la edad media. Compilación, estudio, traducciones y notas* is still awaiting publication.

Jean Charles Payen was Professor of Medieval French at the University of Caen, France, from 1965 until his untimely death in 1984. He authored numerous publications, among others *Le motif du repentir dans la littérature française médiévale* (1968), *Alard de Cambrai, "Le Livre de philosophie et de moralité"* (1970), and *Le Moyen Age: Des origines à 1300* (1971; completely revised new edition entitled *Le Moyen Age: Des origines à 1430*, 1982). He is widely known for his work on the different literary genres in the Middle Ages and his essays on their characteristics.

François Suard is Professor of Medieval French at the University of Lille, France. He has published a book on the prose rendering of an epic cycle entitled *Guillaume d'Orange. Étude du roman en prose* (1979). His numerous articles deal primarily with the posterity of *chansons de geste* (he is the specialist of this problem for volume 8 of the *Grundriss der romanischen Literaturen des Mittelalters*) and with the Breton *lai*. Presently, he is a vice-president of the Société Internationale Rencesvals.

Ruth House Webber is Professor Emerita of Spanish at the University of Chicago. The author of *Formulistic Diction in the Spanish Ballad* and a number of articles on the epic and ballad, her main areas of interest are traditional poetry, Spanish medieval literature, and narrative structure.